D1118576

ANIMALS

AND THE MAYA

IN

SOUTHEAST MEXICO

ANIMALS

AND THE MAYA

IN

SOUTHEAST MEXICO

E. N. ANDERSON

and

FELIX MEDINA TZUC

THE UNIVERSITY OF ARIZONA PRESS

TUCSON

The University of Arizona Press
© 2005 Arizona Board of Regents
All rights reserved
∞ This book is printed on acid-free, archival-quality paper.
Manufactured in the United States of America
10   09   08   07   06   05   6   5   4   3   2   1

Library of Congress Cataloging-in-Publication Data

Anderson, Eugene N. (Eugene Newton), 1941-
    Animals and the Maya in southeast Mexico / E. N. Anderson
and Felix Medina Tzuc
        p. cm.
    Includes bibliographical references and index.
    ISBN 0-8165-2394-0 (cloth : alk. paper)
  1. Mayas—Domestic animals. 2. Mayas—Ethnozoology.
3. Mayas—Hunting. 4. Human-animal relationships—Mexico—
Chunhuhub Region. 5. Indigenous peoples—Ecology—Mexico—
Chunhuhub Region. 6. Animals—Mexico—Chunhuhub Region—
Nomenclature (Popular). 7. Names—Mayan—Mexico—Chunhuhub
Region. 8. Forest degradation—Mexico—Chunhuhub Region.
9. Chunhuhub Region (Mexico)—Social life and customs.
10. Chunhuhub Region (Mexico)—Environmental conditions.
I. Medina Tzuc, Felix, 1940-. II. Title.
    F1435.3.D64A63 2005
    636'.00972'67—dc22
    2004015055

    Publication of this book is made possible in part by the proceeds of
a permanent endowment created with the assistance of a Challenge Grant
from the National Endowment for the Humanities, a federal agency.

CONTENTS

ILLUSTRATIONS

All photos by E. N. Anderson except as otherwise noted in the individual photo captions.

PREFACE

Quintana Roo, Mexico's southeastern frontier state, is facing a faunal crisis. Game animals are disappearing. So are other animals that depend on old-growth forest. Though Quintana Roo is one of Mexico's least populous states and retains a substantial amount of forest, its animal populations are melting away.

The reasons are straightforward: habitat destruction and overhunting. A rapidly expanding population, needing food, is converting the land to agricultural uses while shooting wild game for subsistence. At the same time, urban expansion and out-of-state investment destroy yet further habitat.

There is serious need for better management of Quintana Roo's wild lands and animal resources. Conservation for sustainable use is not a new concept in the state, and many successful projects, old and new, prove that it is possible.

This book has a specific purpose: assisting such management by documenting Yucatec Maya knowledge and use of animals in the west-central part of Quintana Roo. This book is, therefore, not an exercise in "values-neutral" science. We are committed to providing better treatment and more sustainable management for the rural scene in Quintana Roo. The first author, E. N. Anderson (ENA) came to study Maya use of plants and animals and stayed to help with an ongoing problem. The second author, Felix Medina Tzuc (FMT), as justice of the peace (1999–2002) in the Maya town of Chunhuhub, was and is involved in practical matters related to these wider issues.

Convinced that the primary need in this project is for the maximum possible amount of reliable information, we provide as much factual infor-

mation as we can. Most of the information is about traditional Maya knowledge of animals. We also provide lists of mammals and birds that occur in
the area. We must leave to qualified biologists the assessment of actual populations of animals present, although we can provide informed general data.

The Yucatec Maya have thorough knowledge of the world around them.
Their ethnobotany has been rather well recorded (e.g., Barrera Marín, Barrera Vásquez, and Lopez Franco 1976; Sosa et al. 1985). The combined
knowledge of Yucatec experts runs to literally thousands of plant species.
Hundreds of these have at least two uses; dozens have multiple uses. Soil
science and farming techniques are also well recorded (e.g., Várguez Pasos
1981; Terán and Rasmussen 1994). Animals, however, have suffered neglect.
The few and obscure publications that record Yucatec animal lore are often
marred by inaccuracy. None provides a complete picture. (The Itzaj Maya,
whose language is virtually a dialect of Yucatec, have done better, thanks
to an excellent paper by Atran [1999] and detailed entries in the standard
dictionary of Itzaj [Hofling and Tesucún 1997].) This book covers one small
area of the Maya world. Further work is necessary to provide comparative
material.

We have also been unable to find much scientific identification, so far,
for most invertebrates. This is not a problem in most cases because names
are used in a very wide and easily defined way (e.g., the category *kisaay* is
virtually identical to the entomological category Hemiptera). The worst
problem lies with ants, wasps, and bees, for which a rich Maya terminology has not yet been matched with the rather inadequate biological record.

We have succeeded, however, in recording most of the terms widely used
for animals in west-central Quintana Roo; mapping them onto biologists'
categories; and recording basic information about management and uses.
Dr. Eugene Hunn worked with us briefly on the present project, and, in fact,
introduced us to each other. His well-known work on the Tzeltal Maya of
Chiapas (Hunn 1977) is comparable to our work.

Our joint work began with that introduction, in early 1991. We worked
together during the first half of that year. In 1993, ENA made a brief return
visit, then returned again in 1996 for another six months, during which time
FMT served as field assistant and general source of expertise. A close friend-
ship developed. This, in turn, led to so much discussion back and forth, and
so many field hours spent examining the cases in question, that our knowl-

1. *Western Quintana Roo: Looking westward from the top of the thirty-meter-high pyramid at Altamirano, south of Chunhuhub. The forest cover is broken by small fields; the town is hidden under tall fruit trees in the middle distance.*

edge and observation base became inseparably merged. Subsequent annual visits, and three months of further work in fall of 2001, cemented the bonds. This book, then, is a joint enterprise.

Our joint effort consisted largely of field work—many hundreds of hours spent wandering in the forests and fields of west-central Quintana Roo. We were based in the town of Chunhuhub, FMT's home.

Chunhuhub was a thriving town when the Spanish arrived, and remained so through the colonial era (Jones 1989). It was destroyed in the War of the Castes, in the mid-1840s. In the early 1940s, settlers from the east moved into the vacant land, and a town was formed, with Juan Xool Uitzil as the most important leader. (The Xool family is still the largest in town.) They settled on the old site, around the ruins of the colonial church. People flooded in not only from other parts of the Zona Maya of Quintana Roo, but also from Yucatán state, especially the nearby parts. Culturally close to the Quintana Roo Maya, they were easily assimilated. The folk classification system has been maintained as a typical Maya system by these immigrants from all over the peninsula.

By comparison with the Maya communities of the henequen and orchard zones of Yucatán, this eastern part of the Maya world has maintained a fierce independence and a self-confident pride in Maya traditions, including linguistic traditions such as folk classification systems. Many of the Chunhuhub families are descendants of the Cruzoob and have not forgotten it. They recall that their immediate ancestors fought the entire Mexican government to a standstill and were able to set terms for peace (Sullivan 1989 provides important observations on this sentiment). Moreover, active Maya groups in Felipe Carrillo Puerto (Chunhuhub's *municipio* seat) and Peto (just across the border in Yucatán) are working to increase cultural pride and awareness.

The Maya of Chunhuhub are peaceful today, feeling that they can succeed economically in the modern world, and that economic efforts are more appropriate than rebellion. Nonviolence is a major value; there are few more peaceful parts of Mexico. The language and culture are flourishing. Thus, it is still possible to learn a great deal of ethnobiological lore, and not only from aged traditionalists. Young, modernizing, well-educated men and women of Chunhuhub are often excellent consultants, since they have self-consciously kept the lore alive and worked at learning it. Of course, not all young people are so motivated, but Chunhuhub is still overwhelmingly a farm town, and the immediate needs of agriculture, forestry, medicine, and hunting would be adequate to keep ethnobiological knowledge viable for the foreseeable future, even without the active interest in learning it for its own sake.

Chunhuhub includes 14,330 hectares (ca. 33,000 acres) of ejido land. Like most Maya communities in Quintana Roo, Chunhuhub is incorporated as an ejido, a community that holds its lands in common and parcels them out, each year, in assemblies or through other official ejido channels. Since 1993, ejido land has been subject to privatization, but most Maya ejidos—including Chunhuhub—have steadfastly refused to do this. One neighboring ejido that privatized its lands suffered from disaster as individuals' parcels were mismanaged. This ejido serves as a cautionary example.

We ranged widely, but tended to concentrate on the southern part of this land, where Don Felix's orchard and milpa lie, and where the forest is thickest, wettest, and most remote. Very frequently, we had as companion Don Jacinto Cauich Canul, of Chunhuhub, or Don Adriano Dzib and his family, of Presidente Juarez; often also Don Pastor Valdez (ENA's landlord in town) or other experts and authorities. Frequently, we met others in the field and talked to them about plants, animals, and hunting. Both of us did further work on our own, seeking out and questioning other experts, in town and in the field.

Chunhuhub—"wild plum tree"—is a town of some six thousand people. It is the largest and most prosperous town in the area and thus is a center for many small rural ejidos in the neighborhood. It is established in the band of fertile soil that is found at the base of the hills of the central Yucatán Peninsula. Where these hills give way to flat land, runoff has deposited rich farmland, and Chunhuhub occupies this position; its ejido lands are half in the hills, half on the flat.

Because of its size and number of hunters, Chunhuhub has relatively serious animal conservation problems. On the other hand, its prosperity is shown in the number of domestic animals and the consequent amount of meat available to the citizens.

No Maya town is typical. Compared to many other Maya towns, Chunhuhub is richer, more educated, and more dynamic. It is stable, peaceful, and has a high standard of health and health care. Yet it remains quite traditional. Maya is the common language (outside the town center, with its stores and offices). Subsistence agriculture is still common. Income is generated largely by sale of fruit, and secondarily of animals, maize, and other agricultural products. Traditional uses of plants and animals are still widely known. The town's excellent technical junior college (Cebeta) makes Chunhuhub a major exporter of educated-person power, but the community is still largely a farm town, closely tied in to the forests and fields of Quintana Roo's internal frontier.

The Maya not only concern themselves with animals for instrumental reasons; they also like, even love, both tame and wild animals. Traditionally, and to a great extent still, they regard animals as fellow members of a wider society. In Maya religion, animals have a status as spiritual beings and as social persons—not human persons, but persons nonetheless. They communicate with humans and share with them a conscious participation in a sacred cosmos. Younger Maya today have moved away from that cosmos: Their tangible world is no longer sacred, and, for many of them, religion itself is lacking in deep importance. In Max Weber's terms, they have suffered much "disenchantment" (Weber 1963). Yet many or most of them retain a deep love of their natural environment and of animals.

The landscape of Quintana Roo is a creation of Maya shifting agriculture as much as it is a creation of limestone soils, summer rain, and tropical climate. Thus the plant and animal life is not an undifferentiated mass of natural resources lying around for the taking. It is a culturally influenced creation. The landscape itself is a cultural construction in a literal sense. Under these circumstances, the animals of Maayab (Mayaland) form a true heritage, a heritage that is both cultural and natural.

Protection of heritage is a recognized function of governments. The Mexican government has been a world leader in saving prehistoric sites and historic cities, elite and folk arts, music and drama. INAH (Mexico's Instituto Nacional de Antropología e Historia) has been successful in preserving much of this. We hope that Mexico, and Mexico's friends in the international arena, will recognize the forests and wildlife of Quintana Roo as deserving of protection, just as the great Maya cities are.

The forests and their denizens are part of the great heritage of humanity. Saving them is a vital economic issue, but more, it is a moral issue. The people of Quintana Roo, to say nothing of visitors from elsewhere, draw from the natural world not only income, but also personal and spiritual welfare.

ACKNOWLEDGMENTS

We are grateful, first and foremost, to Barbara Anderson and Elide Uh May, and to the rest of our long-suffering families; and to our frequent companions Jacinto Cauich Canul and Pastor Valdez, and their wives and families. We have also received wonderful cooperation and assistance from Eugene Hunn, Mario Jimenez, Adriano Dzib and his family (especially Aurora Dzib), Andres Sosa, and dozens of other expert consultants in the field. In the urban and academic world, we (more specifically ENA) have had occasion to be deeply grateful to Myra Appel, Scott Atran, Arturo Bayona and Adriana de Castro, Betty Faust, Scott Fedick, Salvador Flores Guido, Arturo Gómez-Pompa, Gerald Islebe, Juan Jimenez-Osornio, Francisco Rosado May, Lidia Serralta, Karl Taube, and the anthropological and ecological authorities at Universidad de Quintana Roo, Universidad Autónoma de Yucatán, the Plan Forestal of Quintana Roo (notably A. Ehret Duhne and Gilberto Avila), and Ecosur (formerly CIQRO), and to an anonymous referee who provided valuable linguistic information. We are deeply grateful to Christine Szuter, Allyson Carter, and Melanie Mallon for editing and all manner of related assistance.

We are particularly grateful to Eugene Hunn, who not only introduced us to each other and helped us in the field, but also read over the manuscript with meticulous care and suggested dozens of changes, which have been adopted.

A Note on Language and Transcription

Field work reported here was conducted largely in Spanish. ENA's Maya is by no means fluent. FMT is completely bilingual, being extremely fluent in both languages and using them equally readily. Most of our consultants, however, were more fluent in Maya; many were monolingual. FMT thus often served as translator, though ENA conducted a great deal of field work on his own, in Spanish eked out with fragmentary Maya. Obviously, it would be desirable for native speakers of Maya to extend the present work. No doubt this will soon occur, for the Maya are rapidly turning to formal education as a way to advance themselves, and ethnobiology is a very popular subject for research in the Yucatán. Maya researchers such as Edilberto Ucan Ek (who has worked with many of us in the field; see Atran et al. 1999) have already contributed much.

Maya has been transcribed in various ways. There were several versions of the hieroglyphic writing system of ancient times. The Spanish experimented with various systems of writing the language in Roman characters. Recently, a reasonably simple and uniform system for writing any Mayan language has gained ground throughout the Maya area. This system, agreed to at a convention in Guatemala in 1988, is now rapidly becoming standard in Mexico. In particular, leading Maya scholars and writers such as Hilaria Maas Colli now use it. Thus, it is the system used here.

In this modern system, letters are pronounced as in Spanish. Thus, for instance, *j* represents the /*h*/ sound. (Maya /*h*/ is much softer than Peninsular Spanish *j*, but that is a minor point.) *X* indicates the /*sh*/ sound, as it did in old Spanish and still does in Portuguese.

Glottalization is indicated by an apostrophe ('). Glottalized consonants (*k'*, etc.) are pronounced with a slight explosive sound. A glottal stop between vowels is heard as a slight catch, like the catch that distinguishes "unh-unh" meaning "no" from "uh-huh" meaning "yes" in English. In fast speech, the glottal stop is dropped.

Doubled vowels indicate vowel length. Thus, in *aakach* (horsefly), the *aa* in the first syllable is dragged out about twice as long as the *a* in the second.

The transition to the new spelling system is far from complete. Moreover, place names and other such standardized words are written according to the commonest of the earlier systems, the one that became more or less standard by the end of colonial times.

Thus, everyone who wishes to read even a few words of Maya has to learn two different systems. (If you are serious about Maya linguistics, you have to learn about a dozen systems.) In the standard old system, *c* wrote the /k/ sound; *k* was glottalized /k'/; dz was glottalized /ts'/; other glottalized consonants were indicated by doubling *(pp, tt)*. Z was /s/; *h* was /h/. Vowel length was not indicated at all. Doubled vowels were not long vowels, but glottalized ones: *aa* meant /a'a/. (Sometimes even this was not indicated, when ordinary pronunciation elided the glottal stop.) And there were other minor differences.

Place names have to be read accordingly. Chunhuhub, in the new system, would be Chuunjujub'. Dzula, next door, would be Ts'uula'. Calkini would be Kaalk'ini'. But nobody is going to change the spelling of hundreds of map designations, so we are left with multiple systems for the foreseeable future.

One often thinks of T. E. Lawrence—Lawrence of Arabia—who wrote to his editor: "Arabic names won't go into English. . . . I spell my names anyhow, to show what rot the systems are" (Lawrence 1935, 25). Many modern writers on things Maya seem to have taken this leaf from Lawrence's book. The majority of these writers do not know Maya and just transcribe the words as they find them in whatever source they are using. Needless to say, this compounds confusion to the point of madness. Imagine the plight of a Maya child trying to learn to read his or her own language. Fortunately the current system is gaining currency, and Maya may be standardized at last.

Quite separate from the problems of spelling are the far more serious problems of accurately transcribing Maya in the field. In particular, long vowels (and glottalized double vowels) are routinely shortened in fast speech. Thus, it is often difficult to tell whether a given syllable has a long vowel or a short one. Moreover, there are dialect differences in this, and sources differ. Thus, for instance, I hear *ooch* (opossum) as having a long *o*, but dictionaries (though not Bricker, Po'ot Yah, and Dzul de Po'ot 1998) give it a short *o*. This may be a dialect matter, or just my idiosyncratic ear. The most accurate dictionary of Maya, Bricker, Po'ot Yah, and Dzul de Po'ot's *Dictionary of the Maya Language As Spoken in Hocabá, Yucatán* (1998), often records slight differences from my hearing, usually in the direction of longer vowels than mine. I have usually corrected to their usage when even a few Chunhuhub speakers conform to it, but there are some genuine differences between Hocabá Maya and the Maya spoken in and around Chunhuhub. Since I am interested in recording spoken Quintana Roo Maya, I indicate actual spoken pronunciation, with variants. Readers should remember that any and all long vowels are shortened in rapid speech. Thus, spellings may become arbitrary, especially for words never before written down. For comparative and philological purposes, one wants the "correct" form, but for the purposes of this work, the ordinary spoken form may be more useful. An analogy would be to recording English "harrier" for comparative purposes, but writing it as "'arria" if recording Cockney dialect. The accommodation reached in this work should be considered a way station. Ongoing research into Quintana Roo Maya by scholars such as Valentina Vapnarsky will soon revise the whole picture.

Glottalization is also problematic, though less hard to hear and more consistent than long and short vowels. The wasp named *bobote'* (to my hearing) is *bobo'ote* in the standard Maya dictionary *(Diccionario Maya Cordemex* [Barrera Vásquez 1980], now reissued as *Diccionario Maya Porrúa)* and *booteh* in Bricker, Po'ot Yah, and Dzul de Po'ot 1998. These differences make no linguistic sense and appear to be simple free variation on the part of consultants. (FMT frequently talks about bobote'; there is no question of a mistranscription here.) Again, these may be dialect differences or just the Maya tendency to elide glottalization of vowels in rapid speech.

Tone is a major problem. Tone is phonemic in Yucatec, but tones differ from dialect to dialect. Chunhuhub, being about half Quintana Roo Maya and half immigrants from various parts of Yucatán state, has inconsistent and conflicting tonal usages. Individuals have acculturated partly to each other's usages, learned words in each other's dialects, and so on. We have thus not transcribed tone in this work, pending much more thorough analysis—in more homogeneous communities—by trained linguists (we hope to arrange this in the future). Stress is very light in Maya words. We have not marked accent here.

Yucatec is very close to Itzaj and Lacandon (Lakantun), languages (some might call them well-marked dialects) spoken south of Yucatán in tropical Mexico, and somewhat less close to Mopan, spoken in and around southern Belize; the four comprise the Yucatecan branch of the Mayan languages. ("Yucatec" is a Spanish word, not a Maya one, and thus should not be respelled "Yukatek," as some recent sources do.) Much comparative material on Itzaj is available, thanks to work by Scott Atran, Charles Hofling, and others, and some on Lacandon. Mopan, farther both linguistically and geographically, has not been examined for the present work.

ANIMALS

AND THE MAYA

IN

SOUTHEAST MEXICO

Chapter One

IN THE FIELD IN QUINTANA ROO

Mexico's Yucatán Peninsula remains one of the great forested areas of the world. Outside the towns and the burgeoning tourist complex around Cancun lie vast stretches of rich green woodland. These grade from thorny scrub in the dry northwest to tall rain forest in the southeast. Between these extremes lie extensive second-growth forests, which usually shed some or all of their leaves in the dry, hot spring.

From the air, one sees that these long plains and hills are patterned in squares: some sharply defined by recent clearing and burning, some vaguely defined by subtle differences in the age and species of trees. The entire Yucatán forest has been cultivated for thousands of years by the Yucatec Maya. Tracts of two to ten acres are cut, burned, and planted, then abandoned after a few years, as weeds take over or soil fertility declines. Over the millennia, Maya agriculture has had a huge impact on the forests (Fedick 1996). Fruit trees and other useful plants are protected when the rest of the forest is cut. Nitrogen-fixing plants prosper differentially in the depleted soils of old fields. Long-distance dispersers have an advantage in colonizing isolated fields. Vast wildfires, of the sort that devastated uninhabited parts of Quintana Roo in 1989, after Hurricane Gilbert, are inhibited by the countless small firebreaks and cleared spaces. Without the latter, much of the northern Yucatán would be a savannah—as is proved by the continued existence there, until recently, of certain savannah birds.

Much of the peninsula has been seriously overcultivated, or converted into permanent field and pasture. However, in the vast interior, most areas remain as they have been for a long time: "managed mosaics" (Fedick 1996) of fields and various stages of regrowth, from brush and grass to centuries-old forest.

Through much of the year, the land is brilliant with flowers. The intense gold of *taj* (sunflower, *Viguiera deltoides*) along the roads can be so bright that one must literally don sunglasses to drive past it. Whole forests of *ja'abin* (*Piscidia piscipula,* a locustlike tree) can flower at once in spring. Lianas twine the roadside woods with brilliant yellow, magenta, purple, white, and blue.

Throughout this land of varied plant life, wild animals persist. The fields open the land for those that love second growth, such as deer and peccaries (small wild piglike animals). The forests still retain a few monkeys, jaguars, and other rare creatures—though, in these days of shotguns and rifles, very few remain outside of the deepest forests. Hundreds of species of birds flash in and out of dense canopies. The Yucatán Peninsula is a birdwatcher's dream, and indeed ecotourism—not least by birders—is a significant source of income.

The economy is flourishing, but many are still poor. Animals thrive in the "managed mosaic" of fields and forests, but habitat destruction, hunting, agricultural expansion, and tourist activity are reducing animal populations.

In the midst of this green land lies Chunhuhub, a farm town of some six thousand people. Almost all of them are Yucatec Maya. Most live by farming—either subsistence cultivation or commercial growing of fruit, maize, and vegetables. Chunhuhub is one of the major suppliers of the vast maw of Cancun. The maize of the street vendors and the papayas and mangoes of the exclusive four-star hotels both started their life, in many cases, in Chunhuhub's broad and fertile fields.

Chunhuhub is the central town for the least developed part of the Zona Maya: the large area of central Quintana Roo where the Maya held out longest against the Mexican government, and where they still hold much control of the land. The town is a center of education, administration, and marketing. Many of its citizens are descendants of the rebel Maya who kept Quintana Roo independent for decades. Others have moved in, over the last sixty years, from eastern and central Yucatán state. A few come from farther afield, but very few indeed come from outside southeastern Mexico.

By rural tropical standards, the town is far from poor. A few families live in genuine want. Many more live adequately, but in an almost cashless economy; they still grow or gather what they need. Many, however, have broken this barrier and have developed prosperous farms, or become teachers, or sent children to town as skilled workers and professionals. Yet, affluence of "northern" style (whether one means northern Mexico or the northern lands in general) evades most of the population. Land is becoming exhausted; game is overhunted. The future is cloudy. Education is the great hope.

Though more fortunate than most, Chunhuhub is broadly typical of the small towns of Quintana Roo. This state, Mexico's southeastern corner and Caribbean coastland, is being pulled in two directions. Riches pour in from the tourist industry but often go to out-of-state interests. Development has its costs, and these are all too often paid by the local poor rather than by those whose actions entail the costs.

The explosive growth of Quintana Roo's tourist industry, especially in and around Cancun, has led to the state's becoming a magnet for migration. Population growth stands at more than 8 percent per annum (INEGI 1994, 15). Chunhuhub's municipio, Felipe Carrillo Puerto, is growing at about 4 percent. Such rapid population expansion—most of it due to in-migration by adults, rather than local births—makes planning and conservation difficult. Increasing pressure on the environment is matched by increasing pressure on existing institutions. Laws, enforcement systems, and local moral systems must change rapidly to keep pace with changing conditions.

MY PERSPECTIVE, BY E. N. ANDERSON

Under such conditions, much of what happens to the environment has no economic justification. A great deal of devastation occurs simply through error, or because of forlorn hope. Land has been deforested unwisely. Waters have been polluted because urban growth happened faster than anyone could (or would) expand the enforcement of sanitation codes. Vast areas of Quintana Roo that were highly productive forests a generation ago are now wastelands of weeds and thorn scrub.

It is meaningless to debate whether population growth or outside investment is "guilty." Current damage to the environment of Quintana Roo is a single process, in which population growth and investment, subsistence agriculture and commercial development, are mutually reinforcing. Assigning blame to one or another sector of the population or economy does nothing but divert attention from this fact.

The most obvious problem is how to manage Quintana Roo's natural resources such that they will support the present population and the far greater population that will, in the immediate future, depend on them. A part of this problem is the question of how to save the state's biodiversity and its beautiful and species-rich forests and wetlands. They already serve as sources of precious woods, rare medicinal plants, highly nutritious foods, and other locally important commodities—all of which could be, but are usually not, managed sustainably. Moreover, ecotourism is rapidly developing, converting the forest into a major economic asset. In the future, surviving forest areas will be more and more necessary as genetic reserves, breathing spaces for an urbanized and polluted land, and recreational resources for local citizens.

Such valuation does not do justice to Quintana Roo's natural beauty. To anyone who has lived in the state, valuing Quintana Roo's forest for its immediate economic return seems rather like valuing Rembrandts and Van Goghs solely for the canvas they are painted on.

No one is more appreciative of the beauty, wonder, and power of the forest than its indigenous inhabitants, the Yucatec Maya. Holders of the land for thousands of years, they developed there (and in neighboring areas) one of the great civilizations of the world. From 200 to 800 A.D., most of what is now Quintana Roo seems to have been more intensively settled and exploited than it is today. This was true especially in the southwestern part, today the least developed area of the state. Here, the ruins of vast cities thickly dot the limestone plains and ridges. Calakmul, just across the state line in Campeche, covered more than twenty-five square kilometers. Margaritas in Quintana Roo may have been comparable. Kohunlich, Dzitbanche, Ramonal, Coba, and many other sites held thousands or tens of thousands of people.

This civilization, the Classic Maya, collapsed around 800 A.D. Small, scattered sites remain common through the Postclassic, and the Spanish found a large population when they first reached Quintana Roo. Environmental degradation, caused by the agricultural and hydrological activities necessary to support the huge population, may have contributed to the decline—as it certainly did at Copan, Honduras (see Paine and Freter 1996, and references therein). Certainly, it is difficult to imagine the fragile environment of southwestern Quintana Roo supporting a large population for long. Today, massive clearing has led to invasion by bracken fern, which is almost impossible to eradicate. The forest does not soon grow back once erosion and bracken infestation have taken over. The land is abandoned.

Don Felix is less concerned than I by the skyrocketing population growth of Quintana Roo. With a growth rate of almost 9 percent per year (INEGI 1994, 15), Quintana Roo will have as many people in 2200 as the entire world does today—if present trends continue. Obviously this growth rate will not be sustained.

The speed of growth is overwhelming the environment and every plan to save it. The best conservation plans become obsolete almost overnight. Yesterday's sustainable level of hunting is today's holocaust, as the population of hunters multiplies geometrically.

Population growth has been concentrated in the cities, specifically in Cancun, which has grown from nothing to well over half a million in twenty-five years. This runaway urbanization has its own problems—notably pollution of Laguna Nicte-Ha, where sewage treatment has been minimal.

The other focus of population growth has been at the rapidly expanding edge of colonization in the interior of the state. Countless small settlements have been spawned, as population growth in large, established ejidos becomes unsupportable due to the rapid shrinking of the per capita shares of land and resources. Thus, for instance, Betania was born when Protestants and dissidents were expelled from Xocen, Yucatán (Terán and Rasmussen 1994, supplemented by my own findings); Presidente Juarez was settled by Protestants from in and around Chichimila in the same area. Chunhuhub has spun off its own daughter settlements, such as Margaritas, a beautiful ejido in the high forest to the south. New settlements continue to form as these forest towns rapidly increase in population. Every new settlement becomes the center of a rapidly expanding circle of cleared and overhunted land in which game is rare.

Some settlements are much more conservation-minded than others. Margaritas, for instance, settled by the intelligent and responsible Jimenez family, still has some animal-rich primary forest right at the edge of town. But even Margaritas has cleared a great deal of forest and hunted some species of animals into rarity.

The Quintana Roo forest is not a virgin land that must be preserved in some pristine, inhuman state. On the contrary: It is the product of thousands of years of farming. Slash-and-burn agriculture, carefully attuned to the local environment, has produced a particular kind of forest. Fruit trees and—significantly—wildlife food trees are carefully preserved. Other trees that flourish are those that love to invade old fields. The animals that survive are those that do well in a dynamic, ever-regrowing environment. Many are specifically those that fatten on milpas and abandoned milpas, such as White-tailed Deer, Collared Peccaries, and coatis. It was this symbiotic relationship with humans (hunters and all) that created what an early Spanish visitor described as "an infinite number of game in all the land" (Salazar 2000 [1620], 48). Humans participate and live in this wonder of biodiversity. This is not a "wilderness," except perhaps in the literal Old English sense: "wild-deer-ness," place of wild animals. It is a human-ordered world, a world in which "wild deer" and humans sustain each other (cf. Linares 1976). At least, they used to sustain each other, and they could again.

2. E. N. Anderson (center) and Felix Medina Tzuc (farthest left) in a recently cut milpa, Chunhuhub. (Photograph by Gabriel Medina)

It is obvious to the outside observer that Quintana Roo—like most of the world's forested tropics—is facing a crisis and will have no large animals in another few years unless desperate measures are taken. These must include some attention to controlling runaway population growth and settlement. The Mexican government already pays much attention to making birth control available to everyone. Posters announcing birth control and the benefits of small families abound in rural health centers. People are listening: We heard a great deal about the issue, all positive. In our experience, most young families plan to limit the numbers of their children. There seems a great deal of hope that the "demographic transition" is coming rapidly, and fully voluntarily, to Quintana Roo. Further economic development, and progress in making birth control means available, will slowly bring the birth rate down.

This leaves the problem of in-migration from other states. Most migrants go to Cancun, but large numbers of farmers, particularly from neighboring states but also from Tabasco, Veracruz, and even farther afield, have settled in the south and west. Having little vested interest in or knowledge of the Quintana Roo environment, some of these newcomers are indifferent to conservation. Even Maya from Chiapas may be irresponsible forest users, prompting sour remarks from the Yucatec. To their enormous credit, the immigrants are usually quick to pick up conservation ideas, and very assertive about acting on these ideas. We talked to many staunch animal conservationists from Tabasco and other states during our investigations in Manuel Avila Camacho, Tres Garantias, and elsewhere (to say nothing of Chunhuhub). The question of how to accommodate migration is vexed and will probably be dealt with at the local level.

More pressing than population growth, especially in the short run, is the need to control hunting. On this, all older Maya seem to agree. Hunting has recently spiraled out of control in Quintana Roo, leading to the extirpation of almost everything edible that is within easy reach of a road. This problem is even worse elsewhere in the peninsula; an excellent general assessment by Marmolejo Monsiváis (2000) makes depressing reading.

Also to be considered is habitat destruction. Traditional shifting agriculture is a significant problem, but, by itself, it would be manageable; Quintana Roo's agrarian population is still small enough to allow fallowing of land and regrowth of forest, if land use were still traditional. The problem is that hundreds of thousands of hectares have been cleared, at one time or another, in schemes—mostly extremely ill-advised—for agriculture or cattle raising. Most of this land is now waste. Unlike the small, forest-surrounded clearings of traditional slash-and-burn agriculture, these huge cleared areas do not grow back to forest. They suffer from soil erosion and degradation; they have no stumps or seeds to regrow the woods. They grow thorn scrub, weeds, and tenacious nonnative grasses. For all practical purposes, they are lost to productive use. They are too degraded in fertility to be profitably recleared. They do not produce the many wild medicinal plants, food plants, insects, and animals of the forest.

Fortunately, Quintana Roo has not suffered as badly as most of the tropics. This is because the state has been blessed with relatively enlightened leadership, and, especially, with Maya protectiveness of their land base. The vast majority of Quintana Roo's lands are still forested. Many of the forests are in excellent condition. Many are in reserves: biosphere reserves such as Sian Ka'an and Yum Balam, and ejido reserves such as the magnificent rain forests of Caobas and Tres Garantias. Management of old-growth forests for sustained-yield selective logging is now a popular and widespread option, if not yet perfect on the ground. This story must be told elsewhere, but it is to the credit of Quintana Roo's citizens that the state is now one of the best-forested areas in the tropical world. However, the forests have been saved more effectively than the animals. If the larger animals could fully occupy their forests, they would probably be dozens of times as common as they are, judging from comparative figures from elsewhere in the New World tropics.

The tragedy of the Third World is not that the natural environment has been lost; the tragedy is that the loss has accomplished nothing (to paraphrase Geertz 1963, 143). At one time or another, bureaucrats with no experience on the ground have thought that Quintana Roo could grow rice (without alluvial valleys), sesame (without the soil and climate that sesame needs), cattle (without good pastures, except very locally), and other crops. Yet the same bureaucrats have almost totally failed to enforce even the existing laws protecting game, let alone to take initiative to work for sustainable management. Sustainable forestry has finally come to Quintana Roo, but sustainable game use remains an idea confined to very few fortunate communities. The people who suffer from ill-planned schemes are the local countryfolk. The bureaucrats who design these schemes duly get promoted (based on so-and-so many hectares opened for cultivation and so forth). The people on the ground lose the forest and its products, lose the game animals, and lose the soil.

In many cases elsewhere in the tropics, one can assign a great deal of blame for Third World degradation to First World economics. The world system, increasingly interlocked, devastates Third World forests for customers in the rich nations. This is not an adequate explanation in regard to Quintana Roo's wild animals. Indeed, the only successes in saving animals have come through international conservation efforts and ecotourism development. Tourism has, however, brought its own problems; rapid development of the Cancun area has eliminated plants and animals there, and roads have opened the whole state to outside pressures.

Moreover, international economics and national politics lie behind the rapid expansion of population, and some of the pressure on the resource base. The parents or grandparents of my friends in Chunhuhub were isolated, almost wholly self-sufficient forest farmers. Today, Chunhuhub is directly affected by honey prices in Germany, timber shortages in Korea, and, of course, the labor market in the United States. Two Chunhuhubians have made it to Los Angeles. Cancun has brought new incentives for market gunning and poaching. Deforestation, the destroyer of animal habitats, is also brought about partly by desires to export valuable woods, expand fruit production for export, and create mass tourism zones. Last, and most important of all, the increasing power of multinational corporations, multinational agencies, and the centralized national government of Mexico are all steadily eroding Maya power, and thus their ability to control their resources—and even their motivation to try.

This progressively limits the ability of the autonomous Maya communities of Quintana Roo to enforce their traditional conservation rules—especially on outsiders. There is more government interference in local resource management and less chance of stopping it. Such interference often goes against Maya interests. More insidiously, it gives younger Maya a feeling of powerlessness. More are leaving for the cities. Fewer are following the example of their recent ancestors and fighting for their land. Those few, however, show great tenacity. They also display a striking ability to shift their tactics from guerrilla fighting to political organization and public relations.

In the end, only increasing democratization and accountability on the part of Mexico, and increasing ability to work with local communities, will save the Maya and their forests. Some successful templates exist and will be discussed in due course.

So Quintana Roo, like the rest of the world, is as buffeted by international political-economic gales as by Caribbean hurricanes. The winds blow hot and cold for conservation. International attention to biodiversity and rain forests is balanced by national and international pressures to "develop" at all costs.

The choice is not between wildlife and jobs. The choice is between a world in which wildlife and jobs exist, and a world in which neither exists. This cannot be stated too often or too strongly. *Human survival in Quintana Roo—* outside of the hothouse of Cancun—*depends on maintaining the natural resource base.*[1] (See also Marmolejo Monsiváis 2000.)

To Don Felix and me, the birds, insects, mammals, and other animals of Quintana Roo, down to the tiny arthropods and worms, are a series of miracles. The whole picture—the panorama of Ocellated Turkeys, coatis, heliconia butterflies, singing Spot-breasted Wrens, and the rest—is one of the most magnificent things I have ever seen. To me, it is a personal tragedy when a family of White-breasted Wood-Wrens loses its home; how far more tragic to see millions of animals destroyed for nothing. Don Felix feels this even more strongly, in proportion to his longer association with the land.

For the sake of the Maya and the other country people of Quintana Roo, for the sake of the animals themselves, and for the sake of those of us who care about the incomparably valuable heritage of beauty that the Maya have preserved and created in the Yucatán: *May these animals be saved.*

The story of Quintana Roo and its environment is being told elsewhere (Anderson 2000, 2001, N.D.). In the present work, we focus on animals.

This personal introduction serves two purposes: first, to say something about my share in the investigation and my work with Don Felix;[2] second, to provide my own personal slant on what we found. In particular, I want to separate my own views, colored as they are by years of international experience with animal resource management, from his, colored by more local but far deeper experience.

I met Don Felix in 1991. When I returned in 1996, I found him and his family in straitened circumstances. Their harvest had failed two years in a row. The 1994 harvest had succumbed to drought. In 1995, a bumper crop of maize, beans, and oranges was almost ready to pick when Hurricane Roxanne slammed into central Quintana Roo, devastating everything in its wake.[3] Most of the maize and oranges were destroyed. The maize that was not destroyed was quickly attacked by insects and mold. By early 1996, the family was living on weevily maize and sweet potatoes. I promptly added him to the expedition payroll. After the family fortunes recovered somewhat, he found a good use for the added income: He ran for mayor of the town, on a long-shot liberal-populist ticket (a campesino running against two engineers). He lost but did surprisingly well. He later became justice of the peace (1999–2002) in a reform administration in the town. With his colleagues in town government, he can take credit for a dramatic reduction in public drunkenness and rowdiness, and a notable increase in prosperity, order, and public amenities.

Don Felix is a few days younger than I am. We share a great deal, including love of the woods, interest in animals and their doings, and interest in traditional Maya culture. We also share a particular sort of individual spirituality that gives us closely similar personal and religious attitudes toward the wild, coupled with an open, inquiring mind toward all that is observable there.

We differ on minor points of religion. I do not believe in the supernatural abilities of witches.[4] Don Felix does; he has seen and dealt with witches. Moreover, he cites the Bible in this regard, to which my only answer is that the Bible does not say the witches were *effective.* Don Felix prefers Adam and Eve to what he knows of Darwinian theory; I differ. We also differ in certain useful ways that make us complementary in the field. For one thing, Don Felix is an extrovert and a natural-born politician, while I refuse to chair so much as a three-person committee.

Much has been made, in recent anthropology, of the anthropologist as outsider, seeing the people he or she "studies" as some sort of exotic Other. This has not been my experience in Chunhuhub. The town is so much like the small farm towns in which I was raised in the United States that I felt at home from the first. I found the same warm but quiet hospitality, the same talk about corn and hogs and the weather, the same sly poker-faced humor. I cannot see the Maya of western Quintana Roo as "others." In turn, I was accepted without much comment. There are those who distrust outsiders (as there are in the United States), but even they have always been polite to me. And for every one who distrusts, there are many who have welcomed me and become close friends—as close and deep as any I have. Hence this book: not a project of anthropologist and informant, but a collaboration between friends who share a deep interest in Quintana Roo's animal life.

We spend a great deal of time in Don Felix's traditional pole-and-thatch house, talking. Some of the more focused and coherent sessions have been translated for this book. I was trained in systematic, formal data gathering, but as time goes by, I find myself getting further and further from it, and more and more quiet in the field (note the near absence of my voice in the interviews). I have found that once the field worker shows real interest in a subject and finds real experts on that subject, the experts will talk on their own, and if anyone needs to ask questions, they will question each other. I am aware that I lose some systematic rigor this way. What I lose in rigor I gain, many times over, in actual information—and I can (and do) always check and recheck later.

One bit of relatively formal elicitation was done with pictures and recordings. Eugene Hunn (a much more systematic worker than I) began this; we took Don Felix through *Aves de México: Guía de Campo* (Peterson and Chalif 1989; this is the Mexican edition of *Field Guide to Mexican Birds*, Peterson and Chalif 1973), and through Louise Emmons's *Neotropical Rainforest Mammals: A Field Guide* (1990). Subsequently, Dr. Hunn recorded Chunhuhub birds with a small handheld parabolic recording machine, and we played them for Don Felix, who could instantly recognize and name every note (including obscure night birds that we recorded during an all-night stay in the forest; see Hunn 1992).

Neither of these was a substitute for field work. The names derived from pictures had to be confirmed through field work and interviewing—a slow process since many birds are rare and hard to find. It is difficult to recognize birds from a picture. Maya, like other forest peoples of the world, are more apt to know birds from their calls, songs, and behavior than from their physical appearance. Moreover, the pictures in Peterson and Chalif and in

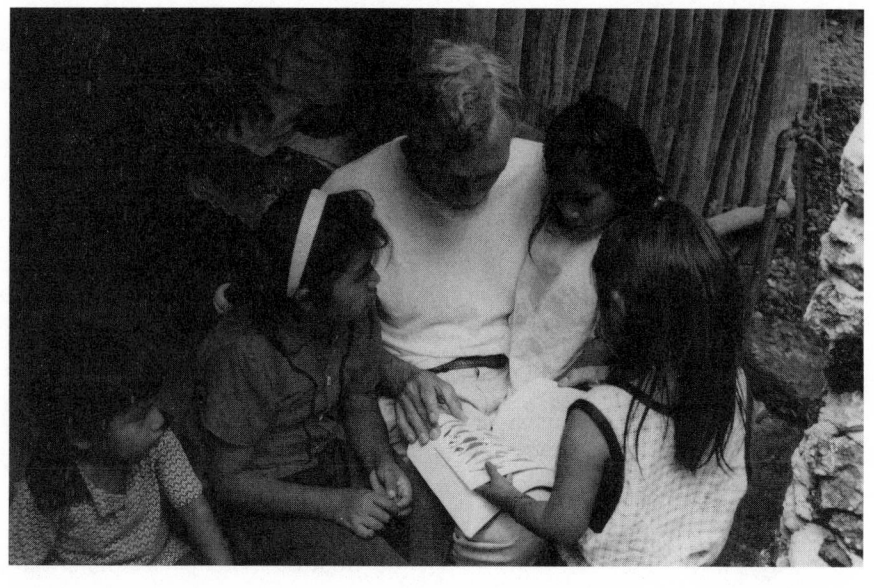

3. *E. N. Anderson going through a bird guide with Maya children. (Photograph by Tracy Franklin)*

Emmons are not to scale, so that Don Felix could not tell whether a brown bird was large enough to be a *k'ok'* or small enough to be a *yankotij*. In particular, rare, obscure, and poorly known birds could not be named from a plate. We simply had to go find them in the field, watch them, and discuss them with each other and any local authorities we could find.

We feel we have a quite comprehensive, thorough, accurately identified, and rigorous account of mammal and bird names. Other animals fare much worse. Lizards are usually called by general, vague, and overlapping names, making precision impossible. Insects are usually more clearly named, but there is much to be done with identifying scientifically the species of wasps and bees.

Since many of the animals discussed herein will doubtless be extirpated even sooner, it seems necessary to report now on our field work. Many of our field experiences will not be replicable by the time this book is published.

Don Felix's life story, and the discussions of hunting and of wasps, were recorded, transcribed, translated, and edited by me. Don Felix then edited further. We have edited heavily, correcting obvious errors and removing the many repetitions, especially the "filled pauses"—few Mexican Spanish speakers, Maya or otherwise, seem to be able to record a text without countless repetitions of *pues* and *así* to fill up what would otherwise be conversational gaps.

The final writeup of this information has been my responsibility, but the views are shared. Much of the actual wording is Don Felix's. I have transcribed several particularly interesting taped sessions. These provide a flavor (weak, without the dramatic voice-tones and gestures) of Don Felix's exquisite narrative style. I can only wish I were able to match the skill of such brilliant translators of Maya oral literature as Allen Burns (1983), Paul Sullivan (1989), or the Tedlocks (Tedlock 1993).

Obviously, the references to the scholarly literature are all my doing, and I take full responsibility for the inevitable errors, omissions, and inadequacies of representation that creep through in spite of my best efforts. Similarly, I must take full responsibility for the final writeup, complete with the inevitable errors, shortcomings, and inadequacies that must beset any endeavor that seeks to capture a living language on a dead page.

I have, however, kept literary discussion to topics or realms of thought that Don Felix understands and talks about. This does not mean that high theory is absent; Don Felix has his own sophisticated theories of life. He has never heard of Max Weber, yet, staunch Protestant that he is, he understands, lives by, and talks about the ideas that Weber captured in his discussions of the Protestant ethic and of disenchantment. Don Felix often sounds as if he had been reading *The Protestant Ethic and the Spirit of Capitalism* (Weber 1930) all his life. Weber would surely be delighted to see his insights holding true in a world so far from fin-de-siècle Germany.

The theoretical ground of this book is cultural and political ecology (see Anderson 1996 for a full theoretical statement of my views). I differ from Julian Steward (1955) largely in being dubious about large-scale abstractions (such as his "multilineal evolutionism" and his rather reified ideas of culture and the state). I also have found that privileging a material-economic "cultural core" does not work. I am agnostic about privileging any sector of culture. I find economics, politics, religion, language, and other sectors of human endeavor all worthy of attention. All can be causal determinants; so can the natural environment. Which one is the driver of the others is an empirical question, and one I am not ready to solve. I take the classic anthropological position of holism: human action is a single thing and must be understood as such. We can look at it through glasses labeled "politics," "economics," or "ecology," but we are in the position of the blind men studying the elephant: we cannot conclude anything accurate unless we compare notes and try to envision the whole animal.

I stand with Andrew Vayda and Bradley Walters (1999) in urging attention to all factors that impinge on a process or situation. However, I disagree with their rejection of political ecology; politics does seem crucial and is often the nexus of action in an environmental event. Don Felix's penetrating and exceedingly insightful discussions of local events and politics show that he shares a similar view; in fact, his political ecology has greatly influenced mine.

I am more or less closely associated with the recent tradition of and political ecology that is represented by the work of Michael Kearney (1996), Susan Stonich (1993), Betty Faust (1998), Thomas Sheridan (1988), and the *Journal of Political Ecology*. We are concerned with how small local communities (often indigenous ones) negotiate resource management, and with how they are dealing with the rapid expansion of economic and political horizons that is summarized in the terms "transnationalization" and "globalization."

The various investigators who work in the vineyard of political ecology have found that local communities benefit in some ways, suffer in many, and somehow manage to cope. They have developed a political ecology that is aware of politics but holistic; they look at phenomena ranging from biology and geology to local resistance through tradition and verbal art.[5]

There is another, different sort of political ecology: a "victim" literature that turns all local communities and indigenous peoples into mere helpless pebbles beneath a road-grader. (A consequence is that the writers feel they have to take charge of these poor helpless victims and lead them to a better future. Often, the writers get surprisingly rich in the process. The victims rarely do.) That literature does not reflect the complex reality of Maya towns in Quintana Roo, or (I suspect) any other indigenous communities. Resistance, creative coping, bending with the wind, out-migration, developing new types of farming, and many other strategies are well-known and oft-used alternatives to being crushed. Chunhuhub has done very well, so far, from the global economy. It could do much better. It could also crash, but at least it will not go down without a fight. The Maya are fully aware of the problems they face and have so far proved to be able to cope creatively and successfully with most of them.

Determining why indigenous peoples once did as they did, and why and how they now choose what they choose, requires close study of many variables. This introduces my other immediately relevant working theory: practice theory, as defined by Bourdieu (1977, 1990) and others. Practice theory has been tailored to ecological research by Endre Nyerges (1997), and applied to Maya linguistic research by William Hanks (1990; see chapter 5). I find isolated-individual models (such as those of neoclassical economics) and models based on grand abstractions (culturology, structural Marxism) inadequate, both as guides to field work and as tools for analysis. They just don't work. Individual actors are not isolated; academic abstractions do not act. Studying actual practice, on the ground, and understanding it in the terms of the Maya themselves before subjecting it to academic theories seems to me to be absolutely necessary. In particular, individuals interact with each other and with the environment, and they interact on the basis of what they know and believe. Much of their knowledge is traditional—the knowledge described in this book—but much is new and is being learned from television and radio and newspapers as well as from older farmers or religious leaders.

Interaction for resource management is not a dispassionate matter. It is emotional, and it has religious and mythic overtones for the Maya. Dealing with modern political systems also arouses passions. Thus the study of cultural ecology in Chunhuhub cannot be confined to studies of "rational choice" and the like. It must involve emotions and their cultural construction in religious and social systems (Anderson 1996).

Much of this book consists of traditional Maya knowledge, written down and more or less systematized. Of course, the result reflects something of the particular systematizing tendencies of the authors (primarily FMT), but we have done our best to capture widely shared understandings.

This said, theory can return to its quiet niche. The attentive reader aware of recent trends in cultural and political ecology will find most of them addressed in the following pages, but addressed unobtrusively, that they may not break the flow of country talk.

MY LIFE AND TIMES, BY FELIX MEDINA TZUC
(RECORDED, TRANSCRIBED, EDITED, AND TRANSLATED
BY E. N. ANDERSON)

I was born in 1940 [or 1941]. My parents lived in Andres Quintana Roo, near Tizimin, Yucatán; they were countryfolk, farmers. By the time I reached five or six, or seven, I was working in the milpa. I saw that they cultivated and sowed. They planted things such as *macales* [native Yucatecan yams]. In those days, around 1946 and 1947, everything grew well. The macales grew huge. One would fill a basket. In a basket they put one. I saw how it was brought in. I asked what it was; they said it was a macal. They also grew sweet potatoes, bananas, manioc, beans, and lima beans.

When I was ten, I started school. There I learned to read and write; I was in school for two years. At twelve I stopped because my parents had a cart with six mules, which my brother dedicated to carrying maize for the countryfolk. In those days it cost sixty centavos to carry a sack of maize ears [from the field to town]. The cost rose slowly till it reached one peso. So in 1952 or '53 I left school and proceeded to help my brother, as assistant carter, helping him every day. I didn't see my parents changing their work. As soon as I opened my eyes in the morning, I could see them working at what they always did, making milpa. They sowed everything for food.

At fifteen, I was working with them in the milpa—with my brothers and parents—felling forest, chopping brush, learning all that. I learned all they taught me. They began to teach me what the plants were called. I would ask my father, and he would tell me, so I learned all the names of each plant. My father knew them all. Or I would ask my mother. At eighteen, I worked more—I had reached the age of full adult work. So I was born in Yucatán, grew up in Yucatán, did my military service in Yucatán.

When I was twenty, my parents came here. They came alone at first, to see what the place was like, here in Chunhuhub. My father came first. He liked it a lot here. So, in about a month, he came back to seek us out in Yucatán, and we moved here. I was young—a bachelor. I lived in Chunhuhub and liked it very much—I liked the way the people worked, how they lived, their manners, how they treated each other.

My parents began to work in the fields, and I with them, making milpa. So, year after year, we made milpas, and got good harvests. From the 1960s through the 1980s, the harvests were good. The farmers didn't live like rich people, no, but they had a comfortable and tranquil life, because they had everything. If you sowed beans, you got a good harvest of beans. If you sowed limas, you got them. If you sowed maize, you harvested enough. But after that, from around 1988 and especially after 1990, things began to change. [Hurricane Gilbert in 1988 was followed by a long cycle in which droughts have alternated with destructive storms.] You would sow and get nothing. The harvests were lost. The cost of living rose. All that the poor needed went up in price. Everything cost more; 1985 was a particularly bad year for price rises of merchandise.

In those years, we lived in San Juan [a tiny hamlet, now vanished, about ten miles south of Chunhuhub; all its inhabitants moved to Chunhuhub]. We saw the situation was very tough. The harvests were scarce, even though the soil there is very rich. At least it gave something—about half of a good harvest. Around the town, people were getting nothing at all. But we sometimes got up to a good harvest.

I lived there [San Juan] for twenty-five years, with my parents and the rest of the family. I always enjoyed knowing the plants and learning the names of plants and trees. Then, I lived with my mother, and she knew a great deal. My father-in-law also knew much about plants and trees, so I would ask him. Not only did I learn the names, I learned what plant cured or served other purposes. I would learn: Such-and-such is a curing plant, it cures such-and-such disease.

When my parents died, I remained there alone with my wife and children. I have unfortunately lost two sons.

So today things are difficult. There are no jobs and no help from the government. The countryfolk have to struggle to find some way to maintain themselves. How to clothe your children, your wife—it's hard to see how to do that. The countryman lives economically. But, before, it was not like that. The countryfolk lived more happily. All that they sowed, they harvested. Today, no; you sow and get nothing. If there isn't a flood, there's a drought.

Take this year [1995–96]: What happened to the harvest? The hurricane came, hit us, flooded all the milpa, destroyed the harvest. Very little was left. The previous year [1994, a historic drought in Quintana Roo], I made five hectares of milpa. There was much sun, and the harvest was lost. I got nothing, not one grain of maize. All the work was lost. The countryman can only stay there with his arms crossed; there's nothing left to hope for. The countryman's hopes are in the harvest. We have to keep hoping and go on with life.

Now as to my marriage: I married at twenty-one or twenty-two—I don't quite remember. My wife is Doña Elide Uh May. When I was twenty years old I came here and met her here. I liked very much her way of walking, of speaking—her behavior. So we were married. So, right up till now, it's been good, thank God, thirty-three years married to her, for the love of God.

She was born here, right in Chunhuhub. She was born the sixteenth of September, 1946. She was from a family of good people—I liked her parents, her grandparents, her brothers. They were very good to be with, and they accepted me as one of the family.

We were working in San Juan. Suddenly we had a son, our first son. All went well—the boy was healthy. Then, suddenly, in two more years there was another son. The first son was Angel, the second, Gabriel. [Angel is now a policeman in Felipe Carrillo Puerto; Gabriel lives next door to his father and farms with the family.]

My ancestors never saw a doctor. They used herbs only. And they lived better, knowing all kinds of plants. The parents of my father-in-law were particularly knowledgeable. They had knowledge from the really ancient people. The ancients died at 100 or 110 years of age, and even up to 115. My grandparents lived many years.

But now things are harder. . . . When the children were healthy there was no problem. But then they come to get sick. Sometimes, with a few home remedies, the child gets healthy again. But when they are sick, all one's savings go. The father is very loving, very caring; when the child is sick one has to do something, and when two are sick, there's twice as much expense. It can occur that one has nothing and has to ask for loans. Sometimes people say yes, sometimes no. People have to have much confidence in you before they'll loan you money. When my mother was alive, she would loan me a hundred pesos. Sometimes my wife had to go from San Juan as far as Peto. [This is about eighty kilometers, a long and arduous journey in the old days; but only recently have there been competent doctors closer.] There were no doctors nearby. There was a doctor named Don Abelio Tax; a good doctor, the doctor for our children. When they were sick, we would take them to him and he would cure them. Those two had asthma. Totally congested—that congestion is terrible. It's not easy to find medicine for it. We knew some remedies. We would see a lady there in San Juan—Doña Chita, the wife of Don Teodoro. And when the doctor didn't cure them, I know a kind of plant that is good for asthma: *bakeak'* [*Psychotria microdon,* a plant containing alkaloids]. She explained to my wife how to use this plant. For two months, we gave it to them daily.

Then, in a year or so, we had a third child. That complicated the situation. When all three were sick, things were worse. A father worries for his children—he worries a great deal. So, once more, "Ay, mama, lend me a hundred, or lend me two hundred," every time my children were sick. This was Arturo. He died at nine months in San Juan, of a sickness that came instantaneously—no one knew what it was.

His younger brother was Alejandro. After Alejandro came another brother, the one named Efrain who is now in Cancun. Then came another, who is now dead, named Denis. He died at eighteen, on the seventh of November, 1995. He died in a vehicle crash near Felipe Carrillo Puerto. He was a painter. He painted, he drew all that we wanted. It was a real loss. Then there came another, a girl named Daisy. Then another named Angelica. Then another boy, named Isaias. The last born we named Mirla. And with that we completed our family. [Daisy, Angelica, and Isaias are now married. Isaias lives with his parents. Mirla celebrated her *quinceañera* in 2000, moved to Tulum in 2001, and works there; she married in 2002.]

I have three daughters-in-law and seven grandchildren. [Twelve as of 2002, and two new sons-in-law and a new daughter-in-law.] My daughters-in-law are Angelina Gonzalez, the wife of Gabriel; Doris Gongora, wife of Angel; and Clara, the wife of Alejandro, who is in Cancun. The situation here is difficult; there is no work; people have to go to Cancun, or to Chetumal, to look for work.

Of the ten children we have had, how many sicknesses they have suffered! And how much energy it's taken. How many times to the doctor. When my mother was alive, she helped me. I would say, "Mami, I have no money, I need some. My children are sick." She would say, "Yes." And my wife would take the children to Peto.

So we lived for twenty-five years in San Juan. There my children grew up. At first, we lived economically. When the children came, we had animals: pigs, chickens, bees, horses. We had milpa. But little by little we sold

4. Tsiimin *(horse) carrying maize from the field.*

all. The children would get sick, and we'd have to sell two pigs, or three. It all went like that—to pay for treatment. My wife took the children in; my role was to find the money. People loaned it to me, or I had to work in another place. To raise ten children, all that the father saves is gone when they get sick. It's difficult to raise children. But they're so wonderful. But to raise them from little ones takes a lot of work. I would get sick.

Then their mother got sick and had to go to Chetumal. It cost more than two thousand pesos. She almost died. I had to give blood, 1,600 grams of blood—I found that my blood was equal to hers, the same type. With all this, we were ruined.

And then I got sick: aches in my ribs and lungs. I had to go to Mérida with my cousins. I got well, but it cost me. It cost around a thousand pesos—a lot of money. It was from a fall. I fell eight meters, from a tree. There was a pair of scissors that hit me. I didn't feel it at the time. Five years later, when I got a cough from the flu, I felt it. I got a pain and my ribs wouldn't function. It was from a trauma that formed and got blood in it, according to the doctor. It cost a lot to cure, and I almost died. I was very thin; I couldn't eat—what I tried to eat I would throw up. My stomach wouldn't accept it. I improved slowly over four months. Then I could eat tortillas again.

I've fallen several times from trees and lost a lot of blood. Now, I'm fifty-five years old and have many lumps. At this age, it's harder to work. At twenty-five, I could work for two. Sometimes when one works, following one's nature, God helps. But when there are children, sicknesses, and advancing age, it's difficult.

[Fortunately, in 1999 Don Felix was elected justice of the peace, a post affording a good salary. The family is now fairly well off and has built a masonry house.]

Chapter Two

THE MAYA AND THE ANIMAL WORLD

For countless thousands of years, the land that is now Quintana Roo has been the scene of intense interaction between Maya peoples and local animal life. No one knows when the Maya entered the region, but the continuity of culture and agriculture over the last four or five thousand years implies that the Maya may have been here that long. However, it is now generally believed that the Maya peoples radiated at some point from the highlands of Guatemala (Coe 1996). The Yucatec were probably among the first to reach the northern lowlands, where they have been the sole indigenous occupants for a very long time. Yucatec (with its sister languages and dialects such as Itzaj) is quite divergent from other Mayan languages, a fact somewhat concealed by the degree to which words have been borrowed back and forth within the family.

Slash-and-burn agriculture in the Yucatán is at least five thousand years old, and civilization (as defined by the presence of huge agglomerations of people and monumental agriculture), at least two thousand (Coe 1996). This long human presence has had profound effects on the environment. These have been covered elsewhere (Anderson n.d.; Greenberg 1992). In brief summary: Intensive slash-and-burn cultivation, with selective protection of fruit trees and industrially useful trees (such as thatch palmetto), led to the development of a special type of forest. Most of the trees in this forest fall into one of three types. First are the leguminous trees, which, partly because of their ability to fix nitrogen, flourish on worked-out, abandoned soils. Second are the trees that are natural invaders of opened and burned lands. These range from the ever-present *chakaj (Bursera simaruba)* to the valuable mahogany *(Swietenia macrophylla)*. Third are the trees selectively preserved: wild fruits such as sapote *(Achras sapota), k'aniste' (Pouteria campechianum),* and *waya (Talisia olivaeformis),* and useful plants such as thatch palms (*Sabal* spp.).

A mosaic of such forests and regrowing milpas is ideal for many animals. White-tailed Deer, in particular, feed in the milpas, take refuge in the dense thorny woodland that invades abandoned fields, and may wander into the higher forest for safety or to forage for fruit. Pacas (or *tepescuintles, Agouti paca*), essentially frugivorous, increase in proportion to the number of sapotes, k'aniste', and other wild fruit trees, and they too come into the milpas to eat squash and other preferred foods. Even deep-forest animals like White-lipped Peccaries probably benefit from the increase in fruit trees. Many other animals prefer the managed environment (see also Greenberg 1992; Jorgensen 1993; Linares 1976). Certainly, as long as large tracts of mature forest are left, biodiversity increases by increasing the number of habitats and the speed of nutrient turnover. In a mature forest, a great deal of nutrients are locked up in the trees, turning over slowly.

On the other hand, increasing population pressure leads to shortening the milpa cycle. This has well-known negative effects on soil structure and fertility, forest diversity, and the ability of slow-growing trees to recover. It degrades animal habitat. Current agricultural practices are devastating much of the forest of neighboring Yucatán state and affect many parts of Quintana Roo.

This seems to have happened in the Classic Maya period, as indicated, for example, by modern lizard distributions: Relict populations of open-country lizards exist in areas now separated by vast forests, implying that much of the peninsula was once open country, allowing these lizards to spread (Lee 1980, 1990). Mayanist J. Eric Thompson is said to have remarked that we should not imagine the Classic Maya landscape as all open fields with "jaguars confined to game parks." Apparently, that is exactly what we should imagine.

Consider the case of hollow trees. Milpa agriculture at low densities produces a vast supply of them, because many large trees are killed but not burned up by the milpa fires. These hollow trees become incredible resources for wildlife. Woodpeckers, parrots, flycatchers, kinkajous, and countless other animals colonize the holes. Particularly important to the Maya are the many species of wild bees that colonize standing or fallen hollow trees and produce honey that was once a vital subsistence resource.

Too-frequent clearing and burning eliminates the hollow trees. Being already dead and often rotting, they are burned by subsequent milpa fires. The young forest, too, is entirely consumed, producing no new hollow trees. Thus, as FMT has noted during his life, a catastrophic reduction has occurred in the populations of wild bees and other important hole-nesters. Woodpeckers can dig their own holes, but kinkajous, owls, parrots (who can excavate dead rotting wood but not fresh wood), and other creatures must go without homes.

Too-frequent cutting and burning also leads to deaths of the wild fruit trees, in spite of efforts to preserve them. They need time to recover from fire scars. Young, thin-barked trees, in particular, seem to be suffering from frequent milpa cutting.

Quintana Roo's soils are more fertile than those of the stereotypic rain forest, but they are thin and fragile. Exposed to sun and rain, they erode quickly, or, in areas of alluviation and sedimentation, they degrade as clay washes in and as organic materials break down into acidic muck. Sizable tracts of extremely fertile and quite deep soil build up along the base of the chain of hills that runs through Chunhuhub and neighboring ejidos. However, the general run of soils in the area degrades after too-frequent cultivation. The nutrient situation thus becomes steadily poorer for wildlife.

The above description raises the question of how frequent is "too frequent." The best tracts can be cropped continuously or fallowed for a very few years so that trees can crowd out the weedy grass. The average tract on hilly land (with shallow but fertile soil, and many leguminous trees) can recover in ten to fifteen years to some sort of cultivable level; by this time the forest will be around ten meters high. In another twenty-five years, the forest is substantial, with trees up to twenty meters high and a meter thick, and is ideal for wildlife. On level tracts, soil is often much worse, and the forest may require forty years for recovery and two hundred years to reach a highly productive stage. Two adjoining milpas may differ very sharply; if one is on fertile alluvial soil, and the one next to it on low-lying acidic clay, the one may take five years and its neighbor fifty years to regenerate enough to be recropped. Traditional Maya are exquisitely attuned to judge soil quality by its appearance and by the vegetation that grows on it.

The ideal mix for maintaining biodiversity would probably involve large, unbroken tracts of mature forest (for brocket deer, White-lipped Peccary, and other forest-dependent game species, as well as for many trees), alternating with smallish tracts of land cut for milpa on long rotation cycles. The Maya traditionally cut one to four hectares for a milpa and keep their milpas as widely separated as is reasonable. This is the condition that held in Quintana Roo until the last generation, when population growth and government schemes led to the rapid cutting of vast areas.

Even now, however, the carrying capacity of the Quintana Roo forests for animal life is truly amazing. Nongame species, including most of the birds, exist at high population densities. The Chunhuhub area, for instance, has over 260 species of birds, many of them exceedingly abundant. However, cutting of forest, spread of nonnative grassland (which supports few native animals), and spread of young and relatively unproductive woodland (often deficient in fruit trees) is reducing avian numbers and diversity.

Maya uses of animals are many and various. In what follows, we present some overview of the pattern of use. (We also provide accounts of uses of animals under the species descriptions in appendix I.) Maya maintain large numbers of domesticated animals and also draw on a wide variety of wild ones. The ordinary Maya household maintains several species of small livestock. Drawing on the forest is becoming less frequent as hunting becomes unprofitable, but it is still rather important for many families. (More detail on domestic animals is provided under the specific animal names in appendix I.)

The typical Maya rural family maintains its permanent home in a town or village. This home is situated within a *solar* or *jardín familiar* (both being Spanish terms for "household garden"). This is an enclosure, usually surrounded by a low wall of dry-laid stones, and covering several *mecates*. (A mecate is twenty-by-twenty meters; the word is derived from a Nahuatl word for a measuring cord. The Maya equivalent, *k'aan*, which has the same meaning, is now rarely used.) Household gardens in Chunhuhub range from two or three mecates to a hectare or more in size.

By far the commonest animal kept in such compounds is the domestic fowl. Chickens have proved extremely tough under rural Maya conditions, enduring heat, disease, and animal predators. Moreover, chickens are always available when a small feast is desired. One can kill a chicken without any great effort or any great loss to the household economy. Other

5. *Typical Chunhuhub garden, with gardener in traditional Maya dress.*

poultry do less well. Ducks flourish where there is enough water or moisture. The Muscovy Duck is preferred. Wild Muscovies are found, rarely, in swampy lakes of Quintana Roo, but the domesticated form spread from South America, apparently in pre-Columbian times. It may have hybridized with local wild birds. The Mallard Duck (domesticated in the Old World and brought by the Spanish) is rare. It usually enters the picture in dilution, so to speak—hybridized with the Muscovy. (Barnyard hybrids of these species are common but do not occur in the wild, at least not locally.) Very few families keep European domestic geese, another Spanish introduction. They are kept more as a curiosity than for utility.

The other native dooryard bird is the turkey—not the native Ocellated Turkey of Yucatán (which, contrary to some claims, has never been domesticated), but the Mexican Highland Turkey, which is the source of all domesticated turkeys. These birds, adapted to dry highland conditions, do not thrive in the Yucatán. They are very sensitive to diseases, especially Newcastle Disease, a recent introduction. Turkeys seem to have been declining over the centuries as chickens waxed commoner, but Newcastle Disease has tremendously accelerated the process. Fewer and fewer families are keeping turkeys. Formerly necessary for Maya rituals, turkeys have been almost totally supplanted in that role by chickens.

Among mammals, the pig and dog take pride of place. Both swarm in the village, wandering free among the lanes. The streets of Chunhuhub abound in potholes, and these are used as wallows by the pigs. A committee on health and sanitation was formed in 1991 and inveighed solemnly against the hordes of free-ranging pigs. No change was noted. The villagers knew that the pigs eat the garbage and weeds along the roads, and are, in fact, the main sanitation facility of Chunhuhub, as of other villages and towns of the area.

Individual families differ greatly in their desire to keep pigs. Most have none. Others have a few. Some raise large numbers, supplying the town market. However, the main supply of pigs for the local sellers of *cochinita pibil* (pig baked in an earth oven) is the local Cebeta (technical school). It maintains a modern, sophisticated, and well-run pig-farming operation as part of its agriculture training program.

A few families in the village keep sheep. One man, a simple, gentle soul, is primarily a shepherd, herding his little flock through the grassier parts of the town fringe. The sheep of Quintana Roo are of a rather mixed origin but overwhelmingly of a brown, hairy appearance. They are raised only for meat; wool sheep would not do well in the climate, and sheep milking is not a local practice. They appear to be a mix of ancient Spanish and North African strains. The Maya, and indeed most Yucatecans, do not normally eat lamb; the market is an urban one, primarily people of either Lebanese Arab or central Mexican origin. However, sheep eating is spreading, now that the animals are there to eat. Goats are very rarely kept. Jaguars are still common enough to make sheep and goat keeping a chancy occupation in remote areas.

Large livestock are primarily cattle. There are some half dozen sizable cattle ranches, none with more than a few dozen head. Several families keep one or a few cows. Cattle ranching does not pay well. A huge effort is required to convert the forest to pasture. Trees constantly reinvade. The extremely dry spring season is inimical to grasses. Nor are cattle useful or easy to feed in the household garden. Cattle pay better in the natural savannahs south of Chunhuhub, around Vallehermosa; here, a thriving ranch economy exists, inspired to some extent by migrants from central Mexico. Even there, much of the forage is coarse saw-edged grass.

Horses, mules, and donkeys were once vital to the local economy, but they have been replaced by bicycles, and increasingly by trucks, buses, and autos. Chunhuhub has very few horses, a burro or two, and no mules. A few horses still work, carrying maize in from the fields or firewood from the forest. Local ranches sometimes keep horses for riding. In the Vallehermosa area, horses are standard working animals, and Maya cowboys ride with the aplomb and skill of their famous north Mexican counterparts.

Collecting feed and fodder for animals is a serious and important activity. People must be able to identify the best feeds and the alternatives for times when the best are not available. Horses, in particular, face problems in the Yucatán, where the little grass that grows is tough and saw-edged. They subsist almost entirely on leaves of *ramón* (*Brosimum alicastrum;* the Spanish name literally means "horse-forage").

An entire book could be written about animal forages in Mayaland—and has, in fact, been written: the superb and richly detailed thesis of Luz Elena Acosta Bustillos (1995), dealing with Xocen (a community described by Terán and Rasmussen 1994, and studied also by Bruce Love and others). In Chunhuhub, animals live mostly on weeds and human leavings. Dogs live on stale tortillas and other scraps. Pigs eat almost anything: cull fruit, roadside weeds, and garbage. Sheep browse the roadsides.

Pet keeping is almost universal. Maya love animals—a fact remarked on by almost all visitors to the Yucatán. Every family has its dog, or, more often, dogs. These are mixed in origin and have been subjected to merciless natural selection in an environment high in disease and low in available food. They are small, slender, delicate-looking animals but incredibly tough and tenacious of life, whether the challenge is mange, parvovirus, or an enraged peccary. Intelligent and easily trained, they make excellent hunting and watch dogs. Cats are rare. Chunhuhub has an astonishingly low rodent population, giving cats little useful work and nothing much to eat.

Wild animals of every sort are coveted and loved. Pets observed in the town include pigeons, doves, parrots, parakeets, a Great Curassow, chachalacas, cardinals, buntings, sparrows, monkeys, squirrels, deer, peccaries, coatis, pacas, and (domestic) guinea pigs. In towns nearby, we have seen pet lizards and even crocodiles. In the past, keeping large animals such as deer and peccaries was considerably commoner than it is today. After observing the depletion of game throughout the area, we began to encourage owners of such animals to breed them, and we encountered some enthusiastic responses; however, attempts usually failed because of lack of proper facilities. In other parts of the Yucatán, pet keeping is common enough to be a serious drain on the populations of some species, especially parrots and monkeys.

Animals are normally treated with tenderness and care, but families differ considerably in this regard. It must be remembered that life is terribly hard for humans, let alone animals, in rural Quintana Roo. People who must drive themselves mercilessly do not always have the opportunity (physical or psychological) to spare their animals. Dogs, for instance, are almost never gratuitously abused but are rarely indulged either. They are left to shift for themselves. Sick or injured animals have little hope of professional care, since veterinary services are hard to come by and exceedingly expensive (in Maya terms). Home care is often provided, however. FMT and his family have experimented considerably with first aid, ranging from care of wounds to use of laundry soaps and herbal remedies in attempts to control mange. Through this they have developed a stock of effective remedies that cost nothing.

As in the rural United States, many an animal that was a pet in its youth is slaughtered for food when it matures and becomes unfriendly. Most families faced with such a situation will sell the animals rather than killing them themselves. Often, especially with deer (which often turn genuinely dangerous and uncontrollable on maturity), some effort is made to find a buyer with adequate facilities to keep the adult animal alive.

The gentleness toward animals is striking. We observed the careful protection of a nest of baby rabbits, even though it was in a young maize field. (Rabbits love to eat young maize plants.) We could match this account with dozens of similar ones.

Urbanized communities in Quintana Roo sometimes provide a sharp contrast. We have visited villages in the Cancun orbit, and elsewhere, in which boys thoughtlessly kill harmless birds with slingshots, abuse dogs for amusement, and pull lizards apart just to pass the time. Such sadism is very rare in the Zona Maya. Tendencies in such directions are stopped by more responsible children or adults. Unfortunately, increasing stress on fam-

6. T'uul *(rabbits): This is the rabbit nest that was carefully covered again and left.*

ily and community ties, and increasing encroachment by urban society, provides both the models for cruelty and the stresses that tend to call it up.

However, the traditional attitudes mesh with more modern urban values enjoining kindness and protection for animals. These latter values have been actively propagated by local educators, such as Arturo Bayona and Adriana de Castro of the Econciencia workshop in Felipe Carrillo Puerto. Thus, urban influence is by no means an unmixed curse for the animals of Chunhuhub. In particular, we note a rapid change among teachers. Older teachers (mercifully, most now retired or near retirement) often modeled older urban values that permitted unregulated and lawless hunting, indiscriminate pet keeping without proper care, and callousness in general. Younger teachers today are aware of conservationist and ecological values.

In short, the Maya house compound may have very few animals—dogs and a cat or other pet—or it may be a virtual zoo, with cattle, pigs, dogs, and other domestic creatures as well as a wide assortment of wild animals kept as pets. People may treat their animals with uncaring neglect, but more often they treat them with nurturing affection.

Animals are chiefly of value as food. Meat is greatly liked and highly valued. Pork and chicken are the common meats. One or two cattle are slaughtered every weekend in Chunhuhub, and beef is then available; sometimes cattle are slaughtered at other times, for large festivals. Turkeys are rarely eaten, sheep never. The Maya are relatively narrow in their dietary tastes, avoiding sheep (though this is changing), horses, donkeys, most reptiles, most insects, and many other foods often eaten in other parts of indigenous Mexico.

Pork is extremely popular. All parts of the pig are eaten. In purchasing cochinita pibil, the diner specifies how much muscle meat, liver, brain, and so forth is to go into the mix. One cook even catches the blood and makes it into blood sausage, using the intestines. People are not usually so thorough in consuming other species.

Typical dishes stretch meat by cooking it with a good quantity of beans (as in *frijoles con puerco,* beans with pork) or mixed vegetables (*puchero, caldo, cocido,* and other mixed vegetable and meat stews). If meat is eaten simply boiled *(ts'anchak),* it is cut small and boiled in considerable water, and the meat eaten with the broth. The meat is further stretched by being eaten with tortillas. Eggs are popular and are usually scrambled. Sizable pieces of grilled meat are luxury items. Cochinita pibil is one way that large pieces of meat are eaten, but they are also eaten as tacos, the meat being folded in a tortilla.

A typical meal consists of a large number of the small Maya tortillas—ten per meal is the standard ration for a farm worker—with beans, vegetables, and a bit of meat or eggs. The ordinary rural worker of Chunhuhub derives about 75 percent of his or her calories from maize. This is the same percentage as one finds attested by carbon ratios in ancient bones (cf. White 1999), and, later, reported by Benedict and Steggerda (1936) from Chan Kom and by Peraza Lopez (1986) from Ichmul (near Chunhuhub). More well-to-do or urbanized Maya of Chunhuhub consume more white bread and sugary sodas, and (if adult and male) beer, but they usually still derive at least 50 percent of their calories from maize. The typical meal is eaten around the hearth *(k'oben)* with the fingers. A small piece of tortilla is torn off, held in a spoon shape, and used to pick up beans or stew.

The result of all this is that, although meat is generally available and part of the usual diet of all but the poorer families, four ounces of meat per day is a fairly liberal ration by Chunhuhub standards. Many people get no more than an ounce. At festivals, or after a butchering or a successful hunt, people get significantly more. Still, except for the relatively well-to-do citizens, the main sources of protein are maize and beans. Animal foods contribute vitamins and minerals, but sometimes not enough; anemia is common among women, and so nearly universal among pregnant women that the town clinic routinely prescribes and provides iron pills for them.

Another animal food, honey, has declined in importance over the years, for reasons that will appear in the following chapter. Other uses of animals are few. Hides are no longer routinely prepared, though they may be sold. Animals are no longer used for work or traction, except for a few horses used as beasts of burden on occasion.

Wild animals, like tame ones, are most useful as food. Fishing is practiced where there are lakes, as at Rancho el Corozo, where the lake produces *bocones* (introduced *Tilapia*). Hunting deserves a chapter of its own (see chapter 4). Other uses exist. Some animals, notably hummingbirds and nightjars, are used in magic. Some animals are omens: calls of owls and nightjars often portend evil (as in cultures around the world). Some animals have calendric functions: the loud spring song of the *juiiro* (a bird, focally the Bright-rumped Attila) reminds the cultivator to clear and plant the fields.

Also important is the aesthetic function. Maya countryfolk take enormous delight in just seeing animals. The beauty of birds and the delightful songs of some of them are greatly appreciated. Most Maya woodsmen and woodswomen feel a certain family feeling about the animals of the forest—something like the feeling they have toward pets. It is satisfying and enjoyable simply to see agoutis, squirrels, or spiders going about their appointed rounds. FMT has frequently expressed wonder and delight at the incredibly complex and intelligent-seeming behavior of the leafcutter ants that are so common in the American tropics. The strange appearance of the praying mantis often stimulates comment; the animal is known as "giver of strange dreams" *(ts'awayek'* or *ts'awayak').* The *weech* (armadillo) is a never-failing source of amusement.[1]

Animals serve as subjects of widely known folktales, moral and otherwise. (See, for example, under *sakpakal* in appendix I; see also Andrade and Maas Colli 1990–1991; Bowes 1964; Terán and Rasmussen 1992; Maas

Colli 1993; Pacheco Cruz 1958; Redfield and Villa Rojas 1934; de Rosado 1992 [1946]). It should be noted that many of the tales in the Bowes, Maas Colli, and Pacheco Cruz volumes are "fakelore," the productions of romantic Mérida litterateurs. Many of these reek of patronizing racism. It is not always easy to separate genuine but heavily rewritten folktales from purely literary creations in these works. At the other end of the spectrum, the Dzib collection (Terán and Rasmussen 1992)—bilingual in Maya and Spanish—is particularly commendable for the extreme care and accuracy of the writers and editors and the fidelity to traditional Maya themes and storytelling styles. Ironically, and tragically, it is unavailable today.

On the other hand, there are many animals viewed with highly negative feelings. By far the most hated and feared are poisonous snakes. Of these, the most dangerous are the fer-de-lances (*Bothrops* spp.). These are uncommon but widely found and prefer to lurk in the dense grass and weeds of regrowing milpas. Individuals are most apt to be bitten when clearing such areas. Fer-de-lances are most active in the evening, when people are returning from work in the fields. Tired and unable to see well, people step on them and are bitten. Today, flashlights have provided a welcome relief. One of FMT's main campaign planks, when he ran for mayor of Chunhuhub, was a promise to get streetlights to the fringes of the town so that people would be in less danger from snakes. Fer-de-lances move and strike extremely rapidly and pack a large amount of poison. They have caused several deaths in the area. Naturally, they are killed on sight and have become progressively rarer.

Tropical Rattlesnakes *(Crotalus durissus)* seem very rare in the area, but coral snakes (*Micrurus* spp.) are not uncommon. They are primarily burrowers, coming out in the evening to lie on warm roads. Though highly venomous, they are a minor problem because of their inoffensive nature and the difficulty they have in biting with their small mouths and weak teeth. Coral snakes, however, are greatly feared because several larger and more aggressive, but perfectly harmless, snakes have evolved a coloration that mimics the coral snake. These are lumped with coral snakes, and only veteran woodspeople know which snakes are nonvenomous imitators.

Snake stories have been noted elsewhere; like other rural people, the Maya have countless folktales and tall stories about serpents. Snakes sting with their tails, give electric shocks, fly, take human appearance to delude people, and so on. In Chunhuhub, some snakes—at least the *chayikaan*—can become a *xtabay,* a demon woman. (In Belize, a green snake is equated with the xtabay; this snake is also a Lord of the Forest and a trickster; see Williams 1994, 16.) Other animals qualify as pests rather than serious dangers. The forest is full of wasps, bees, scorpions, horseflies, mosquitoes, and other pests. It is proverbial in the Yucatán that "all the trees have thorns and all the animals bite or sting."

Serious crop pests are surprisingly few. The worst are raccoons and coatis, which can devastate a field of maize. If they become a major problem, they are shot. Deer, peccaries, and other large animals are now too rare to be damaging. Parrots and parakeets are probably the worst avian pests, but chachalacas, pigeons, grackles, and even woodpeckers can present problems. (The woodpeckers drill into the ripening maize ears to get at the seeds.) These pests are controlled with slingshots.

Many insect pests attack fruit, vegetables, and field crops. Crickets, beetles, fruit flies, and other typical pests are minor problems. Leafcutter ants (*Atta* spp.) are more serious: A large colony will defoliate and kill citrus trees in its foraging range. Virtually nothing could be done about these animals in traditional times. Today, the nest is drenched in gasoline and set afire, or, in desperate cases, dynamited. Dynamiting a nest is so dangerous and expensive that it is not taken seriously as a control measure; it seems more a matter of sheer anger and revenge.

Far more serious are the bruchid weevils that infest stored grain and beans. They do enormous damage. Local varieties of maize have hard, resistant kernels and are not usually destroyed unless they are soaked by rain or flood (as they were in the hurricane of 1995). Often, powdered limestone is mixed thoroughly with stored corn ears; it effectively discourages the bruchids. At worst, burning tobacco—or, today, insecticidal fumigants—can be used to fumigate the stored grain, but this is seen as dangerous to the human consumers.

Last among unwelcome animals are the animals of ill omen: owls and nightjars. The shriek of the Barn Owl is a particularly bad sign. Bats seem not to be very significant, but large opossums that make a grumbling noise are often thought to be evil spirits in the guise of opossums—the infamous *bok'ol ooch* (see under *ooch* in appendix I)—and the small mouse opossums are also sometimes regarded as evil. This concept is related to the more general ones of disembodied bad airs, such as *tus ik'* (stagnant, foul air in caves) and *k'ak'as ik'* (or *k'as ik'*, "bad winds," i.e., evil spirits). The bok'ol ooch is often regarded as a bad wind rather than an animal.

Nightjars can be used in magic; the dried head of a nightjar, powdered, can be sprinkled on the head of someone desired as a mate, as a form of love magic. Whole powdered hummingbirds are more valued for this purpose, or a boy may carry a whole dried hummingbird in his pocket to make him lucky in love (this is said to be a central Mexican custom, imported recently). Hummingbirds are also used in good luck charms and apotropaic powders for dusting one's own body. Other, minor magical uses of animals are found under the relevant animal entries in appendix I.

So, for the Maya of the forest fringe, life is with animals. The animals are not mere furniture. They are regarded with warm positive or negative emotion.

There are still, indeed, many traditional Maya for whom the animals are part of the religious cosmos. Taboos against taking too much game, and fears of owls, nightjars, and bok'ol ooch have degenerated into mere superstitions among the young, but among many older people, they are part of a general view in which animals are part of society. Animals are persons, albeit nonhuman persons. They are protected by their rulers, the supernatural *Yuntsiloob* or *Yumilk'aax* (Lords of the Forest; see chapter 4). Humans must deal through ritual channels with these powerful beings. Protective and familial emotions toward useful animals, and fearful emotions toward supernaturally dangerous ones, are part of a whole emotional system that is at once evocative of and evoked by religion. This complex of ideas has been described more thoroughly by Redfield and Villa Rojas (1934) and Terán and Rasmussen (1994), writing from towns where the old ways persisted. We need only stress the highly emotional quality of the bond.

Animal parts also have their ritual and magical uses. The jawbone of a deer or peccary, or by extension a pig, hung in a calabash tree makes the calabash bear better. One family in Chunhuhub regularly does this; both in 1991 and in 1996 there were jawbones hanging from their calabash tree. Quite possibly, this practice has some connection with the myth of the hero twins, in which the intertransformation of human heads and calabashes figures importantly. (See the Popol Vuh; esp. pp. 145–47 of Tedlock's 1985 translation, though there the commodity in question is translated as a "squash.") Bezoars are used in hunting, as will be discussed in chapter 4.

The widespread Native American belief in animal transformations is alive and well in Quintana Roo. Most emotionally and socially salient are *way* (were-animals). These are human witches, male or female, who transform themselves into goats, cats, dogs, cattle, burros, and other creatures. They are termed according to their transformation animal, usually using its Spanish name: *waychivo, waytoro,* and so forth. Surprisingly, though this belief is pre-Columbian, most of the animals of transformation are Spanish introductions. *Way kot*—eagle witches—are reported from Chan Kom (Re Cruz 1996) and elsewhere but seem rare in Quintana Roo.

There are also *wayp'op',* giant werebats (often equated with the eagle witches). There was a white dog that wandered through Chunhuhub several years ago, causing local dogs to howl; it was suspected of being a *waypeek'* (weredog). To our experience, wild animals do not normally become *way.* Supernatural deer and other game animals occur, but these are associated with the Lords of the Forest and are not witches. In the context of *way,* there was, briefly, a ready belief in the *chupacabras,* "sucker of goats"—the dreadful goat-draining giant vampire of Mexican legend. However, as our friend Don Claudio Canul said, *"aquí puros chupacaguamas hay."* ("Here it is just suckers of sea turtles." *Caguama,* lit. "sea turtle," is Mexican slang for a one-liter bottle of beer.)

Animals also transform into each other. The Maya know, from everyday experience, that certain worms turn into butterflies. They are thus willing to credit the story that some snakes turn into deer in fall. They may turn back into snakes when winter or spring comes. Other snakes eventually go to the sea and become fish. FMT once shot a squirrel, went where it was, and found only a snake; he believes that the squirrel actually turned into the snake, though the possibility that the snake came up and ate the dying squirrel remains open. An old hunter related that he shot a deer, tracked it into an armadillo's hole, and found only the deer's liver. This we think was purely a tall story, a form of verbal art in which Maya hunters excel.

The subject of tall stories leads us naturally to snake stories. Throughout the world, snakes are the subjects of exaggeration and worse. In Quintana Roo, stories range from the exaggerated but widely believed to the deliberately silly. In the former category are flying snakes (based apparently on the ability of several snakes to crawl very rapidly through the trees). Also generally believed is the leaping ability of the *wolpoch'* (or *woolpooch'*, *Agkistrodon bilineatus*). The latter, a fat, thick snake known in Spanish and English as a cantil, is known locally only from descriptions; it does not occur in Chunhuhub. It strikes so vigorously that it appears to throw itself clear of the ground, and it is widely believed actually to do so.

Distinctly less likely to be real is the *picasombra* (shadow-biter). This snake bites one's shadow, following which one declines and eventually dies. Some traditional healers can cure the bite. No one seems to see the picasombra, and for most people, it is a joke rather than a serious concern.

Definitely in the tall story category are snakes that give electric shocks with their tails. At one session, in a notably unsuccessful attempt to delude some visiting biology students from the University of Yucatán, a friend of ours explained: "Around here, if you have a sore back, you find a boa constrictor and wrap him around you and get him to squeeze." The story progressed no further due to the collapse of all present into helpless laughter. Such verbal artistry is a fine art in Maya towns. The ever-valuable work of Maya hunter Eleuterio Llanes Pasos (1993) recounts many tall tales as well as many believable ones.

Today, at least, there is no Yucatec equivalent to the highland Maya belief that everyone has an animal spirit companion, the *ch'ulel* (or *chanul*), which resides in a corral inside a local sacred mountain (Gossen 1994, 1996—Gossen's animal doppelganger was identified as a coyote; Hunn 1977; Vogt 1969). There is evidence, however, that such beliefs did once exist. For one thing, the Lacandon Maya, who speak a language very close to Yucatec, have such a concept. The animal familiar is called *onen*, a word not attested in standard Yucatec, but probably related to *onel* (kinship, fatherhood), because the onen is patrilineally inherited and has become something of a clan marker or totem (see Litzinger and Bruce n.d.). For another, the Yucatec cognate of chanul, *kanul*, is a very common surname (Canul), and one older source glossed the plural *kanulo'ob* as "protector spirits" (Barrera Vásquez 1980, 299). Historian Robert Patch has told ENA of finding a note in an eighteenth-century pastoral visit document to the effect that the Maya had a practice of examining afterbirths to determine what was the animal companion of the newborn baby. More research into such documents is needed.

The word *way* seems to have once referred to such a concept (Houston and Stuart 1989).[2] In Proto-Maya, **way* apparently meant "sleep," and *wayak'* (or *wayek'*) means "dream" in Yucatec today—specifically, a strange or uncanny dream (cf. Gossen 1996). In this sense it occurs in the fascinating and significant name of the praying mantis, noted above. The word *way* occurred in Classic Maya. A glyph showing a lordly face partly covered with jaguar skin has been read as *way* (Houston and Stuart 1989). Many figures associated with this glyph are known. Grube and Nahm (1994) provide a comprehensive list of these. Most of them are jaguars or jaguar-beings of some sort, usually labeled with a glyph read *hix,* sometimes with *baalam.* (Also *balam;* in one case, the balam may refer to a puma; p. 692.) A deer snake *(chihil chan)* is noted (p. 693), as well as various deer. Other *way* include monkeys *(maax* and *ba'ats),* dogs *(ok,* now a Chol Maya word for "dog"), Collared Peccaries *(chitam,* the usual cognate of Yucatec *kitam* in neighboring Mayan languages, including Chol), tapirs, coatis, gopher rats (or gopher-and-rats), Gray Foxes, bats, toads, centipedes, snakes, turkeys, owls, and even leafcutter ants. In colonial times, the *way* belief was distorted by Spanish folk beliefs about witches *(brujos/brujas),* and *way* became largely European animals.

7. Ba'ats *(Quintana Roo spider monkey), Chetumal Zoo. (Photograph by Tracy Franklin)*

Classic Maya art is rich in portrayals of masks and headdresses that must represent some spiritual link between wearer and animal. In addition to the humor noted (note 1 for this chapter), there are representations of Maya nobles associated with hawks, owls, cormorants, vultures, and so forth. In the Palenque Museum, ENA has examined four huge vases that show a man's face topped by a snake head, above which is a limpkin (a wading bird whose loud cries announce rain). Presumably, these were powerful spirit guardians. (Compare the bat dance of Guerrero, which involves a mask with a bat above a man's face.) The codices are rich in pictures of deer, peccaries, dogs, opossums, jaguars, snakes, and birds.

In short, the Maya use animals for a wide range of reasons. As will appear in later chapters, they make use of a large range of animals and know a great deal about an even larger range. It seems reasonable that their traditional cosmology involves a strong and emotionally warm interaction with the nonhuman animal world.

Chapter Three

BEEKEEPING

Beekeeping is an ancient Maya tradition, culturally and religiously important (de Jong 1999). Honey of the native stingless bee was a major medical and religious resource until recently, and it still is in some quarters (Terán and Rasmussen 1994). The ritual drink *baalche'*, for example, was made with stingless-bee honey. Bees were venerated; the Bee God (or Descending God) was an extremely important figure—prominent in the Postclassic period art of the site of Tulum, for example.

This ancient and religiously represented association is much more than an economic one. Bees are still regarded with reverence. They are treated with care and kindness. They are, in fact, treated very much like pets—but pets that deserve great respect. Their harmonious social life and diligent toil are the subjects of admiring commentary. Caring and considerate treatment of bees is regularly observed—and, by FMT, regularly practiced.

Yucatán is a leading honey-exporting area in the world. Only China exports more honey than Mexico, and China has a huge land mass to produce it; Mexico's honey comes mostly from the Yucatán. This great productivity is partly a function of the large areas of regrowing fields and second-growth forests—rich in flowers. However, the real reason for the Yucatán's honey productivity is the special relationship of the Maya with the world of bees. It is a case in which religious, spiritual, medical, and affective reasons have driven the economy. Bees are kept and produced for more than narrowly economic reasons.

To be sure, honey has a ready sale at a decent price. However, the hard work, inconvenience, and risk of beekeeping—especially now, with Africanized bees so common—deter anyone not emotionally involved. Most of the younger generation of rural people do not keep bees. Beekeepers, old or young, are those who are really fond of the animals.

Moreover, bees, like other animals, are surprisingly receptive to kind and considerate care. It is hard to know whether bees appreciate human affect, but they most certainly do respond to the extra care and attention that goes with it. At first, ENA doubted that bees understand and respond to human emotions; FMT, and field experience in Chunhuhub, has convinced him otherwise.

Weaver and Weaver, veteran beekeepers who visited Yucatán, tell the following story: "Once we took a visitor to see an apiary of *colecab [Melipona]*; the visitor caught one of the bees at a hive entrance, examined it roughly, and threw it to the ground. One of us let the struggling bee crawl on to his finger, brushed the sand from it, and when it had recovered, let it crawl into its hive. The beekeeper had sat impassively through the entire episode, but then looked at us appreciatively, and said quietly: 'You understand'" (Weaver and Weaver 1980, 17). So would any Chunhuhub beekeeper.

Bees require extreme cleanliness, for example, and cannot tolerate the casual attitude toward environmental sanitation that characterizes much Maya animal rearing. (These points are discussed by Weaver and Weaver 1980; as professional beekeepers, the Weavers were most impressed by this aspect of Maya apiculture.)

Thus, we have a mainstay of the Yucatán economy depending on ancient Maya religious and spiritual values rather than on modern economic enterprise. Indeed, in spite of some genuinely excellent but underfunded government projects, modern economic enterprise is singularly absent from the honey industry—still organized in a bottom-up, rural way, with a conspicuous absence of modern marketing, advertising, product development, and market research—to the enormous loss of the Mexican economy.

Beekeeping is important to many individuals, including FMT. (We acknowledge the help of Andres Sosa and Mariano Yam for what follows.) Many individuals keep a few hives of honeybees *(Apis mellifera)*. A few have huge holdings. Chunhuhub's most industrious apiculturist, Don Antonio Azueta, had hundreds of hives before most of them were destroyed by Hurricane Roxanne in 1995; he had built back up to 180 by the middle of the following year. Old Gilberto Chan used to have about 900 hives, back in the old days, but his descendants are less enamored of the work, though his son David still had 45 in 1996. More typical is an apiary of fewer than 10 hives. People opportunistically take swarms of wild bees when they appear—as FMT did, for example, during our field work in 1996. This balances out the tendency of colonies to die out from adverse conditions.

There were, in 1996, about twelve serious apiculturists in Chunhuhub—people with thirty or more hives. By 2001 there were even fewer. However, they did well from it. Many more had a few hives incidentally to their other activities. Accumulating capital to buy hive boxes is a problem, especially for the smallholders who might be greatly benefited by beekeeping.

One hive typically has nine combs in it and gives ten kilograms of honey per harvest. Harvests come every two weeks in full flowering season. Hives are piled on top of each other, two or sometimes three deep. Two hives in a stack will give only thirteen combs, since one hive is used primarily to rear young. A stack of three produces eighteen to twenty combs.

Honey is collected in giant drums (Sp. *tambor*) that hold three hundred kilograms. These are trucked to one of Chunhuhub's half-dozen honey buyers. The price they paid varied in 1996 from 8.5 to 13 pesos per kilogram. The usual price varied around 10.5 to 11 pesos. In 1995 the price had sunk as low as 5 pesos. (That was before Roxanne; Roxanne not only destroyed hives, it also encouraged army ants, which love humidity and thus do not usually flourish in dry Chunhuhub. Army ants eat larval bees.) Honey ranges in grade from 6.8 down to 3.5; most Chunhuhub honey is near the top in grade.

There are about six honey buyers in Chunhuhub, ranging from small operators to the huge, successful honey enterprise of the García family (who also own the town sawmill and the large Corozo ranch). Honey buying is a simple matter: one buys the honey at 11 pesos (1996 prices; there has been little change since) and sells it to large urban assemblers at around 12. Profits are small per unit but large in the aggregate because of the huge amount of honey produced in the area. We were unable to obtain figures of the actual totals of local production. Suffice it to say that production was enough to make the honey operations extremely profitable in spite of the low profit margins. There is a large cooperative honey agency in Felipe Carrillo Puerto, but it is too far away for Chunhuhub producers. A hive with bees cost, in 1996, 150 pesos, a swarm 70, the bare box 35. The wooden squares in the boxes, in which the bees make their combs, are 6 pesos each.

Honey season is January through spring. By far the most important single honey plant is *taj* (a common sunflower, *Viguiera deltoides,* of which there are two or three local varieties). This plant paints highway sides and deserted milpas a brilliant gold from January into March. During this time, bees produce vast quantities of rich, polliniferous, runny honey. The flavor is not considered so good tasting as honey from other sources, however. By March, the superior honey from *ts'its'ilche' (Gymnopodium floribundum)* delights beekeepers; this tree produces enormous amounts of flowers, and they give a fine product. *Ya'axnik (Vitex gaumeri,* a quality source) and chakaj *(Bursera simaruba)* are also important at this time, as are plants like *jool (Hampea trilobata).* In May comes the spectacular flowering of ja'abin *(Piscidia piscipula),* the commonest tree in the Yucatán and a fine honey source. This is also the season for *jujuub (Spondias mombin)* and other trees. In June, all flowering dies down, but *muk' (Dalbergia glabra,* a thorny vine that is an excellent honey plant with a long flowering season) and other plants are found. The rainy season—summer—is a dead time, and beekeepers must often put out sugar for their hives. Some now put out vitamin supplements. In fall, flowering begins again on various trees and vines. *Xtabentun (Turbina corymbosa* and similar species of large vines and viny plants) becomes important. Xtabentun honey is superior in flavor and gives its name to Yucatán's traditional anisette liqueur—a product, of colonial origin, that was traditionally sweetened with this honey. Then, through the winter, comes citrus flowering, as well as various composites. Avocado and other domesticated trees and bushes are also important in season.

It is doubtful if European bees could be kept in the Yucatán without Maya agriculture; the bees depend, during much of the year, on the plants of milpa regrowth (especially taj) and on orchard trees. The wax is rarely collected, and royal jelly seems not commercialized in the area (it is important in Yucatán state).

Africanized bees work hard and produce much honey, but we can attest from experience that their reputation for savagery is little, if at all, exaggerated. Non-Africanized European bees, locally miscalled American bees, are sought out and cherished. These dangerous bees invaded the Yucatán in the late 1980s and took over from European bees or hybridized with them. Most of the swarms in the peninsula are now Africanized. Some have remained pure, and these are often sought. They can be told at some distance because the Africanized bees are darker; a European swarm, when spotted in a tree, is quickly taken. Africanized bees are quick to sting, and once one stings a person near a hive, the whole hive attacks. Since a full bee outfit ("space suit") costs six hundred pesos (in 1996), most small beekeepers have been forced out of business, and only large-scale apiarists (and a few extremely careful ones—including FMT) can continue to keep bees. Moreover, areas without remote forests and fields can no longer produce honey, for Africanized bees cannot be raised in areas with much human or animal traffic. In some areas, however, Africanization has proceeded less rapidly. In the nearby village of Presidente Juarez, most of the land is flat, floodable lowland, unsuitable for Africanized bees, who prefer forest on drier, rocky ground; and the beekeepers are careful to rogue out Africanized bees. Hence the European bee still prevails there.

The Africanized bees have also destroyed what was left of the native stingless-bee industry. They are said to drive out these small, frail bees deliberately. At the very least, they outcompete them for nectar, and wild swarms outcompete them for hollow trees. Africanized bees are "very hard workers," as Maya apiculturists put it. They produce a great deal of honey, but they are too dangerous to keep in town, and they are difficult to manage and handle. About 50 percent of the bees in the area are Africanized, with the bigger apiarists being more affected, apparently. Various projects for raising and distributing European queens have been tried, with limited success at best. Good queens sell for up to eight to ten pesos.

Moreover, varroa mites—serious parasites of bees—arrived around 1993–94, necessitating great care and frequent treatment. Fortunately, varroa mites appear to be extremely susceptible to tobacco smoke. Burning a few tobacco leaves at the hive entrance provides adequate control. A disease called *loque europea* or *loque americana* requires sulfate treatment. More traditional pests include ants and the tayra *(Eyra barbara)*, a large weasel that is known as "the scourge of beehives" because of its fondness for robbing them. These do little damage.

Formerly, native stingless bees *(Melipona beecheii)* were kept on a large scale in *jobon* (hollow tree trunk) hives. As of 1991, very few stingless bees were kept in Chunhuhub or its area. By 1996, all stingless bees in the area had died out, in spite of a number of governmental and private initiatives to encourage stingless beekeeping. We note a downward cycle: the less support for traditional beekeeping, the less the governmental agencies (which have exceedingly limited resources) can reasonably involve themselves in programs to save it. A major problem has been the shortening of the milpa cycle, which eliminates the hollow trees inhabited by the wild bees. A long cycle favors the bees, since it kills large numbers of trees and leaves them standing, or fallen and hollowed. Too-frequent fire eliminates these large dead trees without creating new ones (the forest has no time to recover and produce a new crop of large trees). The wild bees nest in the commoner forest trees and depend heavily on *tsalam (Lysiloma bahamensis)*, ts'its'ilche', xtabentun, and *sakpakxiiw (Walteria americana)* for food (Rogel Villanueva Gutierrez, pers. comm.). They also draw on many other local flowers.

Stingless-bee honey brings five to ten times as much money per kilo as European bee honey, but even at this price it is not economical for people to raise stingless bees. There are several reasons for this. They are difficult to keep and do not produce much honey. Overly frequent milpa cutting and burning has eliminated the old hollow trees that the wild populations need. Even in the much more traditional village of Xocen, stingless bees are kept by no more than one or two people, for ritual reasons (Terán and Rasmussen 1994; see also de Jong 1999).

Stingless-bee honey is used to sweeten foods and drinks, as well as for medicine (including medicine for magico-religious purposes) and ritual use. It was, until recently, necessary for making baalche' and other ritual offerings. (European bee honey and even sugar are now used.) The honey has a lower sugar content, or, to put it another way, a higher moisture content than European bee honey. It is generally agreed to be far superior in flavor, a judgment with which we concur.

Medical uses have included treatment of stomach problems; diarrhea (for soothing the stomach); hemorrhoids; parasitoses; cataracts and other eye problems; catarrh and throat inflammation; sores on skin, mouth, or tongue; night sweats *(aak'ab k'iilkab);* and other conditions (Medellín Morales and González Acereto 1991b). "Night sweat" is a Maya nosological entity; in Chunhuhub, descriptions of it apparently refer to febrile crisis from major infectious disease, but perhaps include nocturnal heart attacks and the like as well.

Much detail on traditional stingless beekeeping is provided in the literature (de Jong 1999; Landa 1978 [1566]; Redfield and Villa Rojas 1934; Weaver and Weaver 1980). Landa recorded the use of both domestic and wild stingless bees. The watery honey was cooked down to make it more solid. The wax of wild bees was "smoky"; he did not know why (Landa 1978 [1566]:101). The reason was doubtless that the hives were smoked so that they could be taken.

In 1946 came the first beekeepers' convention of the Yucatán (Martinez López 1946). The document emerging from this convention notes that selected strains of European bee had been introduced throughout the twentieth century (many by G. Gaumer), and that a major export industry was already established; the convocants looked forward confidently (and accurately) to rapid expansion of exports to Europe, because World War II had just ended.

Weaver and Weaver found that European bees had come to the traditional villages of central Yucatán state only in the 1950s. Previously, beekeeping had focused on *Melipona beecheii,* the *kolekaab* or *xunankab*—"lady bee"—of the Maya. Stingless beekeepers set up jobon hives on A-frames under thatch shade. Several ceremonies were practiced in regard to beekeeping; most touching is that dead bees were shrouded in a leaf and buried. More important was the *hanlikab* (food of the honey, or food of the bees), a *loj*-type ceremony to feed the protective spirits of the hives; this ceremony is described in detail. (A loj is a ceremony to ask for success in an endeavor, or to render thanks for blessings conferred.) Enemies of the bees included army ants, honey-robbing bees, and hive-parasitic phorid flies *(nenem).* Anteaters also seem to have occasionally gone after these hives. The Weavers report that bees were loved, credited with intelligence and sensitivity, and treated with tremendous respect. The religious association of bees and honey was still very strong at that time (see also Terán and Rasmussen 1994).

The Sostenibilidad Maya agricultural development project, with which we were involved, focused heavily on stingless bees and accumulated a large knowledge base about them. The project also staged a number of workshops at which stingless-bee apiculturists could get together, organize, and share knowledge. Moving spirits were the brilliant young ethnobiologist Sergio Medellín Morales and the veteran bee expert Jorge González Acereto.

The program was quite successful within its limits, even establishing a non-profit company (Yik'el Kab A.C.), but could not do much to reverse the steady decline.

Since the reports of the Sostenibilidad Maya project are now almost impossible to find, it may be worth reviewing them here. Investigators found that stingless-bee raising, as of the late 1980s and early 1990s, was concentrated in the highly traditional southeastern and central-eastern parts of Yucatán state. Here, some 530 or more producers had at least 5,300 hives, each with 3,000–5,000 or more workers. Some hives were noted in northern Campeche as well as central Quintana Roo. Hives produced only one-quarter to one liter of honey per harvest. Rarely was honey or wax sold; most of it went for personal and community use, usually in religious ceremonies and traditional medicine. The system was in decline. Organization, distribution facilities, credit, and modern facilities were lacking. Knowledge was being lost.

Jorge González Acereto and Victor Cámara González found that modern hives of a special design—small and flat—had some advantages over traditional jobon hives but some drawbacks as well. The jobon, being cheap (or free), appears to be here to stay.

Several wild bees were cropped for honey, with at least some attention paid to conserving or managing the resource:

> Bo'ol, *Nannotrigona testaceicornis*
> Ch'a ch'em, *Trigonisca hypotrigona*
> E'jool, *Cephalotrigona capitata*
> Kan-Tsak, *Scaptotrigona pectoralis*
> Mu'ul-kab, *Trigona fulviventris*
> Niit-kib, *Lestrimelitta limao*
> Ts'ets, *Melipona yucatanica*
> Xnuk, *Partamona cupira* and *Trigona fuscipennis* [apparently depending on local use]

(List from Medellín Morales and Campos López 1990, 11; identifications by Jorge González Acereto.)

No evidence was found that any of these had ever been domesticated. (Some *Trigona* and *Scaptotrigona* bees are apparently kept in other parts of Latin America.) Some of the above are known to us as wild bees of the

Chunhuhub area. The *e'jool, tse'ets,* and *k'antsak* occur. Ceremonies noted included the *tsakab,* offering of honey to the gods (Medellín Morales and Campos López 1990, 13).

Several valuable and interesting texts were recorded from Maya elders who kept stingless bees (Conrado de Ucán et al. 1992). A bibliography on stingless bees appeared (Medellín Morales 1991). Particularly valuable was a glossary of bee terms (Carrillo Magaña 1990), notable because it uses a linguistically accurate transcription system, unlike the somewhat casual and old-style usage of most of the reports here cited. Production manuals for ordinary countryfolk were issued (Medellín Morales and González Acereto 1991a, 1991b). A pilot study in Tekanto had considerable success in stimulating production (Medellín Morales and Cruz Bojorquez 1992). Technical and managerial advice was issued (González Acereto and Medellín Morales 1991a, 1991b), and an overall review of the project appeared in 1991 (Medellín Morales et al. 1991).

Sostenibilidad Maya also issued a catalogue of plants used by bees (all species) for nectar and pollen (Silveira Silveira 1990). It listed plants by month of flowering. Thus it provides a complement, rather than a replacement, for the classic (and all too rare) booklet on the subject by Narciso Souza Novelo, Victor Suarez Molina, and Alfredo Barrera Vásquez (1981). Subsequently, an exhaustive monograph by Harriet de Jong (1999) has recorded almost everything that could be recorded about beekeeping in Yucatán. Meanwhile, attempts to commercialize the stingless bee continue.

For a while, it appeared that the stingless bee might provide a way out of poverty for the farmers of Yucatán. It was commonly kept, and much was known about it. Its honey sold for a good price. However, ecological changes (including decline of the forest with its flowering plants), difficulties in marketing, competition from European bees, and other factors have proved overwhelming. Fewer and fewer Maya are keeping bees at all because of urbanization and the problems with Africanized bees. The stingless bee fit in well with the old pattern of isolated small settlements practicing subsistence agriculture. It has not proved well-adapted to large towns, or to the world of specialized commercial agriculture. We certainly hope it will hang on, somehow, but FMT somewhat regretfully confines his attention to European bees—life in a town is for the hardy, wide-ranging, hard-working, and highly productive, whether one is speaking of bees or of humans.

DON JACINTO CAUICH AND DON FELIX TALK
ABOUT WASPS AND BEES

JCC: *Ts'eelem* is a wasp. Its larvae are tasty—good with chile and lime juice. Really tasty also is the *xanabchaak*. Its hive is big. It too is tasty with lime and chile. You toast the larvae.

FMT: The others too—we like to eat them because they are wasps that are eaten. They are not bad wasps. The bad wasps are those you can't eat. The royal hive [*panal real*—the nest of the *ek*] is similar, with the larvae and royal jelly. We prepare it with bitter orange juice or lime juice, and chile—great food! It's a bee or a wasp—either way. It has honey. They go and put honey in the outer part of the nest. They put the honey around so they can raise the young, feeding on the honey. But all wasps are bees, or about the same thing. All have honey around their larvae in the nest, to raise the larvae. [This is an overstatement. We are aware that most wasps don't have honey.] We eat the ts'eelem, the royal hive, and the xanabchaak, but not usually the others.

There is also the *box xuux*. It's good. We toast and eat it. The *ts'ibinajij* [*ts'ibilnajij*], no, because people say that if you eat that you go mad. No one eats the young or honey. The *chuk'utkib* is a wasp that is not eaten. It is very fierce.

JCC: And its hive is very tough.

FMT: Its hive is solid mud; with red dirt they make it. It doesn't burn. It doesn't turn black. And it's always collected. It's a material that does not burn.

JCC: The *bobote'*, how is it eaten?

FMT: The bobote' is not eaten. They are very fierce. They are big and long. We have seen them occasionally, [their nests] stuck to trees. They're blue [shiny blue-black].

JCC: There are other wasps—I don't know if you know them. They stick their nests on trees, too, but are small. They don't grow any larger. But there are some that, if the shoulder of your horse is wounded, if you take a wasp and put in on the shoulder, that will heal it. Because when the shoulder is wounded, it won't heal; but with this wasp it will. You use the larvae; you put them on the wound. This wasp is not eaten.

FMT: The *k'an kub* isn't eaten; it isn't used at all. It stings hard. Of all wasps, the one that stings hardest is the *chuk'utkib*—and the bobote'. They give you fever. When they sting you two, three, four, or five times, oh God, with that, later you get fever. And so much pain!

Another that is strong is the *k'otkanab [k'otkanal]*. The little bell, they call it [from the shape of the nest]. It hits you right away. For sure, when it comes to sting, where it stings, in whatever part of the body, you'll hit the ground, pam! To the ground you go, knocked out for two or three hours! It's a sting, but, *strong!* They say that it compares with the bite of a snake. It's a solitary wasp. Its home is a little bell, roundish. It nests under the leaf of a palmetto, or a maize leaf. The nest is only so big [five–six centimeters diameter]. It holds to this size. It can't get bigger, that little house. Where it's stuck on, it stays there, really well protected. It doesn't get wet, or get in the sun—nothing. There it has one larva. It lays its egg and has one young one. And once this larva has pupated, it goes away. It leaves. When it goes, it has to make its own nest, its *chan* [little] hive. One for one, especially. It finds its branchlet or leaf and goes to live there. And when its larva comes, it goes. It has stung me.

JCC: Me too [points to mouth]. My mouth stayed swollen till I couldn't talk. I had an attack here [points to throat]. My throat was swollen shut. It was like a snakebite.

FMT: It's as bad. It stung me here [points to right side of chest]. The doctor said that if it had stung me here [points to heart], it would have killed me. When it stung me, I fell down immediately. We were harvesting with baskets. I just yelled, "Aii!" and pam! it hit me; and pum! I hit the ground. When my brothers came up and saw me, they said, "A snake must have bitten him." They thought that. But, no, it was a wasp.

They thought, well, he's unconscious. They lifted me up and took me to my house, and there they rubbed me and checked me over and found my heart was still beating. But strongly, "pom, pom, pom," as if it would burst. The doctor said, "It's just a sting, but if it stings you here [pointing to heart], your heart would burst, from the power of the venom. It would burst instantaneously," he said. "And you'd die."

And in an hour or two, when they checked again, I couldn't talk. I wanted to talk but couldn't. My throat was swollen shut. I was all swollen up. I was unconscious. I stayed about three hours like that till my throat opened up. I said to them, "What stung me?" I took off my shirt, and there was a hole there. The sting that nailed me had left a hole. It was a big stinger, like a scorpion's. With a scorpion sting, your tongue swells up, but you can talk. Your whole body swells. But not so much. But it makes a hole. It's a very bad wasp. You have to be very cautious, walking in the woods.

And the ek, the royal hive, that one stings you, but it's like a regular bee sting. [Actually it is much less serious, barely noticeable.] You don't feel it much. You can bear fifty or one hundred of those stings.

JCC: There is another that lives in a hole in the ground, a big one— what's it called?

FMT: *Balankab* [jaguar bee]. There are black ones and red ones. But they too are fierce. They sting hard, to the point where the blood runs out where they sting. They are not like regular bees. The sting of these two kinds of balankab—they can sting up to ten times and the stinger doesn't stay in the sting. In contrast, the regular bees, when they sting, the stinger stays there and the bee dies, because its guts are pulled out. But these wasps, no. They can sting up to twenty or thirty times.

The balankab—the black ones are big, like *sacucheros*. And bam! one stung me once. We were gathering chicle, and we passed above its house— it was in the hole of an armadillo. We passed there and it sensed me. But I didn't see it. When I heard a blow, like "tsit, tsit, tsit," on my back . . . but they had got me, gotten into my pants and on up to my head. Totally. I had to drop my machete, my rope, and my chicle bags, throw all of them down. "Let's go!" And I was breaking through vines, mashing over litter. They didn't stop, either—it was a swarm of them that came after me. And they followed me—Hii!—I ran some five mecates [one hundred meters]. I got away from them. And my brother-in-law Julio too, they stung him. We ran. They are very fierce wasps.

And also the red one, the *chak balankab.* They're super fierce. They get into your shirt, like the chuk'utkib. The chuk'utkib gets into your shirt, after looking for a place to get in. It gets in your shirt and, bam! It stings you like the balankab. [This small wasp normally gets down into an animal's or person's hair and stings repeatedly there in relative safety.] The chuk'utkib puts its nest in the subin tree. I don't know why. [Biologists theorize that this wasp, like the stinging ants that also live in the subin *(Acacia cornigera),* has developed a mutual protection arrangement: The thorny tree protects them and they protect it. In consequence, the subin is the dominant tree in over-grazed land in the area.]

And the bobote' also stings hard. Your blood flows. But no more. You can bear up to ten stings. And the k'ank'ub [k'an kub; "yellow wasp"] too, and the ts'ibinajij. The ts'ibinajij—they're fierce wasps. They come into houses. They like to gather in the thatch. Or under a rock overhang, or under stones. They always nest under stones. [These are paper-nest hornets whose nests are about twelve to fifteen centimeters in diameter.]

JCC: But sometimes they are medicinal.

FMT: Which?

JCC: The chuk'utkib and ts'eelem.

FMT: What do they cure?

JCC: Sometimes when one goes to one's house, there's someone else there. . . . [FMT laughs.]

JCC [laughs]: With these, and not only with these, with others. My uncle said that to cure a person, you have to take your machete and—ts'ibinajij [ts'ibilnajij] and chuk'utkib, and other wasps even more fierce—mix them, burn them, and wash the machete in that. You'll be healed. Or with a *chiiwoj* [*chiiwol;* tarantula].

There are women that do evil, but the man doesn't know what's going on. When he is cured, oh man, he gets really fierce. He's cured well; he has his valor back.

FMT: Jacinto is saying that when some women want to do wrong to their husbands, one can cure it with these wasps. You mix up all the larvae. You make powder with ts'eelem, chuk'utkib, box xuux, and larvae of the subin tree ants—nine of each species. With this, powder is made, and they give it to you to drink. More than once. When a woman has worked evil on you, this will get your valor back. You have to be careful, because these are fierce.

JCC: It's a secret [i.e., a magical practice]. If you have a friend, or an aunt or uncle, you'll be invited to eat, and they'll put this in the food.

FMT: There are many women that didn't care for their husbands. They do a kind of evil. They take away the valor of the man; they know a secret. Well, in truth, women are very astute. They don't say that they're going to do this, but when they do this, then the man has no valor. You can see many things that a woman will do, and the husband doesn't talk or do anything contrary; instead of talking, he cries. Because the woman has gotten rid of his valor. How does he get it back? The man too has his secrets; and this secret is with wasps. [Otherwise, uncured,] when another man comes to your house, you can't do anything or say anything. You can only cry.

Once we heard about Don Santiago Loria—no, Don *Ernesto* Loria. They said that he sought out a woman, very lovely, with blue eyes. He married her. But in one or two years, he had no valor. We were children then, when he told us the story. He said, "Listen: This and this happened to me, kids. Don't be careless."

Sometimes a woman, we say, deceives her husband—he takes her into his confidence and she sometimes goes beyond that. She takes away his valor. Once it so happened to a man. His wife took away his valor. When strange people came to his house, or another strange man was in his house, he didn't do anything about it. At last, it is said that they threw out his hammock, out into the garden, under the mango trees. They threw it out of the house where he slept with his wife so that he would not stop the woman sleeping with another man in the house.

So passed the time. But one day, a friend said, "Listen, aren't you taking any account of what's going on in your house?" "No." "Well, look here, this and this and this is happening. Your woman—When you go out, another man comes in." "It can't be!" "Sure! I've seen it myself. That's why they moved your hammock outside." "No!" "Well, it's so, and you've become like a child. They have gotten rid of your valor, and you stay like a child. The woman says to you 'I'm going shopping.' Then she says to the other man, 'He's like a child; you can do it.' The woman is in command. She has gotten rid of your valor." Thus the friend spoke to the man. "Look," he said, "[You think] 'It's all right.' You go to drink, and it happens. Years have gone on in your house, and [you just say] 'It's all right.'"

This friend took an interest in curing the man. He began to cure his friend. To get back his valor. He got it back and saw what was going on in his house. He said, "Now I have my valor back." When the man came in, he grabbed him and began to beat him with a big vine. He grabbed him, beat him, and threw him out. He said "Scoot! I don't want you in my house. I don't want to see you here." He took his young wife and said, "This young one is no good to me. On the contrary, she messed me over." So, when he got his valor back, he just threw her out.

He said: "You have to be very careful. There are women you can't trust."

JCC: Back to the bees. Bees' honey is eaten. Each class of bee, it's tasty. Like the e'jool, its honey is tasty.

FMT: These are bees whose honey is eaten. Edible.

JCC: They don't sting you.

FMT: No. They are used a lot for providing honey.

JCC: Now the *k'antsak*—its honey is a little bitter.

FMT: It lives in holes. It looks for holes in trees, to make its wax. This wax is used like that of ordinary bees.

J. It makes little balls.

FMT: E'jool, *xi'ik*—

JCC: Just little balls.

FMT: A ball full of honey or pollen. And that is for it to eat. Another is the lime bee.

JCC: The *niitkij.*

FMT: It's called the lime bee because it smells a lot like limes. It makes its nests in small caves.

JCC: But they give almost no honey. They're just lazy!

FMT: They aren't eaten much, the e'jool, xi'ik, *ya'ax ich*, xunankab, the *tse'ets.* The tse'ets is about the same as the xunankab. It makes a lot of wax. Its ball nests are full—storing honey.

My father—many, many years ago, when we lived in an ejido called Tsuluntok [bordering on Don Felix's native village of Andres Quintana Roo, Yucatán], he had more than two hundred hives, which were in hollow tree trunks. They were cut long. In these lived the bees. When he went to take the honey [*castrar*, lit. "castrate," is the rather graphic Spanish verb used for taking honey], he would lower the beds, the jobon as they called them. Each fifteen days, he took the honey. There were some carafes [metal milk cans], like water carafes, but each holding forty or eighty kilograms. For milk or honey. Huge carafes. And there during honey season he had to fill up to six of these big carafes for household use. When I was growing up, I never saw sugar, I didn't know what sugar was. There, it was all honey. Coffee with honey of xunankab bees. Pozole with honey. All we had to eat or drink, with honey. Atole and *xlampas* with honey in them.

JCC: Xlampas is *choko saka'* [hot corn gruel], isn't it?

FMT: Uh huh. Pinole [ground seed meal in water] with honey.

JCC: *Xeche ixi'im* is maize ground up.

FMT: Yes, xeche ixi'im. You grind it raw. No more than soak it for one day or so. Then you grind it. You put it in a bowl or jug.

JCC: It's like rice.

FMT: It's like rice. The maize kernels are broken into little bits. It's tasty. Every so often we would have it to eat.

But with honey, in those days, forty or fifty years ago: When we went to fell woods, there were many of these [hives] in the wild. For sure, wild bees. We would go and bring them in. I saw that when the honey was taken, they used a long wooden pole with a sharp point. They put the point in [punctured the hollow tree where the hive was], and the honey just poured out. They took a bucket and got it. They used some strainers so no dirt got in the honey. And when the honey had run out into the bucket, it was clean. This was for storing in the carafes. It was for consumption. In all—forty-eight or fifty years ago, I never saw or knew sugar. Just honey of xunankab. We didn't have "American" [European] honeybees then. They didn't exist. Finally when I was eighteen, I began to see them. "Let's go get some American bees!" I saw them. But nobody took them.

JCC: People were scared of them.

FMT: They were scared because the bees stung hard. Nobody went after them. They lived in caves and cenotes. And slowly the xunankab disappeared. We began to work just with American bees. I have seen that change. Now nobody raises the native ones. They are very rare. People used to have up to three hundred hives.

And in those days there was very little sickness, because people didn't eat sugar. No Coca-Cola. Just cold water from the cenote. No ice, but the cenote water was cold enough. And clean. At night, for supper, a bowl of atole, or xlampas, or xeche ixi'im. Xlampas is an atole too, well sweetened with the xunankab honey, or that of the *xya'ax ich* ["little ya'ax ich"] or the *tse'ets*. How rich that was! And tasty. With this, we were happy. Lie in the hammock, start up at dawn: Breakfast was another bowl of atole. They'd give you your pozole and a bottle of honey. I saw the workers going to work, off to fell trees or whatever, with their pozole. They ground up their pozole and made balls for taking along, and gave them a bottle of honey. So they went. When they went to mix up the pozole, they put in the honey. They say that wild honey doesn't contain sugar. It isn't like cane sugar. We saw that many sicknesses came in as sugar became common. But in those days I never saw such. The people lived without sickness. Almost no one got sick. [Sober medical records belie this rosy picture of the good old days. The Maya constantly speak in exaggerated terms of the good old days, a widespread Mexican practice satirized in the folk saying, "In those days, we tied up the dogs with sausages and they didn't even notice."] And the honey— I don't know if you've seen the wild honey. It's a food. It has many vitamins. . . .

Xk'eelsej was made also. You grind up the maize, but not very fine. Just run-of-the-mill, in little grains. When you cook it, it forms strips. It stays like rice. It has a good taste. Because you don't boil it [first with lime water]. Just maize. You take the grains off the ear and soak them for a day. . . . [This is cracked corn, like the corn rice of the Philippines; a coarser product than xeche ixi'im.]

JCC: Xeche ixi'im isn't soaked.

FMT: Yes, it is, but not very much.

JCC: There is another thing, *sikli sa'* [squash seed gruel].

FMT: That isn't with honey?

JCC: You don't boil the maize [with lime water], but you [cook it after] sifting, and mix ground squash seeds in.

FMT: I've heard of it, but I haven't seen how it's made.

JCC: You boil the maize but don't cook it much. It's tasty.

ENA: There are no wild bees anymore?

JCC: Because of the American bees.

FMT: And because the forest is gone. Now there is almost no more forest. It doesn't exist. Even little woodlands are rare. In these groves, there are still bees. You can seek out the e'jool, k'antsak, ya'ax ich, xunankab, xi'ik'. The xi'ik' is very rare; it just about doesn't exist. In Yucatán there used to be many.

JCC: It's medicine too, the xi'ik'. If a pimple or boil grows in your armpit, you use the honey or pollen.

FMT: Sweet potato, *iis,* they call it—what the bees put there. Because it's so fine. But it isn't sweet potato, it's pollen.

Ts'eelem: Those wasps are thinner and smaller. They're little ones. And the ts'ibinajij: They're small but a little bigger and thicker [indicates length of about one-half centimeter], and a bit darker. The ts'eelem is a bit whitish. Its wings are whitish and spotted. The ts'ibinajij's wingtips are black. The chuk'utkib's wings are all black and red. It's larger, about a centimeter. And its wings are more yellow or red.

JCC: Like chocolate.

FMT: Like chocolate, its wings. But these bees are thicker. And the—

JCC: Xanabchaak?

FMT: Bigger [indicates two and a half centimeters]. Red and yellow. And the k'ank'ub [k'an kub], yellow. It's like the ts'eelem, but yellow; for this they call it the k'ank'ub [k'an kub]. It makes honey, but only a little. It nests in holes in trees. It isn't like the others.

JCC: The box xuux is fat. [Indicates a bit over half a centimeter for length.]

FMT: And its wings are white, the tips are. But all the body is black. Because of this it's called box xuux, "black bee." [*Xuux* is actually a general term for small wasps, not bees, but Don Felix said *"abeja"* here.]

ENA: But it doesn't make honey?

JCC: No.

FMT: It lives in subin trees and puts its house there.

JCC: What next? Bobote'. Size [indicates three centimeters]. It makes its house on poles. It sticks it to them. And *k'otkanal [k'otkanab]*. It's always big [indicates four to five centimeters]

FMT: It has yellow wings. Each bee is distinguished by its size or color.

JCC: The k'otkanal is about the same in color as the xanabchaak, but it's bigger.

FMT: And the royal hive—it isn't big; they are somewhat short, those bees [indicates about one centimeter].

JCC: A bit fat too.

FMT: A little fat. And spotted, or striped.

Each bee has its own way of making its hive. The ts'ibinajij makes it under a stone or in houses. The ts'eelem hangs its large nest on vines. It is up to a meter through, really thick. And the k'ank'ub [k'an kub], in hollows in trees; in a hollow trunk it makes its wax, its hives. The xunankab too. Not outside, but in holes in trees. The xunankab is like the *joolom* [in size].

ENA: What is a joolom?

FMT: They're bees too. When the sun is hot, they come out. They live here [pointing to numerous holes in the poles making up his house wall—these being the homes of these small solitary bees]. They don't give honey, nothing. I don't like them making holes in the wood! But they're the size of the xunankab. No more than slightly greenish [i.e., they are blackish gray or blackish green]. The xunankab is greenish and striped [yellow]. It's similar to the tse'ets, which is related. The tse'ets also makes nests in holes in trees. I have taken out some pieces. Sometimes there are some pieces of wax, full of honey. You stick a point in and the honey flows out. It's really, really tasty. And so this bee is distinguished—by how it works, where it lives, how it makes its hives, and in what it nests, in what kind of tree.

The box xuux nests on the subin, a ball nest. Like a little hat. No pointed end on it. It enters from below. The lower end has a hole. It's a thick nest.

Another that makes its nest in holes is the balankab. There are the *chak* [red] and *box* [black] balankab. They all live in holes in the ground. But other wasps, no. They live on palms, in poles, in spiny bushes, in things like that. The ek lives so [it hangs a huge paper nest on small thorny trees]. The country people know all these kinds of wasps as well as the American honeybee.

Chapter Four

HUNTING

Hunting remains an important subsistence activity in Chunhuhub and throughout the peninsula (Marmolejo Monsiváis 2000). However, its importance is declining rapidly, along with the game.

Until recently, Quintana Roo was a hunter's paradise. The lush forests supported huge animal populations. Milpa agriculture greatly increased the abundance of the most important game animals: White-tailed Deer, Collared Peccary, Plain Chachalaca, Ocellated Turkey, and paca. These mammals and birds thrive better in a Maya-managed habitat than in mature tropical forest. Minor game animals such as quail, rabbits, gophers, and armadillos also prefer the managed environment.

Unlike most Mexican indigenous peoples, the Maya do not eat many wild species. They eat most large mammals, but they do not like opossum. Most are repelled by raccoons, though they will eat them occasionally, and some people like them. They do not eat small mammals, except for squirrels, gophers, and rabbits. They eat the standard game birds—gallinaceous species and waterfowl—and sometimes other large birds, but they do not eat small birds. They rarely eat reptiles, and virtually never eat amphibians. In parts of the Yucatán, iguanas are popular, but there are no large iguanas in Chunhuhub (possibly—so one person theorized to us—because they were all eaten long ago), and small ones are ignored. Turtles are sometimes eaten. (Some turtles are used for medicine by Maya in Belize; see Carr 1991a.) They greatly relish fish but rarely get them in the dry interior. They never eat insects, except for wasp and bee larvae, which are quite popular. In this they contrast strikingly with other indigenes of Mexico, a point noted and discussed by Ramos Elorduy (1991; cf. Ramos Elorduy and Pino Moreno 1989).

8. Juuj *(iguana), Puerto Morelos.*

One effect is to put heavy pressure on the animals that *are* used. Another is to provide an incentive for raising domestic animals on a large scale.

Traditional Maya agriculture produces a mosaic of regrowth stages, from milpas to mature forest. The game animals feed in the milpas, to the sorrow of the owners. In a milpa that has been harvested and left to regrow, squash and root crops typically persist, to be harvested by both human and animal visitors for another year or more. After this phase, the milpa becomes an almost impenetrable tangle of brush, weeds, and thorny bushes and young trees. It then becomes an ideal refuge for game animals. Moreover, many of these plants provide excellent forage for deer. In about ten years, the milpa regrows to young forest. This is its most worthless stage from the animals' point of view; most of the nutrients in the landscape are tied up in wood or tough leaves, and the young fruiting trees are not big enough to produce heavy crops. At this stage, ancient sapotes and other fruit trees left by the Maya cultivators become vital resources. Finally, after forty or fifty years, newly growing sapotes, wayas, and other important fruit trees and vines are mature enough to provide large crops. (For further detail on milpas and game, see Carr 1991b and Mandujano and Rico-Gray 1991. Also, Olga Linares' classic 1976 article on garden hunting is as applicable to the Maya as to Panama.)

On the other hand, old-growth forest is the preferred habitat of brocket deer, White-lipped Peccary, guans, Great Curassows, and monkeys. Squirrels and agoutis are commoner in older forest. The tapir, always rare and now virtually extinct, seems to have been confined to dense forests near water; at least, this is true of the few surviving ones. They take refuge especially in the almost impenetrable *aguada* forests.

Hunting is carried out primarily with guns. Guns are called *ts'on*, which meant "blowgun" in the old days; we learn from the colonial dictionaries that guns were originally *Kaaxlan ts'on*, "Spanish blowguns." Rifles are particularly common and are normally of small caliber, .22s being very common. Ancient shotguns, some apparently left over from the "rebel Maya" days, are not rare. Sometimes these explode, with unfortunate results.

Maya are crack shots. When ENA first heard of people hunting quail with rifles, he thought his consultants had simply made a mistake in their Spanish. This proved not to be the case. Maya routinely use rifles to hunt small game birds and think nothing of wing-shooting them. It is a point of pride—as well as an economic necessity, since there is a chronic lack of cash to buy ammunition—to kill an animal (large or small) with one shot. This is no mean accomplishment, especially since hunting is regularly done at night in dense forest.

After a certain number of large animals is killed, a gun must be reconsecrated in a *loj ts'on* ritual. Ideally, the proper number is twelve, with the thirteenth animal being parceled out to the whole community in the ritual (Llanes Pasos 1993, 23, 80). This cleanses the gun of the problems associated with so much killing of animals, who are, as will appear below, under the protection of powerful supernaturals. A loj ts'on allows the hunter to start anew. This small ceremony involves chants, ritual foods, and consecration of the gun on an altar table. Forms appear to vary throughout the Maya area.

Bezoar stones, known as *virtudes* (virtues), or *tunich* or *piedras* (stones), are taken from deer. They are then used as powerful charms for deer hunting. They too have to be renewed, usually by finding a new stone rather than by ceremonial renewal. Other charms are often found and used for hunting other species. Canine (or long incisor) teeth—what English-speaking hunters call "eyeteeth"—are also popular virtues, especially for animals that have no bezoars, such as peccaries and pacas. Deer eyeteeth, however, may be used as well (as noted also by Mandujano and Rico-Gray 1991).

The most successful hunting is done at night, often with jacklighting. Hunting is, however, often done by day. Most of this—and, indeed, most hunting in and around Chunhuhub—is opportunistic. Many men carry guns wherever they go and shoot anything that happens along during the course of ordinary daily activities. Given the current scarcity of game in Chunhuhub, this is the only reasonable way to hunt; trips designed specifically for hunting are too unprofitable to be taken very seriously as subsistence activities. Thus, deer are usually taken by surprise. If a deer is known to be in a particular area, it may be stalked, but this is not often successful. (See Mandujano and Rico-Gray 1991 for discussion of deer hunting in the peninsula.)

Successful hunting—in remote areas where it is worth doing—often involves a stand. A platform is made in a tree, usually at the edge of an isolated milpa or near a waterhole. Typically, it is more or less protected and concealed with branches. The hunter may stay there several nights without shooting, to accustom the animals to his presence. Eventually he can pick off animals that come into the milpa to feed.

Much less common, but more fun, is *p'uuj* (or *ch'uk*): beating the bush (Sp. *batea*). A party of men and boys, with dogs, forms a line and crashes through the brush, making as much noise as they can and picking off whatever is flushed. With somewhat more sophistication, the more experienced hunters may be placed in the line of game, and trained dogs are used to drive game toward them. In olden times, a horn or conch shell was used to signal (Llanes Pasos 1993, 80); now, people just yell. Though entertaining, p'uuj is a singularly unsuccessful way to hunt. Birds and animals for miles around are alarmed and flee or hide. It was more successful in an earlier era when game was commoner and less shy. When a jaguar began to devour sheep in Presidente Juarez, a p'uuj for it was organized. Not so much as a track was found. The jaguar was back the next night, eating more sheep.

Opportunistic hunting, and sometimes serious hunting too, is done also with machetes and clubs. Folktales maintain that even jaguars have been taken by machete. More seriously, those men who cannot afford guns can realistically expect to get armadillos and pacas this way. These are nocturnal animals that live in burrows or caves. If they are driven from their holes in the daylight, they can be killed by a lucky blow as they emerge. Sometimes even more wary and diurnal animals, such as coatis, can be surprised and killed with machetes. One successfully bagged paca seen by ENA was taken this way.

Hunting is also done with slingshots, known by their Spanish names *resortera* or *tirahule*. Most slingshot hunting is done by small boys, but adult men do it too, when after very small game. The usual targets are doves, quail, and rabbits. Even chachalacas and pacas are obtained this way, though very rarely.

Hunting relies on a knowledge of *pe'echak* (or *chikaan*): tracks and trails. Maya are excellent trackers. FMT is able to identify and track animals from indications that ENA (who is by no means inexperienced in reading animal tracks) is unable to see at all. Animal calling is also done. "Pishing" and "squeaking" with the lips is well known; blowing on a grassblade held between the thumbs is more effective. Particularly interesting and significant is the use of a leaf held in the mouth. The top edge of the leaf is folded over and held against the top lip; the rest of the leaf remains projecting over the lower lip and acts as a free-beating reed. Tough but thin and flexible leaves are necessary for this—young citrus and ramón leaves are good for the purpose—and every Maya hunter knows what leaves to choose in the forest. A good hunter such as FMT can imitate a variety of animals with incredible accuracy, and can also play popular tunes to while away the hours.

Hunting is also done by means of traps. Formerly, there was a great range of traps and snares (Flores 1984). Currently, the only common method is the *harcon,* or box trap. Bait is scattered under a cage of sticks, propped up with a stick. Birds come to the bait and trip the stick, or a boy stations himself in brush nearby and pulls a string attached to the stick. This method is usually used by boys to snare birds, either for food (quail and doves) or for pets (Indigo and Painted Buntings, cardinals, and other colorful birds). The pets are kept till they die—usually all too soon—or are given or sold to neighbors. There is no organized sale of pet birds, as there is in the Mérida area. Rarely, rabbits and other small animals are caught in box traps (Flores 1984; Hovey and Rissolo 1999). Foot-snaring nooses, famous from the depictions of snared deer in the pre-Columbian codices, are no longer found. Gophers are snared by nooses or twig snares set in their underground runs.

It is impossible today to form any idea of what animal populations would be in an undisturbed Quintana Roo forest habitat. All the forest has been managed for thousands of years. Even long-abandoned areas reveal a suspicious abundance of sapotes, allspice, and other long-lived trees that are selectively left when land is cleared. Moreover, intensive hunting has led to game depletion everywhere, even in the most remote areas. Existing density figures are extremely low. For instance, even relatively thinly populated areas have peccary populations of only six or seven animals per square kilometer, as opposed to twenty, thirty, or even fifty in Venezuela and elsewhere (Gilberto Avila, pers. comm.). This is certainly the result of heavy hunting. We interviewed the people in the study sites, who left us in no doubt on the matter. It is likely that Quintana Roo's habitat is better than that in Venezuela; indeed, it would be hard to imagine a better habitat for peccaries. Until recently, these animals were extremely abundant—a major danger to milpas. We noted a large drop in number of peccaries taken between 1991 and 1996, though there was some recovery by 2001 (Hurricane Roxanne had presumably been a factor in 1996).

As of 1996, game had become rare in Chunhuhub. There was so little successful hunting that ENA was unable to conduct a meaningful survey. Systematic questioning brought essentially no results. FMT, an enthusiastic lifelong hunter, abandoned hunting. His gun was confiscated because he neglected to renew his permit. He decided to do nothing about it, seeing little future in hunting. Shortly before this, he had shot a female peccary and adopted its two small young. One died, but one grew to maturity and then escaped. During her captive youth, Bixa was an ideal pet, smarter and more easily trained than a dog. Don Jacinto Cauich also gave up hunting.

To collect data, ENA took to stationing himself along the road that leads northwest from Chunhuhub on virtually every evening spent in the town. This road transects the best hunting area near the town and is convenient for observation. Individuals were stopped and asked about hunting. In five months in 1996, the following were recorded:

March 2: a man with freshly shot coati and armadillo.

9. Kitam *(Felix Medina Tzuc's pet peccary), Bixa, in 1996.*

March 5: a man and his son, jacklighting with a headlamp, getting an agouti.

In addition, elsewhere, we observed a gopher and (at another time) a paca. We found the remains of a curassow that had been shot, and, at a poacher's stand, some feathers of an Ocellated Turkey that was probably shot but may have escaped. We heard of a few deer, peccaries, and other animals shot in nearby areas, but not in Chunhuhub itself. In 2001 the situation was slightly better—a few deer and peccaries were shot—but remained bleak.

More typical was March 22: We met two parties coming in from different directions after beating the bush. One had nine men with five guns and four dogs. The other consisted of six men with three guns and one dog. The total game observed by these parties was one armadillo—and they missed that! Thus, since the early 1990s, game-animal populations have generally leveled off, at an exceedingly low level, in the Chunhuhub area.

However, as of 2001, peccaries are getting commoner again. Chachalacas, decimated by Hurricane Roxanne, have steadily increased since it passed. Deer are seen rather frequently and still provide an occasional meal.

We found many tracks of peccaries and deer during 2001, but very few of other game animals.

Pacas (tepescuintles) are still almost extinct in Chunhuhub, but ENA observed one shot in 2001, and FMT says they remain, at low levels of abundance. The hunter who shot the paca said that these animals are indeed rare, but deer are *bastante* (frequent).

Agoutis remain but are now rare. ENA saw two recent kills in 2001. One hunter in a remote forest community had the help of his two large hunting dogs, which were in as good a shape as any hunting dog could be. They had the floating gait of superb field dogs. We complimented him on them. He said, proudly, that they were fine at hunting anything—deer, peccary, paca. No laws reached that far into the forest.

We also saw recent kills of coatis that had been robbing fields. In one case, we met FMT's nephew, who had staked himself out to get a coati that had eaten an appreciable percentage of his milpa harvest. Two hours later, he came in with the animal, which we carried to town in our car trunk, along with some sacks of maize. The coati was to be eaten. Significantly, he shot only the robber, caught in the act—not the other coatis in the forest.

10. Chi'ik *(coati), Tabasco.*

Amazingly enough, jaguars are still found. In addition to the sheep-addicted animal in Presidente Juarez, there is one in Margaritas that got six pigs a few years ago.

FMT feels that fewer people hunt today. However, there are more guns than ever, especially in the small forest ejidos, and people feel less constrained by fear of the Yuntsiloob. On the other hand, there seems to be less of the serious, persistent, night-long hunting that used to be a typical activity. The guns are largely used to control milpa pests such as coatis, and to pick off the occasional game animal that shows up in daylight. There is less need to hunt, now that domestic animal meat is common. In some of the smaller ejidos, nearer to forest and poorer in agricultural production, hunting with dogs remains a nightly activity. Dogs are better kept than they were, and many are superb hunters.

In short, hunting is as prevalent as ever, in spite of the waning of the old ways and the coming of a market economy. Game is disappearing fast from the ejidos that still hunt actively. The more vulnerable animals, such as guans and wild turkeys, are long gone from everywhere near human activity. Animals find refuge only in large tracts of roadless forest, between ejidos. (This pattern of refuge in unoccupied zones between populated ones is widely noted for Native America; see Martin and Szuter 1999, 2002.)

Guns have increased in proportion to population, in spite of Mexico's theoretically strict firearm-control laws. Even if each hunter takes no more than is necessary, hunters are now numerous enough to eliminate the game. There are now many hunters for every one deer or paca in the area (and in Quintana Roo as a whole).

Traditional Maya religion and culture, as we have seen, reinforced conservation in many ways. The Maya are one of the Native American groups that have an explicit ideology and practice of conservation. They deliberately forego opportunities to kill animals, in order to ensure better hunting later. In view of recent challenges to the existence of Native American conservation (Alvard and Kuznar 2001; Krech 1999; Redman 1999), it may be useful to document these measures. Specifically, the rules are

1. Do not kill an animal unless you have a good reason. (Maya are strikingly protective toward even insects, and toward pests like rabbits and coatis, not killing them except when a specific individual or group is damaging a particular field.)

2. Do not take for food more than you need for yourself and your immediate family and neighborhood. Selling some meat is permitted, but
only in the close circle of the community.

3. Do not take many animals at one time. If a group of animals is encountered, do not kill all of them.

4. Do not kill more than a small number of animals within a year (but no
set figure is given).

5. Try to minimize the killing of animals in reproductive condition—
subject to the qualification that one can take an animal when need is
great, and one cannot, in the forest, easily tell the reproductive condition of the animal.

5a. When one accidentally kills a mother with young, try to capture the
young and raise them.

6. Do not leave a wounded animal to go off to die and be wasted. Kill
with one shot; if you fail and wound the animal, follow it until you get
it. (This is a serious point of honor for traditional Maya hunters, and
they wax scathing when talking about violators.)

These rules, especially the first five, are believed to be enforced by supernatural sanction. The Yuntsiloob or Yumilk'aax, the Lords of the Forest,
enforce these rules. Specifically, one must face Siip (formerly spelled "Zip"),
the Lord of Deer; the Sojol Kuts (or "leaf-litter turkey"), the Lord of Game
Birds; and San Eustaquio, the Catholic patron of forests and game, who is
in fact a yumilk'aax under a syncretistic Christian name. These and other
deities guard the forest and its life.

Unfortunately, as people drift away from the old traditions, they feel less
and less constrained by such rules. Young hunters need to prove themselves
and have not personally seen the crash of game numbers. Above all, they
have grown up in a more Mexicanized world, where traditional Maya beliefs
are fading into the background.

In traditional belief, going back probably for thousands of years,
respectful attitudes and practices were sanctioned by the Lords of the
Forest (Yumilk'aax, Yuntsiloob) and by the Lords of the Animals. The Lords
of the Forest were, and by many people still are, believed to be powerful
supernatural beings that wander in the forest, whistling like the wind. They
protect the forest and its denizens. They strike with sickness and accidents

those humans who use the forests and forest resources wastefully. In addition, each animal species has its chief, a supernaturally large, powerful, and beautiful exemplar of the species. We draw again on the invaluable work of the Maya hunter and storyteller Eleuterio Llanes Pasos:

> The *tates*
>
> The *tates* (*tat*, "father"; *yum*, "master and lord"), owners of the forest, can take away people [cause them to die] when the drought burns up the fields for lack of rain. . . .
>
> The *ik'kuts* or *soholkuts [Sojol Kuts]:*
>
> One can't fool the *yumilk'aaxoob*. If you don't obey their rules, you will be punished.
>
> It was said of the *ik'kuts* or *soholkuts* that, for it, the case is the same. *Ik'* means "spirit, phantom"; *sohol* means "dry leaves, leaf litter"; *kuts*, "wild turkey." This is a turkey of the forest, more beautiful than you could [normally] see or hear singing. It will show itself when you're hunting, to flatter your vanity, but in the end you can't kill it. You don't take account of the trickery. When you lift it from the ground there is only skin and feathers. . . . It flies away, mocking you. . . . Thus the lords of nature punish those with too much ambition for killing the wild animals. The vengeance of the *yum* is sometimes more terrible, even to occasioning your death. (Llanes Pasos 1993, 82–83)

We direct attention also to Don Jacinto's experience (following section) and to Llanes Pasos's stories (e.g., pp. 23–25). There are countless such stories current in oral literature (see, e.g., Terán and Rasmussen 1992). Moreover, similar stories are reported for virtually all indigenous groups in Mexico. Typically, these follow a pattern: A man who hunts too much is out in the forest. He is lured by animals—or captured and taken outright—into a hole leading into a mountain. Here he meets the Lord of the Animals, who directs him in no uncertain terms to cut back on his hunting or even to abandon it. He returns, warns others in his community, and soon dies or is saved by a special rite. Elizabeth Benson's fine book *Birds and Beasts of Ancient Latin America* (Benson 1997, 24, 134) describes this story, with Maya citations. (See also Paredes 1970, 5–7, for a particularly fine version—actually a Mixe-Zoque story collected by ENA's teacher, George Foster.)

A superb account of the Lord of the Deer, which segues into deer lore that parallels most of the above, was given by Felix Tesucún—an Itzaj Maya—to Charles Hofling (Hofling 1991, 136–66).

While the attitudes and practices enforced by such sanctions leave something to be desired (the stories do not, for instance, enjoin protection of females in breeding season), they are unquestionably effective at greatly reducing hunting pressure. They appear, from our experience, to have been invoked especially when game was getting scarce. They also ruled out the senseless killing of any animal, and they ruled out wasteful use of plant resources as well.

Even now, in Chunhuhub, market gunning remains virtually nonexistent—as has always been the case. Traditional attitudes hold strongly that hunting is for subsistence (though this does not ban individuals from selling excess meat from a large deer, or the occasional sale of small animals, within traditional village trading networks). Hunters have usually been good about taking only small numbers of animals. One cannot imagine Quintana Roo Maya doing what Miguel Alvarez del Toro reports from Chiapas in regard to monkey hunting: "There are many hunters, really criminals, who kill dozens, solely for the sadistic pleasure of seeing defenseless animals die" (Alvarez del Toro 1991, 38). ENA has encountered such behavior toward animals occasionally in Mexico and commonly in the United States, but neither of us has observed anything like this in the Zona Maya. Far more typical is behavior of the sort observed by ENA: When one woman of Chunhuhub saw her children thoughtlessly killing butterflies by switching them out of the air, she made them eat the butterflies (Anderson 1996).

In short, in Chunhuhub and throughout the Yucatec Maya world, an explicit conservation ideology is backed up by actual behavior. This contrasts very sharply with the lack of conservation reported in, for example, the more remote and thinly populated parts of Amazonia (Alvard 1995).

In Margaritas, beliefs in hunting magic survive and reinforce conservation. There occurs the belief in the magical effectiveness of deer bezoar stones, a belief that seems almost worldwide. More local—but typical of all central Quintana Roo, at least—is the story of the deer's nose-worm. When one shoots a deer with a parasitic worm in its nose, one keeps the worm alive in a flask by feeding it deer blood.

One hunter asked a bezoar how much he could hunt that day; it would somehow communicate how many animals he could kill, and which species. One day he overhunted its limit. That night, in the forest, a ring of animals formed. One wounded him; he knew he had to throw the stone away. A huge deer appeared from the forest and swallowed it. That was the end of his hunting luck. If only PROFEPA (Procuraduría Federal de Protección al Ambiente, Mexico's environmental enforcement agency) were so vigilant.

Because of such beliefs, and a strong social ethic, the people of Margaritas are saving wildlife—especially their colonies of spider and howler monkeys—and are getting more and more conscious of the need to conserve. Gone are the days when one could kill thirteen White-lipped Peccaries in a day and sell the meat (up to 120 kilograms per animal).

Alcocer Puerto (2001) has recently described similar management practices in Yaxunah, Yucatán. There, people hunt in spite of its illegality but do not hunt during September, the fawning time of the local deer. So the state's laws are disregarded, but the unwritten laws of the community are not (Alcocer Puerto 2001, 85).

For Kantunilkin, Quintana Roo, a superb (but, alas, unpublished) study by Almanza Alcalde (2000) has documented further traditions. All there agree that the game is vastly diminished from the old days (Almanza Alcalde 2000, 103–105). Conservation measures include condemnation of using whistles to lure deer, since the whistles imitate the calls of fawns and thus lure mother deer, leaving fawns orphaned (Almanza Alcalde 2000, 126–30). As in the Chunhuhub area, Siip is believed to be the Lord of the Deer; Almanza cites Landa's famous writings on this matter, which show that belief has changed very little in 450 years (Almanza Alcalde 2000, 131). Siip will punish hunters who overexploit the game, especially if they overuse secrets like deer bezoar stones, eyeteeth, and the small worms *(paka'ach)* in the throats of animals (believed magical there as elsewhere; Almanza Alcalde 2000, 133–35). In Kantunilkin not only the gun requires a loj ceremony, but even the hunting dogs are given a loj, the *loj peek'* (Almanza Alcalde 2000, 134).

As in Llanes Pasos' account, the *sohol kutz* (sic.; Almanza Alcalde 2000, 140) protects the turkeys. It can take the form of any game bird. One can control it with the *yerba sohol,* an herb that shines at night. Again as in

11. Uulum *(turkeys).*

Chunhuhub and its neighboring villages, San Eustaquio guards the forest, and San Jorge guards snakes (a natural role for St. George of dragon fame).

Almanza's community is guarded by four Yum Balam, one at each corner (Almanza Alcalde 2000, 143–4), and these seem to reinforce community morality. Yet they do not prevent a local *jmeen* (Maya ritualist) from turning himself into an eagle *(way pop)* and flying to Canada and the United States to get merchandise for his store, nor can they always stop magical snakes from entering the vaginas of menstruating or pregnant women and causing infertility or worse (Almanza Alcalde 2000, 146). Magic and evil winds are part of the world, often sent as punishment, often sent in spite of the Yuntsiloob.

According to local people, PROFEPA tries to enforce the laws. Theoretically, one can go to jail for killing tepescuintles or deer out of season. However, local countryfolk are seen as subsistence hunters, and enforcement agencies rarely have the heart to jail them. This dubious charity leads to a "tragedy of the commons" (Hardin 1968). Hunters see no prospects for conserving, so they take what they can before the final collapse. They are thus exterminating the game when they could easily be working to help increase game-animal numbers. Conversely, well-to-do urban hunters (mercifully absent from western Quintana Roo) are usually too powerful and rich to arrest. So no enforcement occurs.

During our field work together, in several hundred hours of field time in fairly remote forest areas, we observed only one small herd of Collared Peccaries; fresh tracks of deer, agouti, and paca; and many coatis. In addition, at least one troop of spider monkeys survives in Chunhuhub, in a small area of tall forest with many mature sapotes and other fruit trees. These monkeys preferentially stay in the sapotes. A large monkey troop based in the great Classic Maya ruin at Nueva Loria had, however, been eliminated by shooting as of 2001. The peccary herd and a freshly shot curassow were both at fruiting sapote trees in the remote southeastern corner of Chunhuhub's ejido lands, and were evidently lured by the sapotes from wilder and more remote places.

In 1996, in the extremely rough, thorn-covered hills at the southwestern edge of town, we observed fresh deer bedding and dung right at the edge of town, as well as many peccary, agouti, and even paca tracks. The individual deer in question was well known to local hunters but too wily for them!

In nearby areas less heavily hunted than Chunhuhub, we observed many more animals and evidences of animals. Deer remain fairly common in the most isolated parts of isolated private ranches, but even here they are fading out fast. In various remote areas of fairly old to very old forest, we observed in 1996 four jaguarundis (and tracks of several more), two ocelots, and fresh tracks of a jaguar. Most of the jaguarundis, and the jaguar, were in marshy or swampy areas, where they could take refuge in the vast and impenetrable thorn forests that cover such areas.

From talking to several dozen hunters and woodspeople, and from FMT's own wide experience, we could put together a general picture of animal abundance in the region. Details will be found in the specific accounts in appendix I (cf. also Jorgensen 1993). In general:

Rabbits, squirrels, gophers, agoutis, quail, tinamous, chachalacas, and parrots remain fairly common. Numbers of all these decreased sharply during and after Hurricane Roxanne but were increasing again by mid-1996. None of these are systematically hunted except the agoutis.

White-tailed Deer, Collared Peccaries, pacas, spider monkeys, armadillos, jaguarundis, Great Curassows, and Ocellated Turkeys are rare to very rare in Chunhuhub, persisting in greater numbers in other areas. The more remote the area, the more animals one finds. The armadillos—less rare than the others—were never very common and were largely wiped out by Hurricane Roxanne rather than by hunting pressure. Ocelots are very rare now in Chunhuhub but remain not uncommon in Naranjal Poniente just to the south, and presumably wander into Chunhuhub and occur in other nearby ejidos.

Brocket deer, White-lipped Peccaries, tapirs, howler monkeys, jaguars, and guans no longer occur in Chunhuhub (except for occasional jaguars that wander through from other areas) and are exceedingly rare throughout central Quintana Roo. Brockets and howler monkeys survive in some numbers not far to the south, for example, in the ejidos of Margaritas and Manuel Avila Camacho.

Most, if not all, elders in the Zona Maya today feel very uncomfortable about cutting large areas of forest, because it is so destructive of wildlife habitat as well as of trees. It is well known that small areas grow back rapidly to forest, while big cleared areas tend to revert to weeds such as bracken fern. We have frequently heard this expressed (and, of course, we share the same value ourselves). Families who want to clear eight hectares will clear two four-hectare tracts; sometimes even four hectares will be cleared in two or three parcels. (Cf. Vayda 1996, 19–20, reporting the absence of such knowledge or belief in an ecologically comparable area of Borneo. The Bornean area has worse soil than Quintana Roo, and had a smaller, more dispersed population until recently. Thus, perhaps, no occasion had arisen to learn this bit of ecological lore.)

On the other hand, hunters take any and all animals at any and all seasons. Concern with age, sex, and reproductive status of the animal has not usually been a serious issue—though Alcocer Puerto (2001) and Llanes Pasos (1993, 69) explicitly raise it in the context of traditional conservation ideology. Until recently, there was apparently no need to make it so. Low human population and high animal population permitted hunters to take what they wanted. Moreover, it is far easier, under field conditions, simply to limit the number of animals taken. Seasons are difficult to enforce without game wardens, and observation of the reproductive status of animals is difficult or impossible in the forest, particularly since much of the hunting of larger animals takes place at night.

Today's problems stem from several causes. First and most important is the skyrocketing human population. A smaller and smaller percentage of the population is hunting, but, with Chunhuhub growing from zero to five thousand people in fifty years, the pressure on game resources has become intolerable.

Second, habitat is degrading rapidly (cf. Humphries 1993). Permanent cultivation and cattle ranching produce environments of virtually no use to most local animal species. Moreover, much of the environment is currently in the young-forest stage, which, as noted above, is poor animal habitat.

Third, traditional conservation ideology is breaking down rapidly. It remains strong among people over seventy. It is still a factor to reckon with among most adults. Young people and young adults have little of it. This is especially true of those who have been more influenced by rural mestizo Mexican cultural values. Some, the most alienated, have acquired an image of the Mexican rancher as a person who shoots everything he sees and is far too macho to waste his time thinking about laws, rules, or conservation. This stereotype is far from true of all ranchers. Many ranchers known to us, in Quintana Roo and elsewhere in Mexico, are horrified at such behavior. But Quintana Roo countryfolk have indeed been exposed to both rural and urban "sportsmen" who do in fact act that way. However, traditional conservation ideology is still strong enough to provide a powerful force for game management in such ejidos as Manuel Avila Camacho and Tres Garantias. Even in Chunhuhub, it is still strong and is directly responsible for the survival of the animals that still survive there.

Tragically, market hunting, though almost absent in the area we know, is common in some nearby areas with better game resources and better access to towns. Deer meat is sold in Jose Maria Morelos, and we have even seen it offered openly by a restaurant there, in spite of Quintana Roo's law against the sale of deer meat. The restaurant, just down the street from the police station, once had a large sign on the main road offering venison as the day's special.

It will be obvious to the reader, by now, that enforcement of game laws is virtually nonexistent in rural Quintana Roo. We never found anyone who knew the state game laws (assuming that such exist). Local police and government officials we interviewed could not provide us with specific information about either state or national laws. In fact, Mexico's federal hunting laws are enlightened (see Editorial Porrúa 1995, 207–15). They ban market hunting, taking of females of game mammals, and most other unsustainable practices, and they set strict limits. However, they are not necessarily enforced on the ground (on these issues, cf. Alvarez del Toro 1991, esp. pp. 121–27). SEMARNAP, Mexico's secretariat of the environment, issues a *calendario cinegetico* (hunting calendar) with season and bag limits, but we have never observed an actual document of this kind in the rural Zona Maya.

Part of this is the tragedy of the commons at work. However, deliberate failure to enforce laws is not really a tragedy of the commons but a tragedy of government abnegating its clear responsibilities. Abnegation is at all levels. Ejidos protect their cattle and sheep but not their game, although they own the game (collectively) just as they own the livestock. There is something of the sense of traditional English common law: anything one works on, raises, or creates is one's own and taking it is theft, but anything one does not raise or create is literally "fair game" for anyone.

Private landowners suffer along with everyone else. Ranches are subjected to constant and heavy poaching, to the annoyance of the ranchers, many of whom have traditional Maya values.

The common-private distinction is not particularly relevant here. Ranchers often are well ahead of the ejidos in developing their lands intensively for cash crops and cattle. Competition may force them into this, in which case what we may call the "tragedy of the private sector" is worse than that of the commons. In any case, some ranchers are not conservation minded, in spite of their having theoretical (and, sometimes, really effective) control of their game resources. Far from managing these resources sustainably, they sometimes take on the role they believe is proper for a Mexican rancher, including a dedication to the hunt. Others simply allow their friends and employees to hunt at will. Most Maya ranchers continue to pay some attention to conservation and protection, but their holdings are usually small and hard to protect. Only ranches that are both large and well managed have good game stocks, and even these have far lower animal populations than they could maintain—and, indeed, did maintain in the very recent past.

Playing against these unfortunate facts of life are several countervailing forces. First, and by far the most important, is the rapid change of Mexican popular and official attitudes toward conservation. Until recently, Mexican urban culture had little place for the natural environment. Within the last twenty-five years, Mexico has discovered the environment and is now a world leader in conservation. A generation ago, Mexico had few parks and reserves, and these few were consecrated to recreational and economic use—not to biotic conservation. Today, Mexico has millions of hectares of parks and biosphere reserves dedicated to this purpose. Quintana Roo alone has the vast Sian Ka'an Reserve, the new Yum Balam Reserve worked out in cooperation with the town of Kantunilkin, and many smaller reserved areas. Just across the border into Campeche is the truly mammoth Calakmul Reserve, at 2 million hectares, one of the largest and richest biosphere reserves in the world.

Meanwhile, improved scientific training has created a new generation of biologists and administrators, committed to preserving the environment and its fauna. A major conference on management and conservation of deer in Mexico took place in Chetumal in 1996 (Escamilla Guerrero and Raña Garibay 1996). Here, game farmers from central Mexico, mixed-species ranchers from the Texas border, and biologists from all over the nation rubbed elbows with Maya elders and woodspeople from the forests of Quintana Roo (e.g., Villegas Maldonado 1996). Many important observations about raising White-tailed Deer in northern Mexico and in the Yucatán Peninsula made it clear that these deer are being managed as both a wild and a domestic resource. Valuable information on raising them in Quintana Roo was provided by Remolina Suárez (1996). (The brocket, confined to old-growth forests and little known, has not been so lucky; it is not even clear whether there are one or two species in the state.) Most important, however, were the papers on game management on forest ejidos.

It would naturally follow that this new environmental consciousness would eventually make contact with Maya traditional conservationist attitudes, and such has proved to be the case. However, in Quintana Roo animal conservation, one sees only the first sprouts of what may some day grow into comanagement of resources on a large scale. None of these sprouts has yet grown in the Chunhuhub area.

The most important initiative, statewide, has emerged from the Plan Forestal, the forest conservation and management plan administered from Chetumal (see Murphy 1990). Biologists associated with the Plan Forestal office have begun to work with several ejidos that have small human populations, large areas with much high forest, and large surviving populations of the game species. All these ejidos are in the south-central and southwestern parts of the state, well to the south of Chunhuhub. As of 1996, the ejidos involved in this program are Manuel Avila Camacho, Petcacab, and Nohbec in the south-center, and Caobas and Tres Garantias in the far southwest (on the Campeche border, just north of Guatemala). Biologists, often on their own time, have worked with ejido leaders to develop working plans for successful conservation of game. Alberto Ehnis Duhne and Gilberto Avila have been among the most active of Plan Forestal biologists (Avila 1996 and pers. comm.; Ehnis 1996 and pers. comm.). The most successful ejido in conserving its animals, at this time, appears to be Tres Garantias; the least successful is Manuel Avila Camacho, which has a relatively small and disturbed forest base.

THE TRES GARANTIAS EXPERIENCE

Tres Garantias is ideally suited for conservation. It has an enormous land base (44,520 hectares), half of it under some of the finest rain forest left in Mexico. The neighboring ejido of Caobas is even larger (68,533 hectares) with even more reserve land, and an equally enlightened game policy (though not without controversy, especially in reshooting jaguars with tranquilizer darts; see Niiler 2001). The two are, de facto, a joint reserve. Tres Garantias has a small population (105 ejidatarios). Above all, the population, or at least its leaders, is committed to conservation and sustainable management of resources. Twenty thousand hectares is dedicated to forestry management, of which five thousand hectares is a game reserve. ENA visited Tres Garantias in 1996 and interviewed residents as well as nonresident scholars who know the place well, including Pedro Macarias and Daniel Gonzalez; he has also made use of data from H. Flachsenberg on file with Plan Forestal. There is a useful preliminary study of the birds of southernmost Quintana Roo, including this area, by Figueroa Esquivel (1994).

Much hunting goes on in the ejido, but there is (so far) no detected diminution in wildlife numbers. Some three thousand kilograms of meat per year is extracted (up to fifteen hundred of this being White-tailed Deer). Belief in the guardians of the game is strong among Maya residents, and non-Maya have their own conservation beliefs.

Tres Garantias has constructed a tourist facility consisting of a few small rustic cabins in an exceedingly remote part of its rain forest, near a waterhole. These cabins have electricity, insect screens, running water, and detached shower facilities but are otherwise quite like traditional forest huts. They are found at the dead end of a spine-jarring trail, passable (barely) to four-wheel-drive vehicles in good weather. These cabins are rented for a few days to groups of tourists; arrangements are made through the Plan Forestal office in Chetumal. (This is interesting in itself, since the office staff consists of biologists, not travel agents.) This tourist camp provides an ecotourism experience in the heart of one of the wildest and most untouched places in Mexico, and one of the richest in plant and animal species. Morelet Crocodiles, jaguars, tapirs, monkeys, Ocellated Turkeys, guans, and a vast variety of smaller animals may be observed. Large animals are shy and the forest is thick and trackless; tourists must normally be content with smaller creatures. This tourist facility is popular, in spite of low-key publicity. It attracts approximately two hundred visitors per year—about all it can handle at present.

The Manuel Avila Camacho Experience

Manuel Avila Camacho is an ejido of twelve thousand hectares, some fifty kilometers south of Chunhuhub. It was established about 1970. It has, as of 1996, 192 ejidatarios, representing a population of about one thousand people, of whom about 60 percent are Maya. It is primarily a subsistence-farming ejido, with cash coming from forest products, cattle, and crops, including a little sesame (a rare and declining crop in Quintana Roo). It still has most of the large and vulnerable wildlife of Quintana Roo, including tapir, jaguars, pumas, howler monkeys, and Great Curassows, but the White-lipped Peccary, guan, and Ocellated Turkey have been extirpated.

In cooperation with the Plan Forestal and the forestry biologists associated with it, the ejido became in the mid-1990s a showpiece of animal conservation. However, smaller and more densely populated than the other ejidos with animal conservation plans, it was vulnerable to changes in leadership, and to population increase unless matched by increasing conservation awareness. As of 1996, the Plan Forestal biologists estimated that there are about six to seven Collared Peccaries, ten pacas, and twenty coatis per square kilometer—relatively high population densities for these animals. (In other parts of Latin America, however, peccaries can reach several times this density; see earlier in this chapter.) Deer and other animal populations are harder to estimate.

With the advice of the biologists, the ejido held a public assembly, and decided on hunting rules:

1. No hunting in the forest reserve. (This is somewhat less than half the ejido.)
2. Only the actual holder of a parcel of land can hunt there, except by his express permission. (This has proved difficult to enforce. Isolated ranches with large forest holdings cannot easily patrol their remote borders.)
3. No hunting in areas where the biologists are conducting studies. (Currently, this applies to a small area only.)
4. Curassows are protected. (The ejido is raising them, getting young birds from the federal animal conservation facility at Bacalar.)

Moreover, game taken is recorded, and the figures are duly totaled and processed by the biologists, who can estimate whether the levels of take are

12. K'aambuul *(curassow), a tame bird in Chunhuhub.*

sustainable. At current figures, they appear to be just barely sustainable, except for the deer, which are certainly overhunted. Substantial underreporting would mean that the game is being depleted.

In practice, the rules proved impossible to enforce. The curassows raised by the ejido, in particular, were hard to protect; curassows become extremely tame and confiding in captivity, and released birds are pathetically easy prey for poachers. Illegal hunting was common. When ENA took a field trip in 1996 with a group of biologists and deer experts, they observed poached venison for sale near the ejido entrance road and were even allowed to photograph it and its seller.

Noe González, a village elder, was a central figure in conservation action and was also the head of the ejido police force. He had authority of both the formal and the charismatic kind. The leadership of the ejido was fairly successful in limiting hunting. A voluntary group called Kanan Kee (*kanaan keej*, "caring for deer") was formed to assist. It consists of twenty-two men and is fairly effective. Lorenzo Villegas Maldonado, owner of the Rancho Haleb (Paca Ranch) nearby, was a guiding spirit (see Villegas Maldonado 1996). His small ranch (thirty-six hectares) has nine hectares of forest; it was isolated and hard to patrol, so he felt the need to find security in numbers. Records kept over three years showed a total take of about five tons total, yielding about 1.6 kilograms of meat per person per year.

Tragically, the pressure of poaching, as well as changes in local personnel, led to the collapse of the Manuel Avila Camacho experiment. When ENA returned in 2001, poached meat was again being sold openly on the road. All conservation had ended, and the plans and statistics were forgotten. This indicates the extreme vulnerability of even the best schemes in today's tropical world.

YAXLEY AND EASTERN QUINTANA ROO

The news from other parts of Quintana Roo is bleak. We have personally observed many game animals being sold illegally, alive or dead, along roads. One can almost always observe poachers illegally selling game on the road between Tulum and Felipe Carrillo Puerto; this game is mostly poached from the Sian Ka'an Reserve.

Ueli Hostetler (1997) documented hunting in Yaxley, a village in the Xcacal Guardia complex. He surveyed households, asking them what they killed during 1993. His findings are as follows (Hostetler 1997, 294):

Number of households hunting: 54 (64.3 percent of the households in Yaxley)

Animals killed:
White-tailed deer, 63
Collared peccary, 107
Paca, 126
Agouti, 81
Coati, 233
Chachalaca, 44
Ocellated turkey, 8

Such kill rates, in the densely populated area where Hostetler was working, are unquestionably far too high to be sustainable. The game in the area will not last many more years.

Given current hunting pressure, the animals at most risk of extirpation in Quintana Roo are probably White-lipped Peccary, tapir, jaguar, Great Curassow, guans, and Ocellated Turkey. Brocket deer are in somewhat less immediate danger. All of these species will survive only in large reserves unless immediate and drastic action is taken. In fact, even large reserves offer no permanent protection, unless current enforcement practices are sharply upgraded. As one drives near the Sian Ka'an Reserve along the main highway to Cancun, one observes many people offering game meat along the road; most or all of this game is poached from the reserve. Sian Ka'an enforcement officials have no authority outside the reserve, and those who enforce authority outside the reserve do not patrol Sian Ka'an. Poachers take advantage of this division. Moreover, for whatever reason, police do not appear to apprehend individuals selling game, though sale of most game species is illegal in Quintana Roo.

JEFFREY JORGENSEN'S WORK IN X-HAZIL SUR

Jeffrey Jorgensen, a wildlife biologist, studied X-Hazil Sur, the southerly settlement of a huge ejido (55,295 hectares with some 1,680 people at the time). X-Hazil is just south of the municipio seat of Felipe Carrillo Puerto. It is thus more exposed to outside influences than Chunhuhub. Jorgensen's work documents what seems to be a more advanced stage of the breakdown of traditional conservation attitudes, as well as more ready access to guns and to illegal markets for meat. In 1989–90, he spent seventeen months in the ejido (Jorgensen 1993, 1994, 1998), studying hunting specifically. It should be noted that Jorgensen is a biologist, not an anthropologist, and his mentor was Kent Redford. Redford, a wildlife biologist, was in earlier years a leading opponent of local resource management, rejecting the idea that traditional people practice conservation or have conservation ideology (he has considerably modified his position; see Redford and Mansour 1996). This may have led Jorgensen to overlook what there was of such ideology at X-Hazil Sur; he recorded none. He did record that the Maya of X-Hazil did not kill animals without reason, were protective of harmless and inedible animals (Jorgensen 1993, 99), and deplored the overhunting that was wiping out the wildlife (Jorgensen 1998).

However, the facts, meticulously recorded by Dr. Jorgensen, speak for themselves. He recorded eighty-eight hunts involving the taking of 584 animals, providing 2,700 kilograms of meat. As in Chunhuhub, hunting was usually carried out with .22 and .16.20 rifles. Dogs were used on 17 percent of outings. Coatis and chachalacas tied for most often killed, with 167 individuals of each.

White-tailed Deer provided an average of 32.2 kilograms of meat; brocket deer, 15.6; Collared Peccary, 15.5; White-lipped Peccary, 31.4; coati, 3; paca, 5.8; agouti, 2.8. Birds provided much less, of course: Ocellated Turkey, 3.3; Plain Chachalaca and tinamous, a mere 0.4; and Great Curassow, 3.1 (Jorgensen 1993, 71). Opossums and armadillos were not hunted or eaten.

Jorgensen found only 4.2 game mammals per square kilometer of old forest, 8.4 in garden-forest mosaic, and 3.0 in newly regrowing forest (the least animal-rich formation in Chunhuhub too). Nongame animals were three to four times as common. Game birds reached densities of 11.7, 4.7, and 21.8, respectively (Jorgensen 1993, 138). Almost all of these were chachalacas, which are common in the regrowing forest because they use it as a refuge from which to fly into the milpas. Most (88.5 percent) of the ejido is covered with secondary forest, greatly reducing habitat quality for most animals.

Even squirrels reached densities of a mere 4.5 in forest (probably much lower than Chunhuhub), versus 180 on Barro Colorado Island. (ENA has considerable experience on Barro Colorado. It is a hilly area of poor soil and is far less food-rich than Chunhuhub. The Quintana Roo areas would certainly have more wildlife per hectare if they were not so heavily shot.) Coatis in X-Hazil reached a density of one to four per hectare as opposed to twenty-four on Barro Colorado. Even kinkajous, not normally hunted (but shot—rarely—in Chunhuhub as pests), were less dense than in Barro Colorado. From the personal experience of ENA, Collared Peccaries are exceedingly abundant on Barro Colorado in spite of the very poor food situation; Chunhuhub and, presumably, X-Hazil (even with its large amount of low-quality secondary forest) are peccary heaven but have almost no peccaries.

Jorgensen concluded that only the gophers and chachalacas could sustain the existing hunting pressure (Jorgensen 1994)—a conclusion probably true for Chunhuhub as well (except that, as noted above, Chunhuhub does not even have many gophers). All the larger mammals had clearly been brought to a parlous state. He found the people to "show a general lack of concern for the future or for self-improvement" (Jorgensen 1993, 50), not only failing to conserve their game but even failing to keep their roofs patched. This stands in striking contrast to Chunhuhub. Our experience of X-Hazil is that it is indeed somewhat disoriented by its proximity to the town, and by out-migration of many people, though it seems to have rallied somewhat since Jorgensen's research. Animal life is indeed sparse. Other communities have done better, and Jorgensen has recently provided a thoughtful comparison with some of these success stories (Jorgensen 1998).

Jorgensen was testing Olga Linares's theory of garden hunting (Linares 1976). He found that people did indeed hunt in gardens, and that gardens served as death traps for animals rather than as multiplying grounds. This is evidently a rather new situation, however, driven by the easy availability of guns and the breakdown of traditional conservation ideology. In general, the garden-hunting hypothesis probably holds for the Yucatec (Greenberg 1992). In Chunhuhub today, animals exist primarily in the most remote areas of dense tall forest, but even there they foray out to raid milpas. More to the point, there is universal agreement on the importance of milpas, especially in former times before hunting was so common. FMT remembers well the enormous herds and flocks of animals and game birds that would converge on, and frequently wipe out, milpas as recently as a generation ago. In those days, hunting was necessary not only to provide protein, but, more important, to save the crops.

Don Jacinto Cauich and Don Felix on Hunting

JCC: I was in school, we were studying, and my cousins invited me to go see a beating of the bush. I said, "Sure, but I don't have a rifle." "Come on, I'll lend you mine," said my uncle Marcelino. "Let's go." He lent me his rifle. We went to the beat. By good luck, a deer started up, a huge animal. My uncle asked me: "Is this the first time you've shot a deer?" "Yes." "Too bad," he said, but he didn't tell me why he said "too bad." It was because when you first shoot a deer, you have to look in its mouth and take out an eyetooth. And when one was certain that it had one, when my father cooked the deer in the earth oven, when we took it out of the oven, I took its eyetooth. If you don't get it at that moment, if you lose it, you can't go on and hunt success-fully. You have to pass some time before beginning to hunt again. But when I began to hunt another time, then I had learned it.

When I shot another deer, it had a virtue [bezoar] in its belly. This was round, like a ball. I took it and put it in my pouch, where I put shells for my rifle. Many of my uncles knew how to use this. They explained to me: "When you have shot five or six deer, look inside them, and if there is another bezoar, take it, clean it off, and take care of it. Wait till it's dry, and when it's ready and you can carry it, hunt again. That way nothing will hap-pen. But if you don't know about that, and you just kill deer, you will get sick." I came here and I had good luck hunting. When I got a bicycle, I shot two deer in one place. That was in San Pedro [his father's ranch, later sold when his mother became terminally ill], where I found another bezoar. It shone, really shone. I took it from the paunch. Not all deer have this. It's luck. It lit up things, like a truck headlight—really strong. [Maya believe that shining stones and similar shining objects have great power; for example, the *sastun*, the clear stone or glass object used by ritualists.]

When I came to the point of having killed six deer, I took this thing. [I got the deer] in a road where it entered to eat milpa, and the dogs went in after it. After I took the bezoar, I shot another deer. When you get another bezoar, you take it anew. It is the virtue, the ball they have.

ENA: How many deer have you shot in your lifetime?

JCC: Thirty or thirty-five. And peccaries. Once, when we were coming back, when I was hunting with my cousin, a herd of peccaries crossed our path and we shot four. That was in the track to Colonia Yucatán. There were many peccaries.

People make the loj ts'on ceremony. They kill four chickens, big ones, for luck in deer hunting, to make a *primicia* [lit. first fruits offering, but the standard Spanish translation of loj, regardless of what the loj is for] for taking up your rifle again. If you don't, it's bad. If you kill many deer, it's bad. To hunt anew, you have to pay your dues [to the supernaturals]. It's an act of thanks.

FMT: You have to kill two, three, or four chickens and hold this ceremony. It's a tradition, a custom.

JCC: You use *saka'*. You boil a kilo of maize, or two, and then grind it. It's prepared and put into calabashes. You tie up two poles to hang the calabashes, full of the saka', with a leaf of *ixi'imche'* ["maize tree," a tree with maize-grain–like fruits]. And when you've finished doing this, you leave it for half an hour, then take it down again. You take it the leaf of ixi'imche', and do like this [motions], "In the name of Jesus, in the name of . . ." [Mumbles in imitation of a ritualist's chant].

FMT: [The ritualist scatters it] to the four cardinal points. He knows how to pray in Maya. Then, you leave off using your rifle; after this, when you take and shoot it, next day, it's all new, they say. You can go and shoot several more deer. And when you've shot four or eight or maybe fifteen more deer, you can do it again.

ENA: Is it bad to kill too many animals?

JCC: No, one gets sick, they say, if you go on hunting without renewing your rifle [with the loj ts'on]. My father said that they did that, killing the chickens, boiling them, putting them out on the table. You present your rifle, take the food, there's the rifle.

FMT: Have you seen any strange things out in the forest? Strange lights or mysterious noises?

JCC: For instance, if there are four deer, if four were killed, if you start to think, "I'm going to go to another milpa," there are times when you don't reach it. . . .

FMT: There are people who don't like to let hunters into their milpas. They go and say to a jmeen—I don't know a Spanish word for that; an herbalist—"You know, I want you to do this job for me: I want you to go in my milpa, and put an *alux* [elf] there, so that no one comes in. In case someone enters to hunt, then don't let them stay there hunting." The person then goes and gives life to a small statue [pre-Columbian Maya figurine]. He says: "This is the way I will get to be master. I will go and hit three times the entrance of my milpa, with my machete, with the flat of my machete; I'll hit a tree three times. And then this image will be my employee, to hear this. But with this warning that I give, he will then not frighten me—won't make any noise."

So the master can come in, harvest, collect firewood, and hunt. But when anyone else enters, he doesn't know how to come in the way the master does. He just comes in to hunt. Then, when he hunts, there are noises of throwing things and hitting trees: much noise. So they say. The master, when he comes and takes anything, brings pozole—saka'. He gives a little pozole to the alux, bringing him his little bowls of it. He knows where the alux has his home—under a rock, or in a cave. He says to the alux: "Don't let anyone enter."

I have seen this sort of thing. A man told me about it, when we went once to look for ears of corn in his milpa in Yucatán. We went with my brother. Bam! A stone hit a tree. I was a bit scared. The boy said to my brother: "Let's go, they're going to hit us." Soon, another, very close to us—the tree sounded when a stone hit it. I said: "This scares me." I didn't know what this was all about. My brother began to be afraid too. He said, "I think you're right. They'll hit us. Let's go back." So we went back. At this point the master showed up. He said: "Where are you going? Why aren't you going in to get the ears of corn?" "Well, it's like we're being thrown at. We thought you or someone was trying to hit us." "Oh, don't worry. It's a friend I have here—my caretaker. He takes care of things for me. Do what you please—go on in—he won't hit you." He took his machete and gave three blows to a dry tree—bam, bam, bam! "Let's go!" He said. So we turned the cart around and went to get the corn ears. We got to where they were, and took them, and heard no more noises. "It's a little old man," he said. It was a secret he knew. No one could steal there—no one. If he had lima beans or squash, he'd get all the harvest; no one would take them.

JCC: When I was there in San Pedro, I killed four pacas. I heard another one feeding. I thought I could kill five. But then I heard animals all round me. They closed in on me. There were many, not just one or two. But I believe that God was taking care of me. [I was afraid that, afterward,] when I came to shoot an animal, I'd fall sick. There was a big mahogany tree. In the branches, I heard whistling.

All the animals that I heard closed in on me. There was not a sound—nothing. I remembered all the animals I'd killed. I was going to kill five pacas. I believe I'd passed my limit; it was too many. But when there was that whistling above—nothing! I looked up. What was it? The power of God? But I knew that if I'd killed one more. . . .

FMT: Five is plenty. And God keeps count of what you do. One more and you might have found things frightening.

JCC: I killed four in less than a quarter of an hour. I heard another one feeding. I went to look for it, when I heard it eating—

FMT: Do you have a stone for pacas?

JCC: No, just one for deer. It's enough. I had one for pacas but it disappeared. Who knows what happened to it? It's gone.

FMT: But now you don't hunt pacas?

JCC: No. Nor peccaries. Just deer. I look for their eyeteeth, and for their bezoar stones. Those are smooth and pretty. Really pretty.

FMT: Thirty years ago, pacas abounded. And in new second growth, where there were squashes [still growing after the milpa was abandoned], when you came in at night, there were pacas feeding. And if you went into the woods—at [fruiting] sapote trees you could kill up to ten. In those days they abounded. People took them for subsistence; no one would buy or sell them.

It's a very tasty animal. There is no better meat. It is the finest-eating animal we have here. It agrees very well with us! When you cook in the earth oven and take it out—man, is that tasty, skin and all. It's beautiful meat: white, white. And it has such good flavor. Superfine is that meat. Peccary is good too, but a little heavy. It doesn't compare with paca. Paca has a finer flavor. We often make a *salpicon* [spiced meat dish] of it, and eat it that way.

Today, pacas are very rare and very shy. The few that remain are very wild. It isn't easy to hunt them. In my orchard, they come to eat oranges, but I've tried three times [recently] and haven't shot one. They're too wild.

JCC: There in San Pedro, in the corner, there were peccaries feeding. I didn't want to shoot one. But after three days I shot one. A suckling. I came with a dog. The little dog went there where the peccaries were walking. The little pigs didn't cry; they went "wank, wank, wank." I took my rifle and called, "Ay!" The dog got scared and bit my rifle! He wouldn't let go. It was the will of God. It looked as if I wouldn't get any meat. But finally I shot at the peccaries—there were about fifteen—and killed three. But I didn't eat these animals.

FMT: They say there are secrets for teaching puppies to hunt. As the man in Gavilanes [Don Juan Sanchez] told us: There are secrets for training them. For I too have had puppies and trained them.

He said that you take four leafcutter ants that are carrying *cargo* [leaf pieces], and three without cargo [going the other way for more leaves], and mix them with masa [and make a tortilla] and give them to the pup to eat. And there are other secrets. There's the one I told you: There are some wasps called *chak'at'bej* [ch'akat'bej; at other times he said *chakmoolbej* were used; probably both are]. You take one, catch one, kill it, and mash it in a cup. Then you take some deer blood and mix it in, and then nine chiles of the kind called *sucurres*. So it is said. You cut up those chiles in the cup. Then you take the pup, put him mouth up [lying on his back], and take his nose. Then when he breathes, you throw the blood in. It's spicy and fills his nose. You do this two or three times. He gets used to it and begins to seek out the blood. This secret works because these little animals, these chak'at'bej wasps, are great hunters. They go into the leaf litter. If a spider or crickets or whatever is there become frightened and try to run or jump, the wasp flies after them and kills them. It has to hunt till it succeeds and kills them. It then takes them away for food. Because of this, the wasp is very good for the puppies. These wasps are yellow or reddish. These are real hunters, and nothing escapes them.

JCC: Here's a secret for making a cow tranquil: take water in which one's wife has bathed and give it to the cow to drink. It will stay stupid! Works for horses too.

FMT: How long have you been hunting?

JCC: Thirty years.

FMT: And what rifle do you like best?

JCC: I use a .22 or a .16—it's not at all slow. A .22 is slower. One shot [of a .16] seems like eighteen shots—you shoot fast with this one.

FMT: When you have hunted for deer, did you hunt in the day, or more at night?

JCC: Nobody hunts in the day. Just at night.

FMT: And your brothers didn't become hunters?

JCC: No. My brother, my poor brother Lencho—Alfredo—in his whole life, fifty-three years, he's killed nothing but one peccary! And even that took ten shots! [Maya take pride in killing with one shot.] He shot the animal and it didn't even close its eyes. Over thirty mecates he had to walk after it because he shot it a lot [but it didn't fall]. My father was a hunter. Not with a flashlight either—nothing but the moon, when it was full.

FMT: You never saw phantoms or heard frightening noises?

JCC: No.

FMT: You didn't hear talking?

JCC: No.

FMT: Sometimes there is whistling.

JCC: Nothing spoke to me, but I heard a noise once without seeing anything.

FMT: Strange objects?

JCC: Objects, no; flames, yes.

FMT: Ten years in the woods alone . . .

JCC: Ten years.

FMT: You never saw anything rare?

JCC: Nothing more than this: In front of San Pedro, our ranch, at nine at night, when I went in to the border of the milpa, a light passed—a flame. No higher than the ears on the corn. When it came, I thought it was a light that one of my brothers was carrying. But I waited. Was it an ocelot? If not an ocelot, was it a raccoon? I went another time, always there was that flame there. It was four meters away. I was with my little brother. He asked if it was always there. We didn't know what it was, nor did we go to look.

FMT: I heard much noise once, but it didn't scare me, because I knew it was a noise of birds. I had no fear of a jaguar. I never was scared. The only thing that scares me is a snake.

There really are witches these days. I believe so.

JCC: Yes, there are.

FMT: *Way,* they're called in Maya. *Brujos* in Spanish. I saw one once, at my apiary. A goat came up when I was there alone. This was at two in the morning. It seemed to be up early. It walked on its hooves, making a noise like "pikich, pikich, pikich"; witches sound like that.

I raised my head from my hammock and saw this goat come. The moon was out, and so I saw it come. The door was open. It came up, put in its head to look at me in the corner of my house, began to look. I thought it was a goat. So I wasn't afraid. I thought: If I can catch it, I can take it to my village. So I'm going to go after it. I wanted to take it to raise in the village.

Now, some two miles south, there was a little rancho called Polcitam, with a few families. At three in the morning that rancho began to wake, and I could hear the roosters crow. And this animal heard that and rose up. I lay waiting for it, in the house, in the hammock. It saw this, saw I wasn't asleep, I think. It turned and went off. It went out, walking, eating on the way. A little she-goat, I thought. At dawn I'll catch it, I said. And when that time came, I began to take the road to the village. When I got on the road, I didn't see it. I said, this animal has gone on. I saw it three times and didn't see it again. It disappeared from the road. I went on, running, and returned to see where I could meet it. I didn't encounter it. It was gone. At dawn I went to see if there were tracks where it had been; not one track did I see. At seven in the morning my brother came. We began to talk. "Ah," he said to me, "very near is Polcitam, and there is a family of witches there...." "So! That one in the night . . . ?" "Yep, it was a witch," he said to me. "Don't go back to staying there alone, or sleep there," he told me.

I didn't go back to sleep in that house at the apiary. I didn't stay there. My sister said that it was a witch that I saw there. Then, when I went there, I had no fear of walking in the woods. No fear.

JCC: I came from Chichimila', near Valladolid. I have been here thirty-three years. Here I was married, twenty-four years ago. Now I am fifty-five years old, on the tenth of February. We had a piece of land, but my father sold it. Now, to seek my small beans to eat [i.e., my modest livelihood], I have my workshop [making rough furniture]. When we got rid of the ranch and moved here, I knew nothing of carpentry. Who knows how I learned it. But now I live here and work at it. I had no master, nobody. Just used my head. I've been doing it about twelve years. Wood has gone up in price. It used to be cheap—15 or 20 pesos for a board. Now it's 60 or 70. I sell tables for 400 or 450, a big chair for 120, a regular chair for 75. These days, life is harder than it was.

Chapter Five

ANIMAL NAMES AND NOMENCLATURE

The Maya love to talk about plants and animals. Anthropologists often focus their research on whatever it is that their consultants are most fond of discussing. The Maya, deeply committed to their fields, gardens, and forest lands, are fond of discussing agriculture, animal rearing, hunting, herb gathering, firewood collecting, and associated matters.

Since colonial times, Spanish speakers in the Yucatán Peninsula have found it convenient or necessary to learn Maya names in order to refer to local plants and animals (as well as soils, water bodies, and much else). From early days of conquest, the Spanish, after vaguely and inaccurately misapplying various Spanish names to local creatures, soon found the local names more convenient. The Maya were educated and literate people and outnumbered the Spanish everywhere. Soon the Spanish became bilingual. Even the elite of Mérida spoke Maya. Over the centuries, Yucatec Maya remained the language of the rural world, even as Spanish became more and more important for urban and mercantile matters. Thus the rich Yucatec ethnobiological vocabulary is not only still alive and flourishing; it is also the only way to refer to most plants and many animals of the peninsula, unless one uses international scientific nomenclature.

Today, in many communities, including the area of the present study, most people are bilingual, and code switching is common: Spanish is used to discuss anything relating to modern urban civilization, politics, and government, but Maya is used to talk about agriculture, forestry, the countryside, and wild things in general. Even the most Hispanicized individuals use Maya names to refer to wild biota, if only because there are rarely any Spanish names to use. This is much more true for plants than for animals, but even many common animals have no local Spanish names and are called by Yucatec names even by sophisticated urbanites in Mérida. For instance, the Great-tailed Grackle *(Quiscalus mexicanus)*, the most obvious town bird in Yucatán as in most of Mexico, is universally called by its Maya name, *k'aau* (also spelled *k'au, k'a'au, k'aw,* or *k'a'aw*), even in the Mérida newspapers (where the word is variously spelled). The names by which it is known elsewhere in Mexico *(tordo, zanate, cuervo, graja)* are not locally known or used.

This sparked an interest in terminology that led, as early as the sixteenth century, to the compilation of excellent accounts and dictionaries. Interest has grown with succeeding years. As a result, the Yucatec Maya are probably the best-documented Native American people in regard to ethnobiology. Early work by local scholars, such as Salvador Pacheco Cruz (1958), was followed by major research using modern elicitation techniques. The record is especially complete in regard to plants (see esp. Barrera Marín, Barrera Vásquez, and Lopez Franco 1976; Sosa et al. 1985), but animals have not been neglected. Several studies of local birds and bird names exist (Bowes 1964; Hartig 1979). An excellent but unfortunately unpublished thesis by Efrain Gutierrez provides a comprehensive dictionary of usage in east-central Quintana Roo (Gutierrez 1987). Pacheco Cruz's work is still useful, though some of his scientific identifications are wrong.

Especially valuable were the contributions of the great linguist and philologist Alfredo Barrera Vásquez and his biologist son, Alfredo Barrera Marín. Not only did they perform incredible labors in documentation and identification, they helped stimulate a vast amount of research, most of it by biologists, including Victoria Sosa, J. Salvador Flores, and Arturo Gómez-Pompa (Sosa et al. 1985; Flores and Ucan Ek 1983; Gómez-Pompa 1987; Gómez-Pompa, Salvador Flores, and Sosa 1987). The Cordemex dictionary, compiled by Barrera Vásquez (1980; now *Diccionario Maya Porrúa*) provides thorough and accurate definitions of many animal terms. Early name uses and bird beliefs are summarized in Alvarez (1980). The original colonial dictionaries themselves, as well as other sources, are now published in modern editions (Andrews Heath de Zapata 1980; Arzápalo Marín 1987, 1996). Unfortunately, many of the animal names in these dictionaries are either not identified or incorrectly identified. Several interesting notes occur in A. Barrera Vásquez's many writings on the Maya, such as his observation that

Maya say the cowbird lays its eggs in other birds' nests as a gesture of magnanimity (1975, 22). In recent years, classics of ethnozoology have emerged from research on related Maya peoples (Atran 1993, 1999; Hunn 1977).

Terminology in the Zona Maya is somewhat different from that found in most of Yucatán state. Actually, the *zona maicera* (traditional maize-agriculture zone) of Yucatán is continuous with the Zona Maya of Quintana Roo, and has supplied many immigrants to it. They are therefore one cultural continuum. Differences begin to appear as one moves west and southwest; the Mayan dialects of the Mérida region or of Campeche state are rather different.

There are, thus, several names attested in the literature that are not found in Chunhuhub. Many of these are of water birds that do not occur in Chunhuhub (such as *pontoj* for "pelican"), but some are simply names that Chunhuhub does not have. Particularly interesting is *kot*, glossed as "eagle" (Pacheco Cruz 1958, 56) and as "red eagle" *(águila bermejo)* in the colonial dictionaries. This bird is interesting for two reasons. First, as implied by Pacheco Cruz and as hypothesized specifically by Timothy King (pers. comm.), this name is very possibly derived from Nahuatl *cuautli*. Second, it is the only native animal that is widely held to be a *way*, a witch's transformation animal (see the colonial dictionaries—Andrews Heath de Zapata 1980; Arzápalo Marín 1996; Barrera Vásquez 1980—and also Redfield and Villa Rojas in Chan Kom, 1934, 179, to determine whether the *way* pop is a variant of *way* kot—as it certainly is in my experience; Alicia Re Cruz recorded *way kot* in her restudy of Chan Kom, 1996). It is impossible now to tell what eagle the kot was. Pacheco Cruz describes it as a small eagle of high forest, an eater of insects, lizards, and small birds. This would fit any of the hawk-eagles or larger hawks. The red color noted in the colonial dictionaries might suggest the Ornate Hawk-Eagle.

However, differences in animal terminology are minor. Even among the Itzaj (modern spelling; traditionally spelled Itzá) Maya of Guatemala, Atran's research has produced names for the commoner animals that are substantially identical to those given here (Atran 1993, 1999, and pers. comm.). However, the new dictionary by Hofling and Tesucún (1997), with its much fuller account of Itzaj animal names, reveals many differences in the names of less common species. Some of these are rather poetic, such as *pay k'in* (caller of the sun) for the Laughing Falcon. The universal Yucatec name *koos* for this bird is apparently unknown to the Itzaj.

The animal lore and nomenclature of the Yucatec Maya is certainly useful but is not limited to the useful. All manner of tiny and insignificant creatures are named. Thus the Maya case is indeterminate between the "utilitarian" theory (Hunn 1982) of nomenclature and the theory of Berlin (1992), who holds that people simply want and need to classify the things of their environment. Maya break down some categories more than others, and there is usually an obvious reason for this. For example, wasps and bees are the subject of a whole classification system, while true bugs are lumped under one name. This is obviously because wasps and bees are valuable and culturally significant—they produce honey and edible larvae, and they sting. Bugs are of little interest. Yet they do have a collective name. Thus, it would seem that both Berlin's *"vis classificatrix"* ("classifying force," i.e., an inferred drive of the human mind to classify things) and utilitarian considerations are active here. The first makes the Maya give names to everything. The second makes them give much more detailed and specific names within certain useful groups of animals.

In ethnobiology there is a range from social-constructionist to realist positions. The former asserts that traditional classification systems reflect society and socially constructed ideas, rather than a reality that is out there in the biological world. This position goes back to Durkheim and Mauss's seminal essay of 1903 (Durkheim and Mauss 1963 [1903]). The realist position asserts that people do attend to biological, natural, and extra-human realities: to things that are "out there," not created by humans, rather than strictly in the socialized human mind. Roy Ellen (1993), Gregory Forth (1996), and to a degree Ralph Bulmer (1967)—all reporting research in east Indonesia and Papua–New Guinea—stress social construction, and Ellen has been sharply critical of narrowly realist models. Conversely, Boster (1987; Boster, Berlin, and O'Neill 1986; Boster and d'Andrade 1989) and Hunn (1977), all writing from Native American experience, seem more prone to assume that people recognize categories that are "real" in terms of formal evolutionary biology. Atran (1990) and Berlin (1992) take a particularly strong position: People are mentally programmed to recognize the multistranded similarities that evolutionary relationships provide, and thus do "carve nature at the joints" (Berlin 1992; Atran's later positions are considerably more qualified and nuanced, due to his prolonged study—including use of psychological experiments, in collaboration with psychologists—of Itzaj Maya classification; Atran 1999). There are two separate realist claims (Atran 1990; Boster, Berlin, and O'Neill 1986; Boster 1987): first, that nature really does have joints, however indistinct they appear; second, that humans everywhere share some commonalities (presumably innate) in thought processes. One need not go as far as Atran and Berlin do to find broad similarities in human cognition. People note the same things, find similar things "salient" or "criterial," figure out similar uses for wildlife, and use broadly similar algorithms in classification. The degree to which this is true remains highly unclear, even speculative; but Atran, Berlin, Cecil Brown, and their various coworkers have established beyond reasonable doubt that the phenomena are real, and that social construction simply does not allow any arbitrary system to flourish. Foucault (1971) recognizes this in discussing the improbability of Jose Luis Borges's burlesque classification schemes. One can see they are fictional without being told.

There is a middle ground that captures the best of both views. Lévi-Strauss (1962) pointed out that traditional peoples have superb knowledge of their environments, a true "science of the concrete," but that their classification systems are also influenced by social factors—and that this is just as true of the French as of the Native Americans. He also noted that there are, within any society, some classification systems that are more realist, others that are more social: for example, in his native French culture, biologists' taxonomy (on the realist side) and breeders' and racers' names for dogs and horses (on the social side; these are highly systematized).

One concludes that both the constructionists and the realists are right. Classification is a social construction, but one that must take account of real natural differences if it is to be of any use at all (cf. Anderson 2001, Atran 1990, Berlin 1992, and literature reviewed therein). The natural differences are there; animals mate with their own species and have mechanisms to prevent hybridization; when these mechanisms fail, it is always along predictable lines: the mistaken matings are with close evolutionary relatives, not with distant ones. Ducks mix with closely related ducks but do not try to breed with eagles.

Native Americans have thoughtfully pointed out that traditional Native American cultures typically recognize nature—in the sense of a nonhuman reality that humans did not create and cannot always control. But they interact with it very differently from Europeans; they continually deal with nature in a highly comprehensive way, regarding animals as both prey and kin, plants as both useful materials and spirit beings, and the world in general as both livelihood and living. This is the Maya pattern, not only in Yucatán but also in the highlands (Lenkersdorf 1996), and I found it also on the Northwest Coast (Anderson 1996).

Since the Maya and contemporary international biologists are both trying to find useful labels that represent some sort of external reality, there are many similarities in the two systems. Since the uses in question are not the same, there are also differences—largely at the level of "lumping." The Maya lump species of flycatchers that are unimportant to them. The biologists try to distinguish all flycatcher species. However, biologists also lump things they do not find salient. Nematologists estimate that the few thousand recognized species of nematodes could probably be split into hundreds of thousands (if not millions) of species, if nematode taxonomy were as developed as avian taxonomy. Thus, even among scientists, one does not expect, and does not find, quite so good a fit between classification systems and natural reality as one would expect from some of the work of Boster (1987; Boster, Berlin, and O'Neill 1986; Boster and d'Andrade 1989) or of Atran's earlier theorizing. Nature has joints, but they are sometimes unclear, and it is often not worth the time required to find them. Thus, any classification system becomes an accommodation to reality, but one conditioned by the needs of the classifiers. Any socially or culturally accepted classification system accommodates the needs of the society. But, since all viable societies have to have *some* contact with reality, all societies have classification systems that recognize many of nature's joints. Thus all systems are somewhat comparable, and all are "scientific" in a broad sense (González 2001). The belief that every culture has its own utterly idiosyncratic system and the belief that every culture shares (to some degree) in a single system that is "true" are alike unsupported by the evidence.

Maya extension of terms fits well with Boster's findings that broad visual similarities serve as primary markers of relationship, and also with Boster's observation that Native American peoples are prone to name birds from their vocalizations. This affects classification; flycatchers, for instance, are broken down as much by vocalization as by appearance. The Maya also consider behavior and habitat in making identifications and classifications. The term *pujuy* (perhaps more accurately *pu'ujuy*, as it is listed in appendix I in this book as well as in Bricker, Po'ot Yah, and Dzul de Po'ot 1998; but we will stick with the normal spoken pronunciation here), for instance, is extended to birds that act like the focal pujuy (a nightjar, or pauraque), but not to other nocturnal birds that are superficially similar in appearance.

Berlin (1992) has demonstrated the similarity of folk classification systems around the world, and the similarity of many systems to modern scientific taxonomy. This he ascribes to a tendency of humans to perceive certain sorts of discontinuities and continuities in nature. It is perhaps more accurate to say that people perceive all sorts of things but interact with humans and with other lives so much that everyone, eventually, tends to realize that some differences matter and some do not.

Overall, the Maya data fit much better with the findings of Boster and his associates than with those of more social-constructionist scholars. The Maya are scientists, not Durkheimian social philosophers projecting their views on an unsuspecting world (Anderson 2000, 2001).

However, different Maya groups, and even different Maya consultants within the same group, classify birds in different ways. This is not so much a matter of failing to perceive relationships as of devising classifications that fit one's own referential and ecological practice (Hanks 1990; Nyerges 1997). This is the cutting edge: the point where social construction influences taxonomy.

It is also worth pointing out that "utility" in the narrow sense originally adduced by Hunn (1982) did not exhaust the reasons why people might want to talk about something. They might want to talk about it only because it is common and has a pretty song, and is therefore hard to ignore if one loves birds as much as the Maya do; thus there are not one but two names for the singularly "useless"—but pretty and songful—Yellow-green Vireo (*Vireo flavoviridis*).

From the point of view of folk classification theory, the Yucatec animal terminology is of interest for several reasons. Yucatec terminology fits well into theories of the evolution and structure of folk ethnobiological systems. It is, indeed, quite typical of a broad class of such systems, resembling (in general features) other nomenclatural systems found among tropical peoples and among many of the heirs of the great Mesoamerican civilizations. On the other hand, it uses fewer and broader "unique beginners" than Zapotec and Mixtec systems seem to do (Alejandro de Avila and Gary Martin, pers.

comm.), and its names tend to be much less complex linguistically than Nahuatl names, which are often whole phrases agglutinated into single words.

The Yucatec system, as used in central Quintana Roo, is of interest also because of the complex and subtle pattern of extension. Most terms refer to a focal animal, or small group of very similar animals, but can be extended to cover other animals that seem slightly less similar. Often, terms are extended very widely, to link animals that have only a slight resemblance. This contrasts sharply with the neat, clean pattern that is reflected in many descriptions of folk taxonomies. We believe that our Yucatec system is more typical than these latter descriptions might suggest. Our prolonged field experience has given us a good sense of the enormous range of extension that terms tend to undergo in actual use contexts. ENA's experience with several other animal nomenclatural systems (including Cantonese, Polynesian, and English) suggests that general, vague, far-extended, and metaphorical uses of animal names all exist commonly in languages throughout the world. This phenomenon has also been noted for the Itzaj by Atran (1999).

The Yucatec system is, unsurprisingly, particularly close to those of other Mayan languages. The structure of Tzeltal and Tzotzil taxonomies has been described in the classic works of Berlin, Breedlove, and Raven (1974) and Hunn (1977). The closely related Yucatec language shares the same structure. The animal taxonomy seems deceptively simple: life-form classes, folk generics, and folk specifics.

Cecil Brown has used many data from these works, and from his own work on Yucatec, in his cross-cultural studies of animal life-form classes (Brown 1979a, 1979b, 1982; Brown and Witkowski 1982). Broadly, there are some simple terms that clearly function as higher-order taxa, as life-form classes are often supposed to do; they include folk generics. The major terms in this set are *ch'iich'* (bird), *yik'ej* (insect, referring mainly to insects with wings and/or legs, not other "wugs" [pests]), *kaan* (snake), and *kay* (fish). However, once we leave these terms behind, problems begin. There are two other kinds of terms that could be seen as life-form categories but that are, strictly speaking, not so.

One is the term ba'alche' (thing of the trees, i.e., wild animal). It is used as loosely as "wild animal" is in English; it is a catchall term, not a proper taxonomic entity. Itzaj has the same word (Atran 1999; Hofling and Tesucún 1997). In both languages, it can mean either "wild animal in general" or "wild mammal" (cf. Atran 1999). The contrast term is *alakbij*, "domesticated animals," with the sense of "animals reared in one's compound." Both terms apply to birds (e.g., chachalacas versus chickens) but seem to be used most in connection with mammals. *Alak* means "to rear animals"; *-bij* is a nominalizing suffix. In standard Yucatec of Yucatán, it would end in *-l*, but Quintana Roo Maya replaces *-l* with *-j* [i.e., /h/] in this linguistic environment.

The other type of problem involves *nook'ol* (worm; Sp. *gusano), aak* (turtle), and some of the insect terms, such as *sinik* (ant). These are all terms that could be seen as broad enough to stand as life-form categories. The problem is that none of these is really very broad in extension. Nook'ol is the most broad of these but is ambiguous because most nook'ol are caterpillars that are known to turn into yik'ej; only a few are nook'ol that never metamorphose. The other terms actually function as folk generics; that is, they are used in the field to refer to evident sets of animals, and they are subdivided by creating folk specifics—simple adjective-noun pairs in which an adjective modifies the generic. By contrast, ch'iich' is never so used; it can only be used to refer to the collectivity of all birds in general, or to undifferentiated mixed flocks or the like. (Kay can be used as a modified noun, but more typically it shares real life-form taxon status: There are many folk genera of fish, and the word kay is not used for them except to refer to a bunch of them collectively, according to my observations in Yucatán and Campeche port towns. See also Atran 1999.)

Mammals, and also many small insignificant invertebrates, are not subsumed under any named life-form class, except in so far as ba'alche' can loosely cover "wild mammals." This is predictable from Brown's model of taxonomic evolution (which indeed incorporated Yucatec data in its formation). There is no need to have general terms for these creatures, for opposite reasons. Mammals are so well known that one usually speaks of them by species name. Domestic mammals in general are also referred to as *ganado* (Sp. for "cattle," including cows, sheep, and goats) or *criado* (Sp. for "raised," used especially of pigs, dogs, and others that are not "cattle").

"Covert categories" *sensu* Berlin (1992), that is, categories that are implicit in the taxonomic scheme but are not named, may exist but are very hard to determine. Sometimes, a category that might be considered "covert" in Maya is routinely named with a Spanish label. It seems the Maya once did have covert categories, and found the Spanish language—with its wealth of mid-range taxa—a godsend for labeling these. A common example is *avispa* (wasp). The Maya *xuux* can be used to cover all wasps, but properly it refers only to a group of small dark ones. Similarly, *t'uut'* (White-fronted Parrot) can be extended to cover all parrots, and that seems to be what was done in the old days, if one had to refer to them all; but actually it means only the single species, and other parrots all have their own names. Thus the Spanish *loro* is now widely borrowed into Maya as a general term for "parrot." At a more general level, *bicho* (insect pest) has been borrowed for a non-Maya concept; the Maya traditionally do not think in terms of "pests," since all animals have their place. Indeed, the Maya, and for that matter many Spanish, often use bicho to mean wug, without the pejorative loading. The Yucatec Maya language has also borrowed Spanish *maleza* (weed) to refer to worthless and undesired plants—a concept and category that does not really exist in traditional Maya thought, since virtually all plants are useful, and few were real pests until the Spanish introduced the tough and weedy grasses that are now the bane of farmers.

It is questions like this that make it necessary for the investigator to live in the field, hearing ordinary usage, arguments, experts teaching non-experts, and "referential practice" (Hanks 1990) in general. We are in no position to approach in thoroughness Dr. Hanks's great study of Yucatec deixis, but we have diligently tried to follow his approach. Language is part of human interaction, and to understand semantic usage one must be involved in a great deal of that interaction. The names listed in appendix I are derived from actual field observation and experience (with very few exceptions), usually with at least two native speakers, and (again with few exceptions) follow-up in detailed interviews back in town. We have refrained from the many experiments and tests used by Atran (1999), not only because of lack of funds and opportunities, but also because we prefer to stick strictly to referential practice at this point in our research. This is, however, not to be taken as any sort of criticism of Atran's superb, even brilliant, work. The need is for complementary studies using different approaches—not for a forced choice between two methods. The methods should support each other, not compete.

In general, the Yucatec Maya system is close to other Mayan systems: Huastec (Alcorn 1984), Tzotzil, Tzeltal, and so forth. It is also quite similar to the folk English, Spanish, and Chinese systems in structure, detail, and concept. This is not true of several nearby Native American classification systems, as noted above, and thus is not to be explained either as a mere reflex of the way the world "really is," or as a peculiarity of Mesoamerican civilization. It seems to be a Maya cultural matter.

Documentary evidence from soon after the conquest makes it clear that this similarity to European folk taxonomies is not simply a function of acculturation to the Spanish system. The early dictionaries cited in the Cordemex dictionary use or imply the system still familiar. Cristina Alvarez's superb synthesis of early ethnoscientific data discloses a biological nomenclature not significantly different from today's (Alvarez 1980). The reasons for the parallel evolution of Yucatec, European, and Chinese taxonomies remain to be elucidated. Brown's evolutionary sequence seems an appropriate beginning, but there is presumably more to say.

However, the Yucatec system is not a neat taxonomy. It is not adequately analyzed by grouping folk species under folk generics. In Berlin's theory (Berlin 1992), folk generics are typified by names like "oak" and "maple" in English, folk species by "white oak," "red oak," "sugar maple," and "vine maple." The species are neatly included under the genera and are regarded as "kinds of oaks" or "kinds of maples" by speakers. Rarely do English speakers face such confusing entities as "Jerusalem oak" (which is not an oak and does not even remotely resemble one—nor is it from Jerusalem; botanists sometimes advise hyphenating "Jerusalem-oak," but the equally ridiculous "Jerusalem artichoke" is never hyphenated). Yet, perhaps English is less neat than this would appear: Is a horseradish a radish?

Yucatec Maya is definitely less neatly taxonomic than Berlin's theory would suggest. There are very few folk specifics. Almost every name is unique. If a name covers several entities that are perceived as different, these entities are not usually given folk-species names; thus *yaj* covers over a dozen small flycatchers, none of which has a specific name. In many cases, birds that are obviously closely related have totally dissimilar names. Parrots were t'uut', *cocha'*, *taadi'*, and so forth, and were hard to discuss collectively until the Spanish word loro appeared. Similarly, pujuy (pauraque) can be extended to cover all nightjars; *che'jun* (Golden-fronted Woodpecker) can cover all woodpeckers; *uukum* (Red-billed Pigeon) can cover all large pigeons; but in all these cases, the other birds so covered each have their own names. The extensions are recognized as messy and problematic, and are now generally replaced by Spanish loan words. Always, it is the most salient (common or visible) bird that gives its name to the class. Outside of the bird world, ants can all be called sinik, though sinik properly means small ants as opposed to the various named varieties of larger ones.

Only some groups are labeled this way, that is, by using a term at two levels of contrast. For instance, there is no term that can be generalized to cover all doves, or all mimic thrushes, or all gallinaceous birds, or all carnivorous mammals, or any group of carnivores (felids, canids, mustelids). Most terms contrast at only one level: They are either highly specific (e.g., *chiik*, "Tropical Mockingbird"; xunankab, "stingless bee") or general, covering a whole group (*ch'uuy*, "hawk"; *kisaay*, "true bug" [Hemiptera order]).

Woodpeckers are divided among three folk categories (all of which lump species recognized by formal biology), while woodcreepers (almost as varied) are lumped into one. This is partly because woodpeckers are obvious, noisy, colorful birds, but also because they had magical and ritual uses in the past, and thus were culturally important to distinguish (Arzápalo Marín 1987). Woodcreepers are inconspicuous and insignificant, and thus are most efficiently lumped under one category.

There are a few cases in which a genuine folk generic is broken into folk specifics; see, for instance, *ch'oom* (vulture) and *ku'uk* (squirrel) in appendix I. However, most situations that appear to involve such a taxonomic breakdown do not really do so. Many species have color varieties, or, occasionally, form varieties; these color names are not thought of as naming folk species in any sense (see appendix I under *k'aaxik'eek'en*, for instance). Everyone recognizes that they are mere color morphs, occasionally occurring in the same litter of animals. Also, this is one place where there may have been Spanish influence on the taxonomy. Colonial dictionaries make it clear that the black and turkey vultures once had different names, and the use of ch'oom to cover four species may be due to influence from Spanish (or Nahuatl—*zopilote* being the only widespread Mexican term for vultures in general).

Yucatec ethnobiological terms are best understood from a broadly focus-and-extension viewpoint (the following discussion is based in large part on

Kronenfeld 1996). Where there are several different-appearing forms covered by one name, there is usually one that is thought of as the most typical one—the one that comes to mind when the term is mentioned. For instance, the mental image of a *ch'el* (or *ch'eel,* as listed in appendix I), "jay," is of a large, bright blue, very noisy bird—the Yucatán Jay. The Green Jay is *ya'ax ch'eel* (green jay—just as in English); it is not the ch'el par excellence. Still less so is the *panch'el,* "aracari" (formerly panch'el apparently included all toucans), which is not really a ch'el at all.

Some terms even contrast at three levels. The Tropical House Wren is the focal yankotij ("one under the wall," i.e., wren); the term is always used to cover all other wrens, as opposed to other small birds. But people use it, in an ad hoc fashion, also to cover other small brown birds that are similar to wrens. Small thrushes, for instance, are sometimes called yankotij. But they may also be called k'ok', through extension of the name that focally belongs to the Clay-colored Robin. Terms like these do not have sharp category boundaries. They tend to expand, like balloons, till they come up against another term. Then there is some negotiation about just where the boundary lies. The extreme is reached with *chinchinbakal,* a very general term used for any small songbird with any yellowish coloring on it.

Some terms have several equally focal exemplars. *Takaay,* for instance, covers all noisy flycatchers with bright yellow breasts. The Social Flycatcher and Couch's Kingbird are both focal takaay, and, for many, two or three other species of similar flycatchers are all equally good examples. The term is then extended, with increasing tentativeness, to other flycatchers.

Another example of extension in action is the elastic use of terms by less knowledgeable speakers. The experts distinguish large flycatchers as takaay, medium-sized ones as juiiro, and small ones as yaj, but to the ordinary person they are all takaay, or at most takaay and yaj. Experts know several types of pigeons, each with its own name, but ordinary people lump all large pigeons under the name of the commonest: uukum. This is a well-recognized way of naming things; it is quite apart from simple mistakes. Chunhuhub Maya woodspeople and agriculturalists hate to admit ignorance of a name and will extend one of the more elastic names as widely as possible. Takaay, for instance, will do for any noisy yellowish bird; we have heard it used for the Black-headed Saltator, though this was clearly a "mistake" from the point of view of the ordinary Maya speaker. However, there is a limit, and an animal that is not much like any named category produces a disgusted response, such as *"Es un bicho, no mas"* ("It's a little pest, nothing else"—i.e., "It's too worthless to have a name, at least one I would bother learning").

Much more interesting is the case of the term *ooch*. This functions as a true folk generic for opossums but is extended also to two other animals that are not at all like opossums: skunks and porcupines. These are explicitly *not* considered opossums or especially opossumlike. The term is used here in a vague sense, roughly, "medium-sized furry animal." But many other medium-sized mammals are *not* called ooch: the tayra, Gray Fox, kinkajou, and so forth. It would appear the term has simply been extended in a few cases and not in others because of pure philological accident.

A more complex case involves names for hawks, eagles, and falcons. There is a general cover term, ch'uuy, that can be used for all of these, though in a more restricted sense it covers only the smaller ones. (Cf. this double use of ch'uuy with the formal systematist's distinction between *sensu lato* and *sensu stricto*.) Several terms are more specific. All these specific terms have foci: common species that are instantly identified, without debate, as the proper core referents of the respective terms. These terms are *ii'* (focally, the Gray Hawk); *keenkeenbak* (small falcons—focally the Bat Falcon); *ek' pip* (or *eek' piip, eek' pip, ek' piip;* small dark eagles, focally the Black Hawk-Eagle); and *jonkuuk* (large eagles; in former times, focally the now-extirpated Harpy). Rarer birds of prey are lumped under these terms, but there is much controversy over just which term to extend. Thus, the Black-shouldered Kite, a recent invader of the area, is sometimes called keenkeenbak because of its long, pointed wings; sometimes ii' because of its size and coloration; and often just ch'uuy. In other words, it has the shape (especially wing shape) of a keenkeenbak but the size and color of an ii', and in very general terms it is a ch'uuy. Thus we have heard, and FMT has participated in, debates about the proper way to refer to this bird. The rare Ornate Hawk-Eagle can be either ek' pip (size and shape right but color wrong, by comparison with the focal species of this term) or jonkuuk (color and shape right but size wrong). FMT finds both these terms sound equally right, according to his sense of the language. The Common Black Hawk, when not just called ch'uuy, can be ii' (size right but color wrong) or ek' pip (color right but size wrong). The Hook-billed Kite, a large bird of prey with several color morphs ranging from pale to black, can be ii' or ek' pip depending on color (or just on the whim of the speaker). It is even conceivable for it to be classified as both an ii' and an ek' pip, treating ii' as a general term of which ek' pip is a subset. However, we have not recorded such a usage. It seems that, normally, animal names are mutually exclusive at a given contrast level. A person may wonder whether a creature is an X or a Y, but the expectation is that it will be one or the other, not both. In some truly borderline cases, one can call a creature either an X or a Y indifferently, but it is still not considered to be both at once in any essential way. (Of course, terms at a higher level, like ch'uuy, include those at a lower level; and there are also synonyms to deal with. In practice, it is not always easy to sort such matters out.)

Still another type of situation is represented by the names *beech'* (quail), *beech' lu'um* (ground quail), and *ya'ax beech' lu'um* (green ground quail). These three birds are not similar and are not related (in either Maya or bioscientific thought). The first is the Yucatán Bobwhite, the second the Black-faced Antthrush, the third the Olive and Green-backed Sparrows (these two being virtually identical). The names merely record a superficial similarity: all are ground-dwelling birds with black face masks or facial stripes. They are thus comparable to our Jerusalem-oak case in English. The Black-faced Antthrush is also known as *tsiiminchak,* "rain gods' tapir" (or, in modern Maya, "rain gods' horse"), for reasons lost in the past. Perhaps the ancient Maya believed that the rain gods rode on antthrushes.

In short, terms can be extended along one or another dimension, according to which dimension the speaker feels is salient at a given time. This is presumably the way in which introduced animals were labeled, such as *yuk* (brocket deer) being extended to include goats. As in the case of yankotij and k'ok', terms are extended until they come up against each other (so to speak), and then there is negotiation about just where the boundary should lie. Many interesting discussions of such terminological matters while away the time on forest trails or long stretches of dull road. Maya, especially those directly involved in forest activities, feel strongly about getting the names right and discuss them as seriously as any group of ornithologists or herpetologists at a professional convention.

At such times, there is much consultation with experts. Some individuals are known to be particularly knowledgeable about animal names. (Others are particularly knowledgeable about plants; still others about soils; still others about house building; and so on.) Such individuals command respect—especially if they also have directly instrumental knowledge, such as hunting secrets or beekeeping expertise. People consult with them and leave judgments on names to them. If such an expert is in a group that is discussing the name of an animal, the final word lies with the expert. Moreover, the Maya, including the experts, are usually very eager to learn new animal names. Experts consult with each other, sharing whatever specialized knowledge they may have. Our quests for names often led to long consultations, and to seeking out individuals with specialized knowledge. Individuals often love learning the names for themselves alone; FMT became fascinated with English animal names and eventually learned a large number of them.

Expertise in these areas is a source of considerable prestige in the community. In the debates over whether ethnobiological classification is strictly utilitarian or is the result of a *vis classificatrix* (Atran 1990; Berlin 1992), prestige is the missing factor. This is probably because most of the debaters come from a culture (modern Anglo-American) in which knowledge is not much respected—especially knowledge of plants and animals. In traditional societies, and notably among the Maya, learning a great deal about plants and animals is one of the most respected of all accomplishments. People diligently seek to learn, both for practical reasons and for reasons of social respect. Among bodies of knowledge relating to animals, hunting competence is particularly admired (see chapter 4). Sheer curiosity is also a factor. There is often little else to occupy an active and inquiring mind in a Maya village, where life tends to settle into a routine of raising corn and hogs.

Sometimes a term is extended idiosyncratically, as opposed to being extended through an out-and-out mistake. There is no real way to tell the difference, since no one has standardized the terms in the fashion of modern bioscientific nomenclature. Maya are undogmatic (sometimes almost to the point of anarchy) about such matters. However, extreme cases are judged with reasonable unanimity. At one extreme, extending a name to cover a new creature that is very similar to the named one is perfectly standard—the recognized way to name new creatures. At the other extreme, anyone calling a vireo an ek' pip or calling a bee a bobote' would be regarded as simply not knowing the words. In between is the case noted above: the use of takaay to cover the Black-headed Saltator. This was clearly a mistake, or at least

13. K'eek'en *(young hog), Presidente Juarez.*

an extremely idiosyncratic usage, but the saltator is a noisy, robin-sized, yellow-breasted bird, like a true takaay. Thus, one can see how it could be classed as a takaay by a somewhat careless speaker. However, no knowledgeable speaker, hearing the word, would expect it to cover a saltator; the knowledgeable speaker would be surprised to find the term extended that way. ENA has much experience with being corrected after using an obviously wrong name. However, we have erred on the side of caution here, labeling some names as "nonstandard" but none as "wrong." We have also, whenever possible, specified legitimate extensions of names.

It should be noted that the whole question of accuracy and standardization of name usage is one that can be addressed only by patient listening and recording. Formal elicitation techniques are useful in this matter also, but there is, in the end, no substitute for listening to actual conversations (see Hanks 1990).

In short, difference in name usage can be due to genuine differences of opinion about how a name is used; or to a tendency to lump poorly known animals under one category; or to sheer mistake. This does *not* show a confused taxonomy, or a failure of "cultural consensus," or a "mere" social construction without external referent, or a "primitive," inconsistent classification as opposed to a "scientific," precise one. It merely proves that the Maya system is a living, evolving one. Writers concerned with inconsistency and individual differences in folk taxonomies (e.g., Sillitoe 2002, and references therein) forget that formal systematic biology has all the same problems. Ornithological authorities differ radically about such things as the numbers of species of Fox Sparrows (*Passerella iliaca*—and other species?) and crossbills (*Loxia* spp.), well-known and well-studied birds. Different books give different lists of howler monkey species (*Alouatta* spp.), lizards, and frogs—to say nothing of such lesser-known groups as ants and deerflies. Differences of opinion are inevitable in taxonomy.

Spanish names used by Chunhuhub speakers seem to have clearer and more sharply defined referents. They are not extended in the broad, creative way that Maya names are. This is true even of Spanish names that have been thoroughly Mayanized, like *wakax* ("cow," from Sp. *vacas*, "cows," the plural having become the Maya singular).

Yucatec and Spanish have been profoundly influencing each other for almost five hundred years. There are many names that are what the Yucatec call *mestiza-Maya*: partly Spanish, or Spanish-influenced. The converse is *hach Maya*, "real Maya." Frequently, there are both Spanish or mestiza-Maya and hach Maya names for an animal.

For example, Spanish names, variously Mayanized, have been borrowed for many introduced animals. Also, the native Yucatec terms for water birds have almost all disappeared and been replaced by Spanish words. Thus, the only Chunhuhub Maya word for "heron" is *gaarsaj*, from Spanish *garza*. The only word for "duck" is *pato* or *paatoj*; the older word *kuts ja'* (water turkey—focally referring to the Muscovy Duck) is not known today in Chunhuhub. (Some books cite the Maya term *ch'iich' ha'*; this is merely a descriptive phrase meaning "water bird.") As noted above, the Yucatec Maya find it useful to borrow broad category terms like loro for parrots, *lagartito* for lizards, and avispa for wasps.

In our list of names in appendix I, we have mixed Spanish and Maya together, because the speakers do. It is unnecessarily pedantic to go through the entire list and separate the Spanish names. It is also, we feel, unnecessarily pedantic to spell them according to a relatively monolingual Maya speaker's pronunciation. It also gives a false sense of the linguistic reality of Chunhuhub, a bilingual town. There are many people in Chunhuhub who call a donkey an *aasnoj,* but many others who pronounce it *asno,* and many—perhaps the majority—who say aasnoj when speaking Maya and asno when speaking Spanish. There are those who call a sheep an *oobejaaj,* but more call it an *oveja* in perfect Mexican Spanish. (Cf. Hofling and Tesucún 1997, who respell Spanish names in Itzaj orthography; but they are making a dictionary, and are doing the appropriate thing for that activity.)

We have included those terms that have been routinely incorporated into local usage (Maya or Spanish). Obviously, there is no purpose in giving the Spanish names for all the creatures listed below, since the purpose of this work is to provide locally used names. Most formal Spanish book-names for birds, lizards, and the like are not known or used. On the other hand, we do not confine our attention solely to terms that have been routinely borrowed into Maya and Mayanized in pronunciation. We also provide other commonly used Spanish terms—largely the useful generics that lack equivalents in Yucatec Maya.

A difference from Itzaj usage (as seen in the published sources) is that Itzaj uses the old Maya prefixes *aj-* for male or large and *ix-* for female or small animals. *Aj-* has disappeared in contemporary spoken Yucatec. *Ix-,* which has shrunk to *x-* in modern Yucatec, is erratically used when the intent is to emphasize the diminutive nature of the animal in question, but it is not a standard part of the name and is not routinely used. One exception is *xtakay;* we list it as *takaay* for consistency, but it is almost always xtakay in actual conversation.

A much more consequential difference is that the Itzaj are alleged (Atran 1999; Hofling and Tesucún 1997) to have many mid-level groupings of species that are covert categories in that they are not linguistically marked but emerge from card-sorts or from questioning about what animals seem related or seem to fall together. We have no clear evidence of such groupings in Quintana Roo Yucatec, except as ad hoc and idiosyncratic affairs. ENA is, frankly, highly suspicious of the alleged Itzaj groupings—especially since they differ considerably between the two authorities cited. FMT is unaware of Itzaj realities but is very conservative about using such groupings in Yucatec.

Discussion with Scott Atran has convinced ENA that the groupings Atran alleges are cognitively real for at least the consultants studied. However, whether they are actually part of Itzaj *folk taxonomy* is another matter. They may be real to *individuals* but may not be part of the *culture* in any verifiable sense. There remains the strong possibility that they are artifacts of formal interviewing techniques. This is precisely why we adopt a practice test and a practice methodology.

We have thus elected to be conservative and deal with higher-order groupings *only* if they are linguistically recognized. (Groupings recognized by extension of a term or by use of a Spanish-derived generic are common among both Yucatec and Itzaj.)

Two philosophies are possible here. The first is to seek actively for covert categories, using various psychological methods, and to recognize every grouping that seems psychologically real. This is the approach of the students of the Itzaj. It has the benefit of finding out a great deal about how individual people (within a culture) classify things, and what points and marks are salient for them. It is adapted to psychological research on cognition. The other approach is to recognize them only when there is proof that they are culturally real and are traditionally reproduced. This is our approach. It is adapted to research on language and culture, on folk classification *systems,* and on folk classification practice—specifically, the interpersonal negotiation of cultural practice and cultural change. In short, each philosophy is suited to—and, in fact, driven by—a particular task orientation. Scott Atran's work with developmental and cognitive psychologists (Medin and Atran 1999) makes the former approach much more useful and practical to him. Our research is on traditional Maya cultural knowledge, and so we adopt the other approach.

It will be noted that we have included some reference to another type of controversy: differences of opinion, in the field, among Yucatec consultants. We have heard (and FMT has taken part in) many discussions about just what animals are covered, and what are not, by particular terms. Higher-order groupings, even clearly salient and well-recognized ones, are subject to constant debate. This fits with Berlin's intuition (Berlin 1992) that the generics are the most psychologically "real" categories, while higher-order groupings are more fluid and less clear to people in most cultures studied.

Partly because of the abundance of such arguments, treating the covert categories recognized in the Mayanist literature as if they were culturally salient, long-established, formal categories is not recommended until further research clarifies the nature of these sets. Similarly, treating our categories as if they exhausted Yucatec ability to categorize animals would certainly be wrong. Individual Yucatecans, like the Itzaj, can come up with relationships and groupings when challenged.

Traditional ecological knowledge can be construed as science, but a science far from that familiar from laboratory and computer (Anderson 2000, 2001; González 2001). This idea has emerged in recent years from a dialogue between the Athapaskan peoples of Canada and a few anthropologists (Cruikshank 2000; Goulet 1998; Ridington 1988; Sharp 1987; Smith 1998; cf. also Whitmore and Turner 2001). The Athapaskans are among those few who lived—and often still live—largely by hunting. Their knowledge system is very different from bioscience but is consistent and well described. Scholars of Athapaskan knowledge confront a system different from their own. They naturally have contrasted the two "ways of knowing" (Goulet 1998).

Athapaskan knowledge is typically communicated either nonverbally (Goulet 1998) or through specific personal stories that make a point (Cruikshank 2000). Abstract linear thinking is not seen as very useful. Hunters attend to dreams, visions, subconscious perceptions, and similar mental acts and processes. A hunter attends to all cues, and integrates them at an intuitive or preconscious level; it is not possible for the conscious mind to attend to all cues that the "bush" presents. A hunter may dream that a moose is in a particular place, then actually go there and find it (Ridington 1988; Smith 1998). His dream served to integrate the cues he had perceived while awake in the bush. Young people learn through experience with elders, and through tales and personal stories used to convey general messages.

The Maya too attend constantly to consciously and subconsciously perceived cues, and often to dreams and visions. They have, also, a hard-headed declarative knowledge that they can discuss in abstract terms. Their science thus provides a useful intermediate case between Athapaskan and modern scientific ways of knowing.

The whole discussion of Maya ethnobiological knowledge as science—not just "TEK" (traditional ecological knowledge) or "folk science" but real science—has been addressed at length elsewhere (Anderson 2000, 2001). Suffice it to say here that Maya natural history is comparable to that of Europe in the late eighteenth century. It has made a long series of remarkable breakthroughs and discoveries. On the whole, broad, abstract, or general theory was lost over the years, to be replaced by theories learned from the Spanish colonists—and, today, from grade-school textbooks. However, the detailed knowledge, and a great deal of background suppositions that could be formalized as theories (González 2001), continues to flourish and develop.

Our species has been wasteful and destructive but has kept the search for truth alive, and has managed harsh environments. We also have to be properly respectful of the other lives on this planet. These truths are among the important things we can learn from the Maya.

Chapter Six

CONCLUSIONS

To quote once again the Spanish missionary-explorer Gabriel Salazar: In the Yucatán Peninsula "there is an infinite number of game in all the land (Salazar 2000 [1620]:48)." Today, there is almost nothing. The Yucatec Maya once described their country as the "land of the deer and curassow." Today, the Yucatán subspecies of the White-tailed Deer is endangered; the more southerly subspecies found in our part of Quintana Roo is rare. The Great Curassow is almost extinct everywhere in Mexico.

Quite apart from other concerns, this extermination of wild game is a disaster for the Maya. They have depended on game to help feed their families for much or all of the last several thousand years. The loss of it means malnutrition for the poor. Also, the Maya not only depend on the animals for quality nutrition; they love and appreciate them.

In 1993, Daniel Navarro listed twenty-two mammals in danger of extinction in Quintana Roo (Navarro 1992). Today, at least one more, the White-tailed Deer, would be added. A few of the animals listed are merely small and hard to find, but most are game animals that have been over-hunted. In the years we have been working together in Chunhuhub, even armadillos, gophers, and agoutis have become rare. Monkeys, not usually hunted for food but shot to get babies as pets, have virtually disappeared. Only Collared Peccaries, which are smart and adaptable, actually seem slightly more numerous than in the early 1990s. Plain Chachalacas have at least stabilized, but other animals are in trouble.

Not only game animals, but also stingless bees (and now even European bees) and other useful animals are becoming rare. Some bird populations are falling. Snakes (especially large ones) and amphibians are markedly less common than they were in 1991.

14. Baby bach *(chachalacas) being raised as pets.*

The habitat in the Chunhuhub area is still almost as good for game as Salazar found it in conquest times. However, habitat destruction in Quintana Roo is serious, especially in the tourist north and the agricultural south. Forest still covers most of western Quintana Roo, and the rest is covered by scattered fields and orchards that supply vast amounts of food for game. The farmers do not always appreciate the use of their crops by wild animals, but usually they like the added meat—a few ears of corn converted into protein is gain, not loss.

Habitat fragmentation by roads, new settlements, and large clearings is beginning to be a problem, however. It has certainly contributed to the decline of animals and is dangerously reducing habitat for jaguars, tapirs, and other large animals. Hunting is easier because of roads. Animals (such as tapirs) that need large unbroken tracts to forage are driven away. Jaguars are deprived of food and take to preying on domestic stock, which leads to their persecution. Roads have contributed to the decline of the Boa Constrictor, which is fond of basking or dallying on roads, a habit leading to its elimination from the vicinity of well-traveled routes.

However, habitat destruction has currently been slowed—not stopped—by a number of factors. First, forest protection has rapidly gained. Second, with tourism established as the great hope for the future among Quintana Roo's elite, there has been a great reduction in the pressure to "develop" agricultural lands at all costs. (Unfortunately, the pressure to develop mass tourism at all costs has its own enormous price; see, e.g., Juárez 2002. But that is a problem, so far, only along the northern coasts.) Third, the employment provided by tourism and the urban economy has absorbed many young Maya, reducing population pressure on the land.

Hunting remains a problem. With United States–style game management, the animals would recover. Thanks to inordinately effective conservation, deer, raccoons, and many other heavily hunted game animals have become major pests in many parts of the United States that are, to use Salazar's inflated rhetoric, infinitely poorer habitat than the Yucatán. Yet, as we have seen, the Maya have a strong tradition of sustainable management of the environment (Faust 1998). How did traditional resource management fail?

Game is owned and managed as a common pool resource, largely within ejidos. As such, it is susceptible to the tragedy of the commons well described by Garrett Hardin (1968). On the other hand, ejidos own and manage agricultural land and resources, forests, and livestock herds communally, and many of them manage these resources very well indeed. Moreover, Maya extended families—often running to several tens of persons—manage land and resources with great care. (On these matters see Faust 1998; Fedick 1996; Primack et al. 1998.)

Conceptually, the problem is not the classic rational-choice tradeoff of individual welfare versus altruism (Olson 1965), but one of long-term individual and community welfare versus a far lesser but more immediate individual payoff (Ostrom 1990; Burger et al. 2001). Individuals know perfectly well that they are depleting the game, and that collective action to save it would ultimately profit everyone.

One must wonder, then, why the tragedy of the commons describes the fate of wildlife but does not describe the fate of trees and farmland. Ejidos are an interesting phenomenon: large enough to be real "commons," but small enough for face-to-face communities to manage.

Farmland management, forest cutting, and logging have all been progressively transformed as population increases. Current institutions are still lagging behind population pressures, but at least there has been a felt need for institutional change, and institutions have indeed changed. Particularly relevant is the success that many ejidos have had in developing livestock herding. When the animals are domestic, they are carefully protected, even though they are owned collectively by the ejido—exactly as the game animals are. Protective institutions do not quite keep pace with changing times, but at least they adjust.

To preserve the game today would be relatively easy. Quintana Roo would merely have to add to the traditional rules the standard modern management tools: bag limits and closed seasons. Mexico does have some game laws. There is also an ecological enforcement agency, PROFEPA, that is now reasonably professional and competent. The game laws, however, are not enforced—let alone strengthened (see Miguel Alvarez del Toro's comments on Chiapas and on Mexico in general; 1991, esp. pp. 124–27). PROFEPA is vigilant about overcutting precious woods—Chunhuhub's ejido government was in serious trouble in 2001 for a minor overcut—but does absolutely nothing to enforce any protection of animals; at least, this is the experience of Maya in western Quintana Roo. Even reserves are not sacrosanct. The huge Sian Ka'an Reserve is openly poached, and the game is sold daily on the sides of Quintana Roo's main highway, but nothing is done. (In the early 1990s, this was related to the fact that certain high officials were among the poachers.) So far as hunting goes, Sian Ka'an is a reserve in name only—a "paper park."

In Yucatán state, by contrast, game laws are now being rather strictly enforced—a case of locking the barn after the horse is stolen, since there are virtually no edible fauna left in that state. Clearly, institutional failure is not due to the inability of either the Maya or the higher levels of government to create appropriate institutions. There is evidently a wider question of attitudes, values, and cultural beliefs underlying the institutional problems.

In support of doing nothing, Maya argue that there is still game, if one goes far enough into the forest. This is true, in that there are a few animals left in the most remote areas between and around ejidos. However, experienced hunters acknowledge that decline is rapid even in such places. Few if any spots in Quintana Roo are free from almost continual unobtrusive scrutiny by Maya woodsmen. Real refuges for the game no longer exist.

This sense of powerlessness is, ultimately, related to the fact that the general Mexican attitude toward wildlife, and the wild in general, has traditionally been negative. Mexico's elite and middle class, until recently, partook of the Mediterranean tendency to view the wild as savage, hostile, and wholly bad (cf. Simonian 1995). Consider the description of the south Mexican forest by a liberal and strong advocate of indigenous peoples, Fernando Benitez:

> The tropical forest is the scene of a struggle for existence of uncommon intensity. The majority of the animals devour one another with unthinking naturalness. . . . The voracity of the fauna has its complement in the voracity of the flora. The forest not only is devoured by insatiable armies of ants, insects, and birds, but it devours on its own, on a scale of spectacular grandeur. There is hardly a tree that is not assaulted and almost asphyxiated by a thick mat of creepers, vines, and parasitic plants. . . . (Benitez 1986, 13; my translation)

He has already foreseen the bright future: "Virgin land, the future great supplier of Mexico . . ." (Benitez 1986, 11). Today, urban Mexican attitudes are changing, and Benitez himself has more recently been an advocate of conservation. However, attitudes change slowly in the rural fringe, and also in the state governmental houses. One notes with sorrow that the recent fifty-four–volume series of indigenous and traditional food ethnographies, issued by the federal government (CONACULTA 1999–2001), includes hundreds of recipes for game without a word about conserving or saving the animals. Until very recently, the Mexican attitude was that all wild things must disappear eventually in the name of Progress, and that therefore one might as well use them unsustainably while they are here. In fact, for many developers of Quintana Roo and elsewhere, the wild should be destroyed even if nothing is put in its place. There are cases in which tracts of forest were cleared simply to get rid of them, with no viable plans to use the resulting wasteland. Government agencies or outside landlord interests were responsible; the Maya do not do this and told us of their shocked reactions.

There is hope, but qualified hope. Captive breeding of animals, local conservation plans, and attempts to work with local ranchers exist (see

Escamilla Guerrero and Raña Garibay 1996). It will be recalled that the Plan Forestal, a plan originally designed for sustainable management of valuable trees (Murphy 1990; Primack et al. 1998), encompassed some attempt to work with animal resources as well.

Recently, a sharp debate has arisen over whether indigenous peoples are conservation-minded enough to be left in or on the lands they have traditionally managed. Idealizers of indigenous people argue that they have always been good managers and should be left in charge of their lands. Biologists and some anthropologists maintain that the ecological virtues of indigenous people are purely mythical—the result of "noble savage" romanticization—and that reserves must shut out indigenous people and be administered by biologists and national governments. This debate was joined in a particularly clear and informed manner in *Conservation Biology* in 2000 (Chicchón 2000; Colchester 2000; Redford and Sanderson 2000; Schwartzman, Moreira, and Nepstad 2000; Schwartzman, Nepstad, and Moreira 2000; Terborgh 2000). If Terborgh's position in this debate were true, the world would be faced with a harsh choice: Force local peoples off their lands, or see the animals disappear.

Fortunately, the problem is more hopeful of solution. Clearly, the Maya (and probably most other indigenous groups) do indeed have strategies for managing and conserving natural resources. These strategies were adequate in the past. Modern changes in demography, weaponry, and environment make the old strategies inadequate. Cooperation between local communities and governments or nongovernmental agencies can produce successful comanagement schemes.

The ingredients of a successful plan are simple and straightforward. They are, first, an interested community that is aware of the need. This is where traditional ecological knowledge and wisdom enter the picture. The more knowledge the community has within it, and the more wisdom it has accumulated about dealing with animals, the better the community can plan. Second, there must be an assertive leadership that is willing to work on the matter and that can control poachers. Third, there must be an immediate economic payoff that makes up for any temporary reduction in game take. Fourth, and most important of all, there must be serious government help, in the form of expert encouragement (and, when necessary, advice) and some enforcement backup. It is this last which has been lacking. Mexico must go a long way in its drive to bring conservation to the grassroots.

In the lack of any government support for conservation, the Maya naturally lose hope that it can be a meaningful alternative. They give up; they adjust to the existing situation. Resignation in the face of adversity may be the best one can do, and Mexican countryfolk are famous for their ability to *aguantar*—to bear and endure anything. However, there is a major crisis at hand today. A combination of Maya ecological knowledge and governmental responsibility would solve it.

The Maya need their animals—for food, for aesthetic value, for ecological stability. The current drift toward disaster can easily be stopped. But it must be stopped within the next ten years, or there will be little or nothing left to save.

THE ANIMAL CLASSIFICATION
OF THE MAYA OF CHUNHUHUB
AND AREA, QUINTANA ROO

Bird names are standardized to follow usage in Howell and Webb (1995) except as noted; mammals to Emmons (1990) and Reid (1997); reptiles and amphibians to Lee (1996) (we have also used Campbell 1998); insect species as supplied by Dr. Jorge González Acereto (more general insect identifications, mostly to family, are ENA's field identifications). Earlier literature has been reviewed, and is sometimes cited, but full analysis awaits publication elsewhere (contact ENA for details; see Andrews Heath 1980; Arzápalo Marín 1987, 1996; Atran 1993, 1999; Barrera Marín, Barrera Vásquez, and Lopez Franco 1976; Barrera Vásquez 1980; Chávez Guzmán 1995; Hartig 1979; López Ornat 1990; Pacheco Cruz 1958; Terán and Rasmussen 1994).

Almost all the names we record have been field verified. Some birds were identified only from pictures in field guides, and inevitably we collected some descriptions of birds not occurring in Chunhuhub and therefore not identifiable, but whenever possible the animals were observed in the field with consultants. (Note that appendix II contains a separate listing of birds, arranged by their vernacular names. This list differs in that only birds observed by ENA in the area are included.) Mammals were not so easy to find in the field as the other taxa, so we observed many in the Chetumal Zoo, with Maya consultants. At worst, we fell back on pictures in Louise Emmons's *Neotropical Rainforest Mammals: A Field Guide* (1990), but effort was made to see as many mammals as possible in the field, and this enabled us to correct some names. Reptiles were also difficult to deal with; the non-poisonous ones were observed in the field, but poisonous snakes were rarely observed by us as a team, though of course FMT has seen countless poisonous snakes in the field.

Comparisons with Bricker, Po'ot Yah, and Dzul de Po'ot's dictionary of the Maya of Hocabá, Yucatán, and with the Cordemex dictionary compiled by Alfredo Barrera Vásquez, are referred to as "Hocabá" and "Cordemex" in the following text. The Hocabá names often differ from mine in slight respects, usually in vowel length. Maya habitually shorten long vowels in the field, and thus the prudent transcriber will use the long vowel if speakers differ. In most cases where the Hocabá dictionary differs from what we recorded, Bricker, Po'ot Yah, and Dzul de Po'ot recorded long vowels and we recorded short ones. These have usually been corrected below to long vowels. In a few cases (notably ii' and *us*), we have definitely heard (and ourselves said) long vowels, but Hocabá and Cordemex both record short ones. Overcorrection may be involved, or there may be some genuine local differences. We have decided to leave the vowels short in these cases.

Tone has not been marked, pending serious comparative study of tone in Yucatán and Quintana Roo dialects of Yucatec. They have major differences in tone and stress (Scott Atran, pers. comm.). Due to the complex settlement history of Chunhuhub, which is about half Quintana Roo Maya and half recent immigrants from Yucatán state, tones are not consistently used by our consultants, and FMT does not regard them as particularly important. Further work in smaller, more coherent communities is needed.

It may be considered worthwhile to append a few notes on ancient Maya animals. Most of our knowledge comes from ancient Maya art, though archaeozoology has made great strides of late. The ancient Maya were sometimes accurate in their portrayals, but their depictions of animals range from the stylized to the merely bad. In particular, many of the pictures in the four surviving Maya codices are so crude that no one can be quite sure what they represent. When one is confronted with a picture that could equally well be a dog, a jaguar, or an opossum, one realizes that something is lacking in the artist's drive toward perfect representation. Fortunately, we have had the benefit of advice from ENA's colleague Karl Taube, an expert on ancient Mesoamerican art.

Particularly important in ancient Maya art were monkeys (associated with the creation myth), dogs, opossums, rabbits, and armadillos. The latter three were associated with ritual clowning and comedy and are still regarded as funny by the modern Maya. Dogs are still regarded as humorous and were clearly so to the ancient Maya; for example, the absurd picture in the

Codex Tro of a dog playing the drum and howling cannot have been meant other than humorously (this picture is so cute that ENA's dog-loving daughter and her husband tiled it into their house floor). In fact, the ancient Maya seem to have been blessed with at least as irrepressible a sense of humor as the modern ones. This has rarely been stressed in studies of Maya art (though see Taube 1989).

A vase in the Bowers Museum, Santa Ana, California, shows humans dressed as a rabbit, a monkey, and a tapir-snouted jaguar; these seem to be more serious characters. The monkey has mythic associations noted in the Popol Vuh. The tapir-jaguar is clearly uncanny and may have associations with death.

Jaguars provided a symbol of power, destructiveness, and royalty. Deer and peccaries were important, with astronomical associations (one constellation was the Copulating Peccaries). There was also a Scorpion constellation, not the same as modern Scorpio in spite of some loose claims to that effect (Love 1994, 95–6, and pers. comm.). The sky also possessed a turtle and a rattlesnake (Love 1994, 95–6), and probably other fauna.

Among birds, the Ocellated Turkey and the cormorant were important. The former seems to be a symbol of land; the latter is certainly a symbol

15. Sak aak or jicotea *(slider turtle).*

of water. Ducks may have been a symbol of the wind; the Aztec Wind God Ehecatl has a duck's bill (Karl Taube, pers. comm.). Herons, especially egrets, are also commonly shown and obviously associated with water. In the Palenque Museum are four large urns, excavated recently at the site, which show unmistakable limpkins *(Aramus guarauna)*. These tropical cranes are ideal symbols of water and rain because they live in extensive marshes and give loud, beautiful calls when rain and storms are commencing. All four vases show the same iconography: the limpkins are shown in their assertive display, above a snake's head, which is, in turn, above a human face. The Palenque Museum identifies the birds as *moan,* because the archaeologists believe the headdresses were intended to show the mythical moan bird.

Hawks, eagles, and owls are commonly shown. The hawks and eagles are too conventionally shown to be readily identifiable (cf. Kendall 1992 on the Aztecs). Lurking in the art must be clues to the identity of the mysterious kot, the *"aguilla bermejo"* of the *Calepino de Motul* and the transformation animal of dangerous witches. The owls, some of which seem identifiable as Great Horned Owls, are associated with bad omens, as in modern Maya culture—and, indeed, in almost all cultures in the world. The mysterious moan bird is not like any real bird but seems to be based loosely on the owl. The quetzal, not native to the lowlands, is shown frequently and not very accurately. Parrots, hummingbirds, and other smaller birds appear.

Crocodiles are frequently shown, often in association with water. Iguanas, snakes, frogs, fish, and other creatures appear in Maya art, especially in surviving paintings. The Bonampak murals, for instance, include a water scene with fish of various kinds, some identifiable (e.g., sawfish and rays). Serious research on such art is needed.

The animals of the Maya codices were authoritatively identified and discussed as early as 1910, by the great Mayanist Alfred Tozzer and the equally eminent zoologist Glover Allen. Eduard Seler, in his foundational study of animals in ancient Mexican art (1961 [1909–1910]), identified the more obvious animals. He provides a particularly revealing and interesting discussion of the enormous importance of dogs in ancient Mesoamerican art. They were psychopomps and otherwise associated with the worlds of gods and the dead. It should be noted that Seler tentatively identifies coyotes in ancient Maya art. This is a mistake; coyotes do not naturally occur in lowland Maya areas. The animals he so identifies are apparently dogs. The one playing a drum and howling (Seler 1961 [1909–1910], 500) certainly is.

Seler presents a portrait of the Water Goddess from the Codex Tro, in which the goddess is holding up a jaguar and a peccary and is accompanied by a dog and a strange rabbitlike animal (Seler 1961 [1909–1910], 491). This is one of many thought-provoking indications that the peccary was sacred, or at least cosmologically important, to the ancient Maya. Jonathan Kendall's excellent and accurate study of birds in Aztec calendric art (Kendall 1992) has a few notes on the Maya—alas, all too few.

MAMMALS

Mammals form an unnamed category but are clearly recognized as a natural unit. Furry animals that nurse their young are included. (Note that some Maya consider bats to be birds, but bats are included in this section.)

Asno. Sp.; donkey *(Equus asinus)*. Syn. for *burro* and *aasnoj*. Very rarely kept in Chunhuhub, where the terrain is well adapted for horses and bicycles, and the donkey is thus not necessary.

Baalam. Jaguar *(Panthera onca)*. Rare, surviving only in remote areas. In danger of extinction in Quintana Roo and, indeed, throughout Mexico (Navarro 1992). The animal is shot whenever possible, more because of its extreme danger to humans and stock than for its valuable pelt. A man with trained jaguar-hunting dogs eliminated most of the last few jaguars in the Chunhuhub area. However, a few still occur. FMT found a peccary half-eaten by a jaguar as recently as 1994–95 in Chunhuhub. We walked for half a mile in the fresh tracks of a jaguar in a remote part of Rancho el Corozo. A jaguar came in November of 2001 to the sheep flock of Presidente Juarez and ate several of them. A major hunt was raised, with dogs and skilled local hunters combing the forest. They found not even a track. The jaguar came back the next night and ate more sheep.

Beautiful pictures of jaguars on classic Maya pots and other art objects are common (cf. Robicsek 1981). The jaguar was a "natural symbol" for royalty. See also *chak mo'ol, chakyik'al,* and *tigre*.

Ba'ats (baats'). Spider monkey *(Ateles geoffroyi)*. In most of the Yucatec Maya world it means "howler monkey," but not in Chunhuhub, where there are no howler monkeys. Howlers begin to appear in Margaritas, well to the south, and there they are called *ba'ats*. Note the glottalized vowel; there is disagreement among speakers on that glottalization, as seen in the Cordemex dictionary (Barrera Vásquez 1980, 40), as well as in my data; *baats'* in Hocabá.

Spider monkeys used to occur in Chunhuhub and may still. A large troop occupied the ruins at Nueva Loria, where they could flourish in the protected forest that covers this extensive Classic Maya city. Unfortunately, illegal and unregulated shooting by certain lawless elements in the area exterminated these desirable and valuable animals sometime between 1997 and 2001.

Pet spider monkeys are highly prized and something of a status symbol among some city folk, though the animals make terrible pets; they are mischievous and uncontrollable at best, and they respond to any bad treatment—including the teasing they usually receive—by becoming savage and destructive. See also *chango, maax, mono, saraguato,* and *tuch.*

Baj. Pocket gopher *(Orthogeomys hispidus)*. An uncommon but serious pest of milpas. Eaten, baked or roasted, internal organs and all; only the hair is removed, then the flesh and intestines are pulled off the bones with tortillas and eaten with a squeeze of lime or bitter orange juice and as much chile as one can stand. This is a popular dish, especially if the gopher is fat. On May 26, 1996, we met a man with two; he had captured them in his milpa with wire nooses and was planning to eat them. Kevin Hovey and Dominique Rissolo (Hovey 1997; Hovey and Rissolo 1999) have researched the trapping of pocket gophers in Quintana Roo, providing full details on methods used. The relative rarity of gophers in Chunhuhub was said by one person to be due to their having been eaten almost to extinction.

Berraco. Sp.; pig *(Sus scrofa)*. See also *cerdo, cochino,* and *k'eek'en.*

Bolsa ooch. Opossums in general (Didelphidae). *Ooch* is usually translated "opossum" but actually refers to any medium-sized furry mammal. When one wishes to be specific about referring to opossums, this mestizo-Maya word is used. See also *jo'onka'an* and *ooch.*

Burro. Sp.; *(Equus asinus)*. Though *burro* is the classic Mexican name for the animal, the Maya usually call it *asno*.

Cerdo. Domestic hog *(Sus scrofa)*. See also *berraco, cochino,* and *k'eek'en*.

Chab. Tamandua Anteater *(Tamandua tetradactyla)*. Fairly common but inconspicuous. Exceedingly tenacious of life, being difficult to kill by any means, and very defensive, standing up and swinging its large claws at attackers. It is said to be especially tough on Tuesday (a "bad day" in folk Catholic belief). If one tries to kill it on Tuesday, one will only provoke a savage counterattack. See also *oso hormiguero*.

Chak mo'ol. Jaguar *(Panthera onca)*. Lit. "red paw." ENA suggests that this name originally served as an indirect reference to the animal by hunters when in the field. Widespread in the Northern Hemisphere is a belief that using a dangerous animal's actual name will call it up, and thus in the forest one must use a circumlocution. This pattern of euphemistic naming applies to tigers in Asia, bears in the circumpolar area, and so forth. See also *baalam, chakyik'al,* and *tigre*.

Chakyik'al. Black jaguar. See also *baalam, chak mo'ol,* and *tigre*.

Chango. Sp.; monkeys in general. See also *ba'ats, maax, mono, saraguato,* and *tuch*.

Chi'ik. Coati *(Nasua narica* and the doubtfully distinct "species" *N. nelsoni*—observed and name noted in Cozumel.) The coati is a common pest of milpas; a troop can destroy a great deal of maize, squash, and other crops in a single night. Moreover, the coati is a popular food, here as elsewhere in Mexico. Thus, they are shot when possible. They are hunted with dogs, but coatis—especially old males—can be extremely fierce, and their long jaws and sharp teeth can make short work of the typical Maya hunting dog. They became noticeably rarer from 1991 to 1996, with both shooting and Hurricane Roxanne as causes (as FMT had much occasion to observe). However, they were reasonably common, and back to their old tricks in the milpas, as of 2001. We met FMT's nephew carrying a shotgun to his milpa one day, to stake it out; a particularly tricky coati was stealing all his corn. He returned in a couple of hours, triumphantly carrying the remains of the coati and planning a stew. These animals breed in summer, and large packs of adults and young then roam the forests—and milpas. See also *tejón*.

Ch'omak (ch'umak). Gray Fox *(Urocyon cinereoargenteus).* Known as *gato (de) montes, zorra,* or *zorrillo* in local Spanish. (*Zorro,* "fox" in formal Spanish, means "opossum" in Yucatán Spanish. It seems odd that what was once a gender distinction has now become a species distinction: *zorro* vs. *zorra.*) Common small predator, often seen in daylight, bounding across roads in forest or brushy areas. Regarded as harmless, or even beneficial, because it eats rodents. Its dung, with salt, is used as a poultice for large sores on legs. The Maya word has been translated "coyote" in some secondary sources. It never means this, and, in fact, coyotes do not occur in the Yucatán. (At least until recently. We have now received credible reports of them in Quintana Roo.) If Maya know about coyotes at all, they call them (what else?) "coyotes."

Ch'oo' (ch'o', ch'o'o'). Rats in general. The introduced *Rattus rattus* and the native cotton rats of the genus *Sigmodon* occur. Small rodents are uncommon in Chunhuhub, their place being taken, by and large, by lizards. They are not very significant as pests. (Hocabá records only *ch'o',* but the long vowel is often heard. This being a very often used word, there is little question of mishearing; but there most certainly is plentiful variation in the pronunciation, and individual idiosyncrasies must be noted.)

Chowak-xikin. Mule. Lit. "long ear." Formerly a major means of hauling. Three-mule wagons may still be seen in Yucatán state, but Quintana Roo has gone to trucks. See also *mula.*

Chul ya'. Margay *(Felis wiedii).* Rare in the forest but still occurs locally; considered endangered in the Yucatán Peninsula (Navarro 1992). See also *chuuchul.*

Chuuchul. Margay *(Felis wiedii).* See *chul ya'.*

Cochino (cochinito). Sp.; small pig *(Sus scrofa).* See also *berraco, cerdo,* and *k'eek'en.*

Curí. Sp., from South American language; guinea pig *(Cavia porcellus).* An occasional pet. See also *kulit.*

Danta (danto). Sp.; tapir *(Tapirus bairdii).* No Yucatec Maya name known, the original Yucatec Maya form *tsiimin* having become completely restricted to the domestic horse. In areas with waterholes, lakes, or marshes, this ani-

mal formerly occurred, though it was never common. It has been eliminated by hunting from all but the most extremely remote parts of Quintana Roo and is considered to be in danger of extinction there (Navarro
1992). It still exists in southern Quintana Roo, where ENA was shown fresh
signs of it by Maya woodsmen in Tres Garantias. FMT, however, found
fresh tracks in 2000, and we hope it still exists in or near Chunhuhub.

Ek' much' (e'much', e'muuch'). Gray-phase Jaguarundi. See *kab koj*.

Jaaleb. Paca, tepescuintle *(Agouti paca, Cuniculus paca)*. This large rodent is
the favorite meat of all Maya who have tried it and talked to us. It is white,
delicate, somewhat fat but not greasy, and very rich in flavor. In consequence,
the animal is shot for food whenever possible. However, its nocturnal and
secretive habits have protected it, and it still occurs throughout the region,
up to the very edge of Chunhuhub. It has, however, become rare and is
considered "vulnerable" by Navarro (1992). Pacas are able to jump high and
far and are thus often called *liebre* in Spanish. Pacas den in caves and sinkholes in the limestone, or in burrows among tree roots. They can leap in and
out of quite deep sinkholes. We examined one sinkhole in which the resident paca had to make a one-meter standing leap, straight up, to clear the
entrance. Well-worn trails going in and out of this sinkhole left no doubt
that the paca routinely performed this feat.

Pacas live primarily on fruit, and congregate under sapote, *k'aniste'*,
and other heavily fruiting trees. Judging by trackways, sapote is particularly
favored, which is reasonable since it produces particularly heavy crops of
extremely sweet, nutritious fruit. FMT remembers when one could find ten
to twenty pacas congregated under almost any heavily fruiting tree. Today,
one is lucky to find one or two. In 2001, we observed one freshly shot by one
of the most skilled hunters in the village.

Paca farming has been proposed by Instituto Nacional Indigenista (INI)
and other agencies, and ENA was able to persuade Andres Sosa, a biology
teacher resident in Chunhuhub, to make a beginning by breeding his pair
of pacas, but the experiment failed for several reasons. It remains to be seen
what conditions are adequate for breeding for these wide-ranging, nocturnal, shy animals. They have few young at a time (normally two, but they
can breed twice a year under favorable circumstances), especially compared
to most rodents, but the high value of the meat would make farming a com-

petitive enterprise. The hide was formerly used for the heads of small drums.

Jabalí. Sp.; peccaries in general. In formal and Peninsular Spanish, the word means "wild boar." See also *jahuilla, kitam, k'aaxik'eek'en,* and *zenzo.*

Jahuilla. Local Sp.; White-lipped Peccary *(Tayassu pecari).* Name of uncertain origin, but widely used in southeastern Mexico and Belize. See also *jabalí, k'aaxik'eek'en,* and *zenzo.*

Jijitsbeej. "Faints in the road," a mythical animal that is so tiny and agoraphobic that it collapses and dies in the middle of a road if it tries to cross. Said in other communities to be an insect or something similar (Terán and Rasmussen 1992; Xocen data), but in Chunhuhub the belief applies to the mouse opossum (see *ooch*) or a similar small mammal. Some say that if it reaches the other side, it becomes a huge animal that eats people. It is almost needless to point out that this whole story is largely a tall tale to amuse children, rather than a belief seriously held by many.

Eugene Hunn calls our attention to his findings in Tenejapa, Chiapas. There, shrews are called *ya'al be*: "weakness" + "trail" (Hunn 1977, 208–9). The animals often die or are killed by predators in the road, and, being almost inedible, are left there. The Tenejapans believe that a shrew will attempt to jump over the road in the hopes of becoming a bat; if it fails, it dies. This makes sense of a belief that in Quintana Roo seems unaccountable. Shrews do not live in the forests of central Quintana Roo—at least we have not found them—but the story has probably transferred from somewhere else.

Jool paay (joolij paay). Spotted Skunk *(Spilogale putorius).* Lit. "hole-dwelling skunk." See also *paay.*

Jo'onka'an (jo'onka'anij). Philander or Common Gray Four-eyed Opossum *(Philander opossum).* Uncommon and nocturnal, known by dense woolly fur and mostly naked tail. Obscure, though known; of no local importance. See also *bolsa ooch* and *ooch.*

K'aaxik'eek'en (k'eek'enik'aax). White-lipped Peccary *(Tayassu pecari).* This was the original *k'eek'en,* the name being extended to the domestic pig. (In highland Chiapas, where the White-lipped does not occur, the domestic pig is *chitam,* originally the name of the Collared Peccary—the expected

Tzeltal/Tzotzil reflex of Yucatec Maya *kitam.*) See also *jabalí, jahuilla,* and *zenzo.*

This animal, in danger of extinction in Quintana Roo (Navarro 1992), survives only in the most remote forests of the far southwestern part of the state. It formerly occurred commonly in and around Chunhuhub, but shooting and the destruction of the high forest eliminated it. Unlike the Collared Peccary, the White-lipped occurs in large herds in deep forest, and thus is highly vulnerable. It occurs in reddish *(chak)* and gray *(ya'ax)* color morphs.

Kab koj. Jaguarundi *(Felis yagouaroundi).* Specifically, the light phase, which is of a tan or honey color; *kab koj* appears to mean "honey puma," with reference to the color rather than the feeding habits. The dark or gray phase has a different name, *ek' much'.* Though described by Navarro (1992) as in danger of extinction, this splendid animal is still moderately common in the area under consideration. We saw several animals, of both phases, and not all of them were in remote areas. Trackways are even more often found. Jaguarundis prefer the neighborhood of water, even small waterholes; they often hunt by stalking birds and small mammals coming to drink. They are more diurnal than other cats. They are runners, rather than springers like the puma and margay. When we saw them, they were usually dashing with a rather greyhoundlike gait through forest or marsh, probably in pursuit of prey.

Keej. White-tailed Deer *(Odocoileus virginianus).* Incredibly, a few deer still exist in the area. We have found tracks in most of the remote, forested parts. Indeed, in 1996, we found the fresh bedding ground and dung of one at the very edge of the village; this wily individual was well known to local hunters, who sought it without success. But, between 1991 and 1996, the White-tailed Deer virtually disappeared in the entire area. It was not rare in 1991, and FMT was still shooting a few for subsistence; but by 1996 there were virtually none, except in very remote areas of private ranches with strict trespassing policies. (However, two were shot in a milpa in southern Chunhuhub on or near June 1, 1996, and one was captured alive in 1999 and kept as a pet.) The meat was twenty pesos per kilogram in 1991; by 1996 it was still selling for roughly that price in Jose Maria Morelos, but in the cities it had reached fifty pesos per kilogram and was going up steadily. By 2001 it was too rare for us to find a price, though it was still occasionally shot for food. Remote communities like Margaritas still have a fair number of deer. Conservationist values, universally attested by older consultants and in the literature (see, e.g., Llanes Pasos 1993), have been weakening for decades and are unknown to some of the young. Yucatán state has banned deer hunting, but there was no enforcement of this law as of 1996; there was spotty but real enforcement in 2001. Don Patricio Canto, a mighty hunter in the old days, told our friend and sometime field assistant Andres Sosa that he got up to one hundred deer in a good year and typically seventy to eighty, as did other top hunters (there were never more than six serious hunters at a time in Chunhuhub). These figures are probably inflated.

Deer are now being farmed near Mérida and Cancun, and the Xcaret ecological theme park maintains a captive herd of the Yucatán subspecies, which is serving as a reservoir of an animal that will soon be extinct in the wild.

Deer are believed to turn into snakes on occasion. Deer bezoar stones give luck in hunting (see chapter 4). Deer are believed to recycle water by secreting fluid from their noses in dry times and then swallowing it. The backbone of a deer is called *sibin*. Occasionally this word is used for other game animals' backbones. Otherwise, backbones are simply *bakij pach* (literally "backbone"), except in the case of birds (see the Birds section of this appendix). The prongs of antlers are *jek* (a two-point buck is a *ka jek*, and so on). A many-forked deer is a *nikte'bak* (flowering-tree bone). Deer hides are used for drum heads and occasionally other purposes.

K'eek'en. Domestic pig *(Sus scrofa)*. This animal has become the favorite mammal for farm rearing. It is the ideal human symbiont, living on precisely what humans do not want: garbage, excrement, and weeds. They also eat snakes and harmful insects. Pigs are turned loose to forage in the streets, where they eliminate organic garbage and keep the weeds and pests down. They also eat unsalable fruit and vegetables. Thus vast numbers can be raised with virtually no labor or investment—though some supplementary feeding with maize is occasionally (rarely) necessary. Pork sells for only twenty pesos per kilogram in Chunhuhub, putting meat within the range of all but the poorest people (and even they usually raise their own). See also *berraco, cerdo,* and *cochino.*

K'i'ix pach ooch. Porcupine *(Coendu mexicanus)*. Lit. "spiny-backed animal."

Kitam. Collared Peccary *(Tayassu tajacu)*. The collared peccary is still found in remote parts of the area. We encountered a band feeding on sapote fruit in the far southeastern corner of Chunhuhub's ejido lands in spring of 1996, and FMT has regularly shot Collared Peccaries as late as 1995. Amazingly, it had actually increased as of 2001; we found several trackways. However, overhunting has almost eliminated this animal, exceedingly abundant within very recent memory. Being tough, fast-breeding, adaptable, and fond of second growth and fields, the Collared Peccary is something of a human commensal in Quintana Roo—able to survive, and even flourish, in spite of heavy hunting pressure. However, rapid human population growth has led to an even more rapid escalation of hunting pressure. (It should be noted that the peccary is shot not only for food—its meat is superb—but also because a herd of peccaries is probably the most devastating thing, short of a hurricane, that can hit a milpa. Raccoons are much more chronically thievish but do less damage per foray.) Even the *kitam* cannot withstand current levels of shooting. Still, in 2001, peccaries appeared to us to be commoner than in 1996. Alone among game animals, they seem to be holding their numbers.

There have been efforts (locally inspired by INI) to farm peccaries. A successful small peccary farm exists in San Francisco Ake', north of Chunhuhub. This farm has had up to fifteen animals; it had eleven, in excellent condition and very tame, when ENA visited it in 1996. The animals are sold locally for food. This inspired us to contemplate the possibility of farming peccaries in Chunhuhub, starting with FMT's pet female animal (Bixa); he tried to find a mate for her, but when she matured, she took matters into her own hooves and fled to the forest, where she was unfortunately shot by a hunter.

Collared Peccaries—young ones at least—are ideal pets. From experience with Bixa and observation of many other tamed peccaries, we can testify that, with minimally good treatment, they become tamer, friendlier, and more affectionate than most dogs. They are excellent watch-animals, driving off strange dogs but becoming very friendly with, and even acting like packmates of, their owners' dogs. They are cheap to feed (unless they discover seedlings of valuable commercial plants!) and easy to control, taking well to tying up or fencing. They do, however, become wilder as they mature, and an adult male can be dangerous, with razor-sharp tushes. They breed successfully in small pens. All in all, they would seem to have a bright future as livestock and pets, if any effort is expended in this direction.

This leads to the question of why the ancient Maya did not domesticate the peccary. (Of course, they may have—they almost certainly kept tame ones, as modern Maya do—but we have no evidence for domestication.) We would propose three reasons. First, before modern guns became available, the animals were so common that there was no need to domesticate them. Second, unlike pigs (which flourish on weeds, garbage, and excrement), Collared Peccaries eat food such as maize and thus compete directly with humans when food is short. Third, peccaries produce fewer young than pigs do (even wild pigs), nor do they grow so fast; thus they do not give the high returns to labor that pigs do. A peccary produces two young a year, rarely up to three or four, while a pig can have ten in one litter. Some believe that peccaries—Collared and White-lipped—can crossbreed with domestic pigs. This is highly dubious, since the animals are not even in the same biological family. See also *jabalí*.

Koj. Puma *(Felis concolor)*. Very rare in the area but said to be present in extremely remote forest areas where deer (its major prey) are still found in adequate numbers.

Kulit (kurit). Guinea pig *(Cavia porcellus)*. Rare pet. Maya variant of Spanish *curí*.

K'ulub (k'ulu'). Raccoon *(Procyon lotor)*. Hocabá: *k'ulu'*; Hocabá Yucatec frequently drops the terminal /b/ (cf. *tsabkaan* below, and also many plant names). This animal is considered to be the worst pest, at least among large animals, of milpas. They also take citrus fruit and almost anything else they can get. Nocturnal, secretive, highly intelligent, and absolutely devastating to maize and other crops. Shot whenever possible, but they remain common and damaging.

Ku'uk. Squirrels. Two species:
　Chak ku'uk: red squirrel *(Sciurus deppei)*.
　Ya'ax ku'uk: gray squirrel *(Sciurus yucatanensis)*.
Both are fairly common in the forest, the gray apparently being more common. Both are sometimes shot for food, and sometimes kept as pets. They appear to be less common than formerly, because of hunting and Hurricane Roxanne.

Liebre. Sp.; hare (*Lepus* spp.) Locally misapplied to paca, sometimes also to agouti or rabbit.

Maax (ma'ax). Howler monkey *(Alouatta pigra).* Found as far north as Margaritas, where howlers may be easily heard. The white scrotum of the adult male was described to us. See also *ba'ats, chango, mono, saraguato,* and *tuch.*

Malix. Mongrel dog, mutt. Usually in the mestiza-Maya form *perro malix:* "mutt, mongrel." See *peek'.*

Marto. Sp.; kinkajou (*Potos flavus).* A rare animal, sometimes shot because it can be a pest of gardens and beehives (and of wild bee nests). See also *mico de noche* and *wayu'.*

Mico de noche. Sp.; kinkajou. Lit. "night monkey." See *marto* and *wayu'.*

Miis. Cat *(Felis domestica).* The name is sometimes said to come from the noise "mis-mis," used by Spanish speakers to call cats (like "puss-puss" in English). Hocabá reports *hmiis* for males, *xmiis* for females; the latter is rare, the former nonexistent, in Chunhuhub. Cats are uncommon in Chunhuhub. Since rats and mice are rare, the cats have neither reason for being nor a ready food source. Families sometimes keep them for pets, but poor feeding and care dooms most kittens to an early death.

Mono. Sp.; monkeys in general. The standard collective, Yucatec Maya having no collective term for monkeys. See also *ba'ats, chango, maax, saraguato,* and *tuch.*

Mula. Sp.; Mule *(Equus caballus* x *E. asinus).* Mules are not kept or used in the area, but they are known from Yucatán state. See also *chowak-xikin.*

Ooch. Medium-sized furry animals. Focally, the term refers to opossums. Most opossums are of magical significance; seeing any of the larger ones is bad luck, according to some, though the beliefs appear to be dying out. One throws salt into flame to neutralize their evil (this is an ancient European trick to neutralize devils and ill fortune). The following folk species are known:

Bok'ol ooch (*bok'ol ha' ooch*): Lit. "chocolate-beater opossum." (Hocabá reports "bokol-'ooch, a type of fox," which is neither the pronunciation nor the meaning reported in Chunhuhub and elsewhere.) A large opossum that makes a noise similar to that of beating up chocolate (drink) in a wooden chocolate-maker: "bok', bok', bok'." This creature is usually considered not to be a real animal, but an evil spirit (*k'ak'as ik'* [*k'as ik'*]) or *mal viento*, "evil wind"; Robert Redfield reported this belief for Chan Kom as well). However, FMT has encountered large opossums making this sound and finds them to be ordinary opossums. Old animals make a grumbling noise for aggressive reasons. Those who believe them to be evil spirits fear that a bok'ol ooch in the yard means very bad luck, and they may call a *jmeen* (traditional ritualist) to hold an exorcism rite. This is done by scattering holy water with a rue branch while chanting a prayer.

Box ooch: Common Opossum *(Didelphis marsupialis)*. Lit. "dark opossum."

Joolij ooch (joolil ooch): Small opossums. Lit. "hole-dwelling opossum." Two species are covered by this term: the Mexican Mouse Opossum *(Marmosa mexicana)* and the Central American Woolly Opossum (*Caluromys derbianus;* see Navarro 1992, 7). The mouse opossum is fairly common but rarely seen because of its small size and nocturnal habits. However, it may invade houses, and a population dwells in the ruined colonial church of Chunhuhub. Some believe this animal is an evil spirit like the bok'ol ooch (but less threatening). It is believed to die if it tries to cross a road (like the *jijitsbeej* of Xocen [Terán and Rasmussen 1992]).

Sak ooch: Virginia Opossum *(Didelphis virginiana)*. Lit. "pale opossum."

As a general term, *ooch* applies not only to opossums but also to skunks, porcupines, and perhaps other medium-sized mammals. These are not thought to be part of a natural group at all. The word has simply been loosely extended to serve in this usage. Conversely, the Philander Opossum is known to be an opossum and included in the *ooch* category (or the more specific *bolsa ooch*, see above, for opossums), but its specific name does not include the syllable *ooch*. This provides insight into the very untaxonomic way that what appear to be folk generics are used in Yucatec Maya. See also *jo'onka'an*.

Oso hormiguero. Sp.; anteater. See *chab*.

Oso mielero. Sp.; tayra. See *sa'anjol*.

Paay (paayooch). Skunks in general. Focally, the Spotted Skunk *(Spilogale putorius; see jool paay),* which is locally common. Other species occur; more research is needed on their actual distributions.

Peek'. Dog *(Canis lupus familiaris).* This constant companion of humanity abounds in Chunhuhub. Maya dogs are small and delicate looking, doubtless as a result of millennia of natural selection for survival on a meager diet of low-quality food (mostly maize). They are mixtures of pre-Columbian Mesoamerican dogs with various European breeds; some show identifiable greyhound or whippet ancestry. They are virtually universal in households, as pets, guards, herders, and hunters. In spite of their small size and delicate appearance, they are excellent work dogs. In hunting, for instance, they are easy to train, incredibly intelligent and enduring, and willing to attack animals far bigger than they are. Some hunters have larger animals, specially cared for, and as splendid for hunting as any dogs we have seen anywhere.

Specialized herd dogs in nearby cattle-raising communities such as Vallehermosa often have some Australian sheepdog or cattle dog ancestry. Hunting dogs, however, are ordinary Maya dogs. An individual hunter will operate with one to five dogs; groups of people engaged in *p'uuj* (beating the bush for game) may use over a dozen. Dogs are carefully trained and often specialize in one animal, especially deer, peccary, or paca. Particularly tough ones may become *tejoneros* (coati hunters); coatis are murderously effective at fighting back and require special courage and strength on the part of the dog. Part of the training of a hunting dog can include "secrets" (magical procedures). For instance, a ball of deer blood and crushed velvet ants, held together in corn meal, may be given to the dog to smell and then eat; FMT has tried this with good results. (The velvet ant is a wingless female wasp that is a tireless and merciless hunter of insects. See *chakmool-bej,* under Insects, below.)

Ordinary mongrel dogs are known as *malix* in Maya, or *perros malix* in mestiza-Maya; the Spanish is *perros corrientes* (run-of-the-mill dogs) or *perros callejeros* (street dogs—normally meaning feral dogs). In Chunhuhub, virtually all dogs belong to someone, but in urban areas, about half the dogs are *perros callejeros.* Breed dogs are *perros de raza* (there is, significantly, no Yucatec Maya word for them). The only breed dogs commonly known are large, savage guard dogs: *pastor aleman* (German shepherd), Rottweiler, and

Doberman. It was usually assumed that ENA would have *perros de raza,* back home in California, and some relief was often expressed when he assured the questioners that his dogs were *puros malixes.*

Dogs are well cared for in Chunhuhub and throughout the Zona Maya. If a family's dogs are poorly fed, it is usually safe to assume that the family is not eating well—though there are exceptions to this generalization. Dogs are virtually never deliberately mistreated, though thoughtless children are given considerable license in treating animals roughly. Dogs are petted and played with and usually become tame and familiar; though they are good watchdogs, they are virtually never fierce or vicious. In general, animals are treated well in the Zona Maya—in sharp contrast to the situation in some parts of the Yucatán Peninsula and Mexico.

Pukil (puk, pukil ch'oo'). Mice in general. The House Mouse *(Mus musculus)* occurs as a minor pest but is rare. Wild mice apparently occur, but they are so rare that we have not identified species.

Put'emput'. A small gray rodent, thick-bodied, short-furred, short-tailed, gopherlike or volelike but not a gopher. It possesses gopherlike cheek pockets. Pacheco Cruz (1958) identifies it as *Heteromys gaumeri* (i.e., a pocket mouse), which may be correct. He thinks the name may be used for the *Marmosa* opossum as well, but we have not found this to be the case in Chunhuhub.

Saabin (saabiin). Long-tailed Weasel *(Mustela frenata).* A fairly common predator. It occasionally takes young poultry.

Sa'anjol (saanjol). Tayra *(Eyra barbara).* Called by apiarists *el azote de colmenas* ("the scourge of beehives"), this common and beautiful predator is a real problem for beekeepers. Otherwise it is a minor part of the fauna, keeping to dense brushy forest. See also *oso mielero.*

Sakxikin. Ocelot *(Felis pardalis).* Lit. "white ear." A rare animal. We saw it together on only one occasion, when one crossed a road in the tall and extensive old-growth forest of Naranjal Poniente. We have encountered it independently there, and elsewhere, rarely. It seems never to have become common, and shooting—both for its valuable pelt and to eliminate it from the neighborhood of poultry yards—has exterminated it from all but the wildest areas. See also *tigrillo.*

Saraguato. Sp.; howler monkey. See *ba'ats, chango, maax, mono,* and *tuch.*

Sereque. Sp. (from Nahuatl); agouti. See *tsuub.*

Sinsimito. Mestiza-Maya word for the mythical Bigfoot of Mayaland. These large hairy creatures are considered dangerous on occasion. Their toes are at the back of their feet, heels at the front, confusing the tracker. They live in deep forest and are rarely encountered—indeed, apparently they are encountered only after consumption of considerable amounts of *chakpool* (raw rum).

Soots'. Bats in general (Chiroptera). Many species exist; even scientists have not worked out the ones present in western Quintana Roo. Bats are considered birds by old-time Maya, but school-goers know they are mammals.

Taman (jtaman). Sheep *(Ovis aries).* Lit. "the one of cotton." (More fully, *jtaman,* but the prefix is now not pronounced.) This creative name arose almost immediately after conquest, being attested in the earliest colonial sources.

Tapir. Sp.; see *danta.*

Tejón. South Mexican Sp.; coati. In formal Spanish the word means "badger," but no badgers exist in southern Mexico, where the word invariably refers to the coati. See also *chi'ik.*

Tepescuintle. Sp. (from Nahuatl); paca. See *jaaleb.*

Tigre. Local Sp.; jaguar. Properly "tiger," but universally used for the jaguar in Latin America. See *baalam, chakyik'al,* and *chak mo'ol.*

Tigrillo. Local Sp.; ocelot, extended to other small cats. See *sakxikin.*

Tooloch (tool ooch). Striped skunks *(Mephitis* spp.). The striped skunk is locally rare and usually just lumped as *paay* or *paay ooch* with the Spotted.

Tsiimin. Domestic horse *(Equus caballus).* The original Yucatec Maya meaning, "tapir," is not remembered. The tapir is invariably known as *danta* or *tapir.*

Tsuub. Agouti *(Dasyprocta punctata).* Known as *sereque* in south Mexican Spanish. This animal is the commonest large rodent, indeed the commonest game animal, in the area under consideration. Too small to attract much attention, and successful at escaping hunters, it remains fairly common in less disturbed areas of tall mixed forest with underbrush and fruit trees. However, it has been getting steadily rarer.

Tuch. Spider monkey *(Ateles geoffroyi)*. By extension, monkeys in general. It has a mestiza-Maya form, *tucho.* See also *ba'ats, chango, maax, mono,* and *saraguato.*

T'uul (t'u'ul). Rabbits, wild or domestic. (Sp. *conejo.*) The small cottontail *(Sylvilagus floridanus)* is present, but uncommon, in young second growth with a mix of grass, weeds, and young trees. It is hunted by snares, dogs, guns, and sticks but rarely obtained; it is too fast and dodgy to be worth the effort, considering how little meat it yields.

Domestic rabbits have been widely promoted in Mexico by the government in *cunicultura* programs. The promoters seem never to learn that the Mexican rural household, abounding already in chickens, turkeys, ducks, pigs, and anything else available, does not need a less-efficient and harder-to-raise small meat animal. However, the Maya have enthusiastically adopted rabbits—as pets. Rabbits are considered too cute to kill. Some people reportedly eat them, but most keep them simply because the children love them.

Wakax. Domestic cattle *(Bos taurus)*. From Spanish *vacas;* the plural was borrowed but is now used for the singular. Only some five families in Chunhuhub, and a few more in neighboring villages, keep significant numbers (ten to twenty, rarely more) of cattle. Several more families have one or two. Cattle raising is more developed in the extensive natural savannahs around Vallehermosa to the south. In the Chunhuhub area, it does not usually pay. Forest must be completely cleared and sown to pasture and will regrow at the slightest opportunity. Moreover, few pasture grasses do well under the regime of extremely wet summer and extremely dry spring. Taiwan grass (a large unidentified grass) produces the most and best feed, but it does better with some spring irrigation. Various African grasses are widely grown with varying success. Left to themselves, Guinea grass *(Panicum maximum)* and *estrella* (star) grass *(Cynodon nlemfuensis)* do well, but not well enough to feed cattle at high stocking rates. Native plants, notably waxim *(Leucaena leucocephala),* provide good forage. Feed supplements include chopped Taiwan grass with molasses. All in all, cattle are demanding and difficult animals that do not pay well, and destroying the forest for them is extremely bad policy.

Most of the cattle are various modern hybrids of Indian zebu-type stock, such as Indo-Brazils. They produce lean meat. In the Chunhuhub areas, they are raised strictly for the meat, usually sold locally. Typically, an animal is butchered every weekend—beef is unavailable the rest of the week. Meat sold for twenty pesos per kilogram in 1996. Some superior animals are found, including a 650-kilogram Brahma bull owned (in 1996) by our close friend Adriano Dzib in Presidente Juarez.

In the natural savannahs around and south of Vallehermosa, cattle do very well, and the land is well suited to them. A herding culture has arisen there, introduced by in-migrants from central Mexico. There and elsewhere in savannah country in the peninsula, cattle are milked for cheese production, and thus pay better and are more useful generally than they are around Chunhuhub.

Wayu' (wayuk'). Described to us as a small, dark, nocturnal animal whose call is "wayuuu." Said to be similar to a kinkajou but smaller. Almost certainly it is just a kinkajou, whose call is recorded as "wake-up" in Emmons (1990, 140); Hocabá *wayuk'*, "kinkajou." (Rare word; our speaker did not pronounce the /k/ but may simply have elided it.) See also *marto* and *mico de noche*.

Weech (wech). Nine-banded Armadillo *(Dasypus novemcinctus)*. (Almost always pronounced "wech.") Color variation is recognized: *Box weech* (dark armadillo) and *sak weech* (pale armadillo).

The armadillo is a significant food animal in much of southern Mexico, but it is not much eaten in Chunhuhub, though appreciated when caught. It is regarded by the Maya as an irresistibly funny animal. It can, however, become something of a pest through its burrowing habits; it may dig up a good deal of a milpa in its search for grubs and worms. Armadillos suffered tragic mass mortality from Hurricane Roxanne; they were drowned in their burrows. The population had recovered only somewhat by 2001, the slow rate partly due to hunting pressure.

Xleech. Sow (*Sus scrofa*, female). Here the female marker *x* is a necessary part of the word. It is interesting that this nonnative animal has a native Yucatec Maya name. Possibly the term originally was applied to female peccaries.

Yuk (yuuk). Brocket deer *(Mazama americana);* extended to goat *(Capra hircus),* but the old meaning persists as well. (Hocabá gives *yuuk,* but the vowel seems always shortened in the Chunhuhub area.) Red *(chak)* and gray *(sak* or *ya'ax)* color variants exist, the gray said to be somewhat different in size and habits. This raises the possibility that two species may be involved. Possibly *M. guazoubira* extends north into the area; other proposals have been made. It seems more likely, at this time, that the red and gray forms are simply color varieties. It is a revealing comment on our knowledge of Quintana Roo biology that such a large, formerly common animal is so little known that there is controversy over the number of species present.

In spite of having formerly been common enough to give its name to the town of Polyuc (lit. "brocket's head"), the brocket is now extinct in the Chunhuhub area. It still survives farther south, but overhunting is rapidly eliminating it.

Zenzo. Mexican Sp.; White-lipped Peccary. (From Nahuatl *cenzontl,* "four hundred," because of the huge size of the bands in the days before shotguns; the number is probably exaggerated, but "four hundred" was a general term for "many" as well as a military term for a group of four hundred soldiers—appropriate to an animal believed to be highly aggressive.) Rarely used term, the commoner local Spanish term being *jahuilla.* See also *k'aaxik'eek'en.*

BIRDS

Birds in general are *ch'iich'* (usually pronounced *ch'ich'*) in Yucatec Maya, *pajaro* in Spanish. All birds can be named, but for many—including virtually all the water birds—there are no Yucatec names, and Spanish names are used.

Moreover, there are no names for any of the many winter visitors. Names of resident birds are extended to cover them. For instance, all warblers with yellow on them are called *chinchinbakal,* a name that focally applies to *Euphonia* tanagers and to goldfinches, while brownish warblers are called *yankotij,* a name that focally means the Tropical House Wren. In Yucatán state, by contrast, migrant warblers have a collective name of their own, *ts'ip* (Victor Navarro, pers. comm.). The loss of water bird names in modern Yucatec is interesting. It was apparently in process even when the earliest dictionaries were compiled; they record all the common bird names but have few water bird names. (Some water bird names, such as *pontoj* for pelicans, still exist in Yucatec but are unknown in Chunhuhub because the birds do not occur there.)

A bird backbone is a *bobox*—not, as in most other animals, a *bakij pach*.

Aak'al. Heard once for Cattle Egret *(Bubulcus ibis)*. Normally called *garza blanca* (Sp. for "white heron"). Apparently a nonstandard name, probably applied ad hoc. Not otherwise attested by consultants or in literature. The word means "lake" or "wet place," as in *aak'alche'* (low wet area), and the consultant was presumably referring to a bird of an *aak'al*. See also *garza* and *lukupech*.

Aguililla. Sp.; hawk-eagles and similar large hawks in general. Lit. "small eagle." A general cover term, somewhat wider than the Yucatec Maya words that parcel out the hawk domain. Can include any large hawk or eagle. See also *ek' pip*.

Azulejo. Indigo Bunting *(Passerina cyanea)*. An extremely abundant winter visitor, but, like all winter visitors, it has no name of its own in Yucatec Maya. It is often trapped (with a drop-cage operated by a string) and kept as a cage bird. Indigo Buntings are commonly sold in the bird market in Mérida, but not in Quintana Roo, where anyone who wants one can trap one fairly easily.

Baakenchulul. Pheasant Cuckoo *(Dromococcyx phasianellus)*. Extended to include the Lesser Roadrunner *(Geococcyx velox)* and Striped Cuckoo *(Tapera naevia)*. All are uncommon. The Pheasant Cuckoo occurs in light second-growth woodland, where its call is a characteristic sound of spring. Many, including FMT, can imitate the call well enough to call this usually shy and invisible bird so that it comes into the open and even flies around one's head. The Lesser Roadrunner and Striped Cuckoo are probably newcomers to Chunhuhub. They live in scrubby second-growth brush. This habitat has expanded greatly in recent years, and the Lesser Roadrunner and Striped Cuckoo have apparently come with it. These birds are thus poorly known to the local people. Indeed, the Striped Cuckoo was not noted at all in 1991 and may have arrived since that year; it has certainly increased.

Bach (baach). Plain Chachalaca *(Ortalis vetula)*. Hocabá *baach* is probably correct, but never so pronounced in ENA's hearing. Syn. of the less common *kobi*. This bird remains common in spite of heavy hunting pressure (as noted also by Jorgensen in X-Hazil; Jorgensen 1993). Its loud calls can be heard all around the outskirts of Chunhuhub and other communities, especially in spring. It is most common in hilly areas and in lighter forest. Hurricane Roxanne greatly reduced the population, primarily (we believe) because it destroyed the chachalaca's food supply. The population had rallied considerably by 2001, though hunting pressure kept it from maximizing its increase rate. The bird feeds primarily on small fruits and berries, including hard and sour ones as well as sweet and soft ones. Pixoy berries are a favorite. It also eats young buds and other vegetable matter. Chachalacas are easy to raise and are commonly kept as pets, often when a mother bird is shot for food and her young are captured. The young become very tame and flourish as part of a dooryard flock, living with the chickens. They are raised to adulthood, at which time they usually either escape or are eaten.

Bech'koos. Hawk with a quail-like pattern. Lit. "quail laughing-falcon." We (as a team) have not seen this in the field, but FMT tentatively identifies it with pictures of accipiters in Peterson and Chalif (1989). The Bicolored Hawk *(Accipiter bicolor)* is possible but so far unrecorded in the area.

Beech' (almost always bech'). Yucatán Bobwhite *(Colinus nigrogularis,* often regarded as a subspecies of the Common Bobwhite, *C. virginianus).* This term can be extended to include any quail. This species is common in young second growth, particularly in areas of mixed grass, weeds, and young thorny bushes and trees. It lives in pairs or coveys. It is occasionally caught, usually with drop-cage traps, but is too small to be the target of serious hunting effort. Thus it remains common—2001 was a banner year for breeding, and it appeared commoner than ever. See also *codorniz*.

Beech' lu'um (bech' lu'um). Black-faced Antthrush *(Formicarius analis).* Hocabá, and ordinary speech, *bech' lu'um;* the combining form of *beech'* may regularly be *bech'*. Lit. "quail of the ground," but not regarded as a kind of quail; the extension of *beech'* is based on general similarity (both birds are small, round-shaped, short-tailed ground-dwellers with black face masks). The antthrush is abundant in old-growth forest. Its whistled cry can easily be imitated, luring this otherwise reclusive bird into sight. See also *ya'ax bech' lu'um* and *tsiimink'aax.*

Bujk'aanij. A large-eared owl, not well known in area. Probably another name for the Great Horned Owl (normally *tunkuruchu*).

Calandria. Sp.; properly lark, but (confusingly) used for orioles, and occasionally for mockingbirds, in the Yucatán Peninsula and southern Mexico. See also *chiik.*

Camacho. Local Sp.; cormorant (*Phalacrocorax; P. olivaceus* the only one found in or near Chunhuhub), extended to anhinga *(Anhinga anhinga).* These birds are *mach* in standard Yucatec; *camacho* appears to be a local Spanish–Yucatec Maya blend. (Santamaria 1988 records it as a Campechian word for the Great-tailed Grackle.) See also *jichkal.*

Canario. Sp.; canary, used mainly by Spanish speakers for small yellow finches, such as goldfinches. Hach Maya is *chinchinbakal.*

Chachalaca. Mexican Sp. and also English for the *bach.* Echoic. See also *kobi.*

Chakts'its'ib (chakts'iits'ib). Common Northern Cardinal *(Cardinalis cardinalis).* This is one of the names that are very often extended, in this case to cover other red birds such as the Summer Tanager (*Piranga rubra*—a winter visitor, and like all winter visitors lacking its own name), or to brownish birds of the general size and shape of a cardinal. The name means "the red one that says *ts'i-ts'ib.*" This common, familiar resident of scrubby second growth is occasionally trapped and kept as a pet. It appears to be increasing locally, with its habitat. (Hocabá *chakts'iits'ib;* I doubt this. Cordemex and other sources agree with Chunhuhub usage.) See also *sob.*

Chaxnuuk (tojkaxnuuk, tojchaxnuuk). Ferruginous Pigmy Owl *(Glaucidium brasilianum).* Sometimes extended to other small owls. (Probably from *chak xnuuk* "red old one," or *chan xnuuk,* "little old one.") See also *kooaak'ab* and *tojkaaxnuk.*

Ch'eel. This name contrasts at two levels. Focally, it refers specifically to the Yucatán Jay *(Cyanocorax yucatanica).* It also serves as a generic for jays and jaylike birds. Within it, in this sense, are two (other) folk species:

Ya'ax ch'eel: Green Jay *(Cyanocorax yncas).*

Pan ch'el (**Pan ch'eel**): Collared Aracari *(Pteroglossus torquatus)*. See separate entry for this bird.

Che'jun (cha'jun, che'jum, chu'jun, ch'ajum, ch'ajun). Medium-sized woodpeckers. The focal *che'jun* is a species pair: the Golden-fronted Woodpecker *(Melanerpes aurifrons)* and the very similar Yucatán Woodpecker *(Melanerpes pygmaeus)*. This name is extended to cover similar woodpeckers, such as the Chestnut-colored *(Celeus castaneus)*, but especially the Golden-olive Woodpecker *(Piculus rubiginosus)*, locally rare. The two focal species are common locally. The Golden-fronted was decimated by Hurricane Roxanne, being reduced to a small fraction of its former abundance. It lives in holes in high, emergent snags, and these were largely blown down by the hurricane. (The Yucatán Woodpecker nests lower down and was apparently unaffected.) Also, it eats a fair amount of fruit, and this food source was largely destroyed. It had fully recovered by 2001, and was noisily, joyfully ebullient as ever. *Che'jun* can become a pest in milpas and orchards, pecking into many corn ears and fruit and thus ruining them. However, the Maya usually tolerate this loss. See also *kolonte'*.

Chibilub (chibiluub). Singing Quail *(Dactylortyx thoracicus)*. Sometimes mistakenly used for other birds. (It should be emphasized that this name is not normally extended to other species, and use of it for them is a mistake, not a legitimate extension. The Singing Quail is rather poorly known and similar birds such as the Little Tinamou [see *ke'el non*] can be confused with it.) Rare in tall scrub and hill forest; almost never seen, though the song is often audible at the edge of Chunhuhub. Decreased by 2001, probably due to habitat loss. (Hocabá *chibiluub*. Again, this may be correct in some abstract sense, but it is not the normal spoken form in Chunhuhub.)

Ch'iich'ha'. Water bird. Not a bird name within the taxonomic system but a loose descriptive term.

Chiik. Tropical Mockingbird *(Mimus gilvus)*. Often, and rather delightfully, Hispanicized or mestiza-Mayanized to *chica* (Sp. for "young girl"). One of the most familiar and common birds of gardens and cultivated areas. Its singing is appreciated but it is sometimes regarded as a pest because of its fondness for some cultivated fruits. The standard Mexican term *sensontle* (from the Nahuatl for "four hundred tongues") is not much used in the Zona Maya, where the mockingbird is given its Maya name or lumped as a *calandria*.

Chikbu'ul. Groove-billed Ani *(Crotophaga sulcirostris)*. Loosely applied to other medium-sized black birds, especially the Melodious Blackbird and Red-eyed Cowbird (more commonly *pich'*). Name derived from call. *Bu'ul* means "beans." This common open-country bird is getting commoner as permanent fields and pastures increase. It is usually regarded as a good bird to have around, because it eats the ticks off cattle. See also *kusuy,* a rare syn.

Chinchinbakal. Applied to any small bird with yellow or yellowish colors on it. The focal ones are euphonias (Scrub and Yellow-throated Euphonias, *Euphonia affinis* and *E. hirundinacea*) and goldfinches (Lesser Goldfinch, *Spinus psaltria*). Wintering North American warblers and any other small yellowish birds are lumped under this term. This is one of the most commonly used bird names, and one of the ones most widely and generally extended. See also *canario.*

Chi'pirix. Ladder-backed Woodpecker *(Picoides scalaris)*. This bird is common in the drier forest and scrub. Extended to other small woodpeckers, mainly the Smoky-brown *(Veniliornis fumigatus)*. (See also *tatak'che'*.) The size, shape, and actions of the Ladder-back make it a playful trope for the penis in Maya speech (as *pajaro carpintero,* "woodpecker," is in Spanish), and the mention of the name *chi'pirix* almost invariably brings a smile.

Ch'oom. Vultures in general. This word is one of the few genuine folk generics in Yucatec Maya. Four folk species are recognized:

Batab ch'oom (batab ch'om): King Vulture *(Sarcorhamphus papa)*. Lit. "ruler (or god) vulture." This rare bird nests in the deep forests southwest of Chunhuhub; a pair with a juvenile can be seen fairly often in that area, ranging as far north as southern Chunhuhub ejido lands. It is regarded as ruler of the vultures because it is the dominant bird at carcasses. Some older people believe that it actually directs the other vultures, telling them when and what they can eat, and thus maintains order during feeding. It is also called *sak uus* (which should mean "white gnat," but here *uus* appears to be just another name for the bird).

Box pool ch'oom (Box pool ch'om): Black Vulture *(Coragyps atratus)*. Lit. "black head vulture." Exceedingly abundant. The name is sometimes applied to immatures of the Turkey Vulture.

Chak pool ch'oom (Chak pool ch'om): Turkey Vulture *(Cathartes aura)*. Lit. "red head vulture." An abundant and ever-present resident of the area, usually the first to locate carrion. Nests in caves and rock overhangs; the young are known to be white and fuzzy.

Sak ch'oom: Wood Stork *(Mycteria americana)*. Lit. "white vulture." The Maya appear to have been a few hundred or thousand years ahead of European taxonomists in recognizing the close relationship of storks and American vultures.

The Black and Turkey Vultures are believed to shed bird lice as they pass over, and one sometimes sees people frantically brushing their hair after such a passage.

Chuukij. Scaled Pigeon *(Columba speciosa)*. Uncommon in Chunhuhub; commoner southward and eastward. Occurs in tall old-growth forest. Its nostalgic-sounding call, a sad "coo-oo, oooo," is verbalized as *uuch ca'achi*, "long, long ago." See also *kukut'kib* and *uukum*.

Ch'uuy (almost always **ch'uy**). Hawks in general. The boundaries of *ch'uuy* and *ii'* are highly flexible. In the field, one man had just finished explaining that ch'uuy were white and ii' were dark when he pointed out a Great Black Hawk as a *ch'uuy*. In fact, the terms are often interchanged. *Ch'uuy* is more general, covering the space of *gavilan* in Spanish. *Ii'* is thus often held to be a subset, including only (or at least focally) the *Buteo* hawks, although ch'uuy is used focally to refer to the Roadside Hawk *(Buteo magnirostris)*.

Ch'uyin (ch'uuyiin). Apparently the Rufous-browed Peppershrike *(Cyclarhis gujanensis)*. This name is derived from the call (specifically the loud dawn song, a repeated "chuyin") and refers to the bird as heard. Few if any recognize the bird itself or associate it, when seen, with the call. When seen, the bird tends to be lumped into the *chinchinbakal* category or other very general categories. The call has a wild high quality that makes it an evil omen in other parts of the Maya world. Also called *k'uumil* (the one of the squashes).

Codorniz. Sp.; quail in general. Locally used for the Yucatán Bobwhite.

Correa. Local Sp.; limpkin *(Aramus guarana)*. There is no Yucatec Maya name for the bird. The local name is probably a variant of the more wide-spread Spanish name *carao*.

Ek' pip (eek' piip, eek' pip, ek' piip). Large black hawks in general. See also *aguililla*. Black Hawk-Eagle *(Spizaetus tyrannus)* is the focal exemplar for this name. The name is extended to include other large black hawks, such as the Great Black Hawk *(Buteogallus urubitinga)*. (The smaller Common Black Hawk, *B. anthracinus*, is usually a *ch'uuy*, though sometimes loosely called an *ek' pip*.) The term is also extended, sometimes, to include the Ornate Hawk-Eagle (see also *jonkuuk*), which is similar in shape but not in color to the Black Hawk-Eagle. Even dark-phase Hook-billed Kites *(Chondrohierax uncinatus)* can be called *ek' pip*, though their smaller size normally makes them *ch'uuy* or *ii'*. (The Hook-billed Kite is rather rare in the area and varies in size—males being smaller—and in color.) In short, the term, like other hawk names, is extended according to color, shape, or size, thus creating a vague boundary zone where confusing and little-known hawks like the Hook-billed Kite can be classed under three or four different names with equal ease. In practice, there are familiar anchors— the Black Hawk-Eagle for *ek' pip*, the Gray Hawk for *ii'*, the Bat Falcon for *keenkeenbak*—and a wide range of less familiar hawks that can be clas-sified under several names (more or less according to whim) or just lumped under the general term *ch'uuy*. FMT uses any or all of these terms for the Hook-billed Kite, for instance, and has had many interesting discussions with friends about the proper names for species like the Black-shouldered Kite that are relatively new to the area (see *keenkeenbak*). (And one person once used *ek' pip* for a Squirrel Cuckoo—clearly a mistake.)

Ek'xikin. Yucatán Parrot *(Amazona xantholora)*. Lit. "black ear," referring to the blackish ear patch that distinguishes this bird from the White-fronted Parrot. The bird is common in the area, but far less so than the White-fronted. Both declined about 75 percent in abundance as a result of Hur-ricane Roxanne, but probably more because they left the area (their food was largely destroyed) than because they were actually killed; within a year after Roxanne, they were rapidly regaining their former numbers. However, even in 2001 they were not as common as before Roxanne, and they had declined in other parts of the state. Trapping for the pet trade is not common in

Quintana Roo, and it is much more likely that the problem is destruction of nest trees. Hurricanes, and increasing agricultural clearance, have eliminated most of the old dead trees with large holes that these birds need.

Faisan. South Mexican Sp. for Maya *k'aambuul* (Great Curassow), which is *hocofaisan* in formal Spanish. *Faisan* properly applies to Old World pheasants. The local application of the name has led to continual confusion.

Gallareta. Sp.; gallinules, coots, and similar birds. There is no local Yucatec Maya name for these, and the Spanish name has been borrowed to cover them. Several species of gallinules and rails are present in the area. See the bird list in appendix II. Focally refers to the Common Moorhen *(Gallinula chloropus)*.

Gallinola. Sp.; jacana *(Jacana spinosa)* and rails *(not* gallinules). The jacana is sometimes called *t'eel ja',* but there is no Yucatec name for the rails (either today or in the colonial sources), so the Spanish name is borrowed.

Ganso. Sp.; domestic goose *(Anser anser).* Rarely raised in Chunhuhub, but some people keep them, largely as curiosities. Their "watchdog" value is appreciated.

Garza. Sp.; herons in general. As with many other water birds, these lack a contemporary Yucatec Maya name (although in the past, they were known as *gaarsaj*), and the Spanish word is universally used. Egrets, the commonest local herons, are *garza blanca* (white heron). See also *aak'al* and *lukupech.*

Guinea. Sp.; guinea fowl *(Numidia meleagris).* As with the above two, there is no Yucatec Maya name. The goose and guinea are, of course, introduced. Guinea fowl are very rare in Chunhuhub, being kept by one or two families as curiosities.

Hermitonia. Sp.; unidentified. Described as a small bluish bird that comes in fall migration.

Ii' (i'). Small hawks in general. (Usually i'—very possibly the correct pronunciation, but I tend to standardize toward long vowels when in doubt; Hocabá and Cordemex, however, agree on *i'.*) Focally the Gray Hawk *(Buteo nitidus),* whose call is *iiiii!* Usually includes also the Roadside Hawk *(B. magnirostris).* The Gray Hawk is specifically *sak ii',* "white hawk," and as such gave its name to the Maya city of Saci, now called Valladolid (Yucatán) in Spanish but still Saci (the old spelling is used in place names) to the Maya. Some sources have mistakenly conjectured that the town was named for the White Hawk, *Leucopternis albicollis,* but this bird does not occur in the Yucatán Peninsula. Maya has no term for "gray"; light gray is *sak,* dark gray is *ya'ax* (focally "green"), very dark gray is *ek'* (black). The term *ii'* is often vaguely extended to include most or all hawks, thus becoming more or less a synonym of *ch'uuy.* See also *ek' pip.*

Jaap. Common Potoo *(Nyctibius griseus).* An uncommon or rare (but highly visible and audible) local bird. The name is derived from the call. Those that do not know the name lump the bird with *kooaak'ab* or *pu'ujuy.*

Jichkal. Cormorant *(Phalacrocorax olivaceus).* Rare, possibly nonstandard name. See *camacho.*

Jonkuuk. Harpy Eagle *(Harpia harpyja).* Now extinct in the Yucatán Peninsula, this bird must have occurred there formerly, as the name is well known and is attested in the colonial dictionaries. Descriptions, both modern and colonial, are quite unmistakable; FMT has heard of it, as a bird that takes adult coatis and other large prey, said to have been found farther to the south until recently. The name is often extended to include the lighter hawk-eagles, such as the Ornate Hawk-Eagle *(Spizaetus ornatus),* in which case the Harpy is specified as the *jonkuuk batab* (ruler *jonkuuk*), a name also attested in the colonial sources.

Jonxa'anij. Small orioles in general *(Icterus* spp.). Contrasts with *yuyum* (the other term for small orioles). *Yuyum* build big nests at the ends of branches and similar (the Alta Mira Oriole, *I. gularis,* is the most familiar example), while *jonxa'anij* tend to build theirs in the dense leaf crowns of palms (*xa'an; jon,* or *jom,* means "hollow, hole"; *-ij* is, of course, the locative and attributive ending). The Hooded Oriole *(I. cucullatus)* is the focal *jonx-a'anij,* since it is the common palm-nesting oriole. However, in practice, its great similarity to the Alta Mira often leads to its being usually lumped as a *yuyum.* Sometimes, *jonxa'anij* is used for yellow orioles (three species in Chunhuhub), *yuyum* for orange ones (five species). There are also other possibilities.

Juiiro. Middle-sized flycatchers that have songs that sound like "huiro, huiro, huiro." The name applies focally to the Bright-rumped Attila *(Attila* *spadiceus; luk'* in other parts of the peninsula), whose loud song is endlessly repeated in spring. This song has a wild, beautiful quality that makes it one of the most striking sounds of the Quintana Roo forest (to Maya and to outside visitors). The bird's song is at its height during the season when people are cutting milpa, and the Attila is thus nicknamed the *pak'sak'al,* "cut and plant the brushfield," since its song calls the people to perform that activity.

The name *juiiro* is also used for the Northern Royal Flycatcher *(Onychorhynchus mexicanus),* an uncommon but conspicuous bird of the mid-levels of deep forest, and for the Rose-throated Becard *(Pachyramphus aglaiae),* which occupies a similar role in the drier forest. See also *piix* and *takaay.*

Juj. Blue-crowned Motmot *(Momotus momota).* A common bird of deep forest environments. The name comes from the call, "hu hu." (The bird is called *jutjut* or *pajaro hu* in Yucatán state; one of the street corners in Mérida is called *el pajaro hu*). The Blue-crowned Motmot is rather poorly known to most and often gets lumped under the name *tooj,* which is correctly limited to the Turquoise-browed Motmot.

K'aambuul (typically k'ambul). Great Curassow *(Crax rubra).* Like the turkey, this was common within recent memory. It is now very rare, though still present in the area. It no longer breeds in Chunhuhub but occasionally still visits remote parts of the ejido lands, where it is depressingly vulnerable. We once found a freshly killed specimen, and we have seen many illegally killed specimens sold along roads in other parts of Quintana Roo. There was a locally caught tame bird in Chunhuhub in 1991.

The curassow, like the turkey and guan, will be extinct in Quintana Roo in the very near future if measures such as captive rearing are not taken. Captive rearing is easy and successful and offers hope for the bird. Tame *k'aambuul* wander happily about the Chetumal and Tuxtla Gutierrez zoos. See also *faisan.*

K'aau (k'au, k'a'au, k'aw, k'a'aw). Great-tailed Grackle *(Quiscalus mexicanus).* (*K'aw* in Cordemex, *k'a'aw* in Hocabá; pronunciation of this word varies greatly from speaker to speaker.) This word has entered Yucatán Spanish as *xcau* and is universally used throughout the peninsula for the bird. The usual Mexican names, *tordo* (from the Spanish name of the European blackbird) and *zanate* (Nahuatl *zanatl*), are not used (to say nothing of other Mexican names, such as *cuervo* and *clarinero*). There seems to be a slight dialect difference in the name: it is *k'aau* in Chunhuhub and most other areas, but *k'a'au* in at least some parts of eastern Yucatán state, and in Presidente Juarez (near Chunhuhub), which was settled from the relevant part of eastern Yucatán. The bird itself is increasing along with humans, as it is a human commensal, living on garbage and crops; it can be a major pest of the latter, eating seeds and young shoots. It is abundant in the town and in fields. Hurricane Roxanne killed large numbers in the trees of the central plaza.

Kaax. Domestic fowl *(Gallus gallus).* An old contraction from *Kaaxlan* (Castilian). Originally, the Maya supposedly named it the Castilian bird or Castilian turkey. This was contracted as the bird became universal. The term is not attested in the colonial dictionaries; example sentences in Maya in the old dictionaries use the Spanish word *gallina.* See also *t'eel.*

The chicken has largely replaced the more delicate, disease-susceptible turkey, though turkeys remain fairly common also. Chickens are the commonest domestic animals of Chunhuhub; almost every family with more than minimal garden space has a flock of several birds. However, no large-scale poultry operations exist in the village. Few people keep more than a dozen. Chicken is a common and popular food and has largely replaced turkey for ceremonial consumption, except at Christmas. Even the traditional Maya ceremonies *(ch'a'chaak, janlikool)* usually involve chickens now. The chicken has revolutionized food in Mayaland by providing a really common, easily raised meat source. Many large families with large house compounds and with flock sizes well above the typical dozen can kill a chicken a day.

Disease, pecking, and bad care cause many poults to lose their feathers. This is believed to be the result of the eggs getting too hot. It is believed that a hen crowing like a cock is an evil omen. This Spanish-derived belief probably has to do with hen-feathered roosters.

Katsimix loro. Unidentified. Probably means "acacia parrot." FMT has heard this term for a kind of parrot not found at Chunhuhub.

Ke'el non. Little Tinamou *(Crypturellus soui)*. Rare but well known in Chunhuhub.

Keenkeenbak. Bat Falcon *(Falco rufigularis)*. (See also *kiris* and *piupiu.*) The name is extended to cover the American Kestrel *(Falco sparverius)*, a rare winter visitor, and sometimes to cover other hawks with long pointed wings, including the Black-shouldered Kite *(Elanus leucurus)*. We have been involved in discussions over the correctness of the latter extension. The Plumbeous Kite *(Ictinia plumbea)*, an uncommon migrant (also seen in summer, rarely), presents a problem. It has long pointed wings, but it is large and dark and can be called by this name or simply lumped as *ch'uuy.*

K'eo (k'eew). Masked Tityra *(Tityra semifasciata)*. From the call. This common and obvious bird is one of the better-known local birds, and its name is also widely known. The name can be extended to the rare Black-crowned Tityra *(T. inquisitor)*. *K'eo* (which literally means "skin") is sometimes extended, for this bird, to *p'eelank'eolij* (possibly *p'eela'an*, "striped," plus the bird's name extended by an attributive suffix, but the bird is not striped and the attributive seems unnecessary, so perhaps this is "just a name"). The Spanish name is *puerquito*, "little pig," with reference to the grunting call note.

K'ili' (xk'ili'). Olive-throated Parakeet *(Aratinga nana)*. Usually with the added diminutive: *xk'ili'*. This bird is sometimes kept as a pet, but also sometimes killed because of its fondness for fruit and crops.

Kipchoo' (chipchoo'). Squirrel Cuckoo *(Piaya cayana)*. From the call. A common and highly visible—and audible—bird of all forested areas.

Kiris (kirix, kiklis). Male Bat Falcon, or Bat Falcon as opposed to other small falcons within the wider *keenkeenbak* category. See also *piupiu.*

Kobi (koobi, koba). Syn. of *bach* (Plain Chachalaca). *Koba* in some other Maya areas; this word is the source of the name of the well-known site of Coba, north of Chunhuhub.

Kobul. A name sometimes used for Yellow-bellied Trogons. See also *kux.*

Kocha' (kochak). Red-lored Parrot *(Amazona autumnalis)*. Rare in most of the area but rising to "uncommon" status in deep, tall forest in the southern part of our sphere of activity. Breeds in holes in large old dead trees, and therefore is vulnerable to too-frequent cutting and burning. The young are often taken as pets, being very popular because of the size, beauty, and tameness of the adults. Name sometimes extended to the Scarlet Macaw, which no longer occurs in the Yucatán Peninsula—though it did in colonial times, when it was called *moo,* as all early dictionaries attest. See *kulix.*

K'ok' (xk'ok', k'ook'). Clay-colored Robin *(Turdus grayi).* In speaking, this word almost always is given the diminutive suffix: *xk'ok';* Hocabá *k'ook',* not normally so pronounced in Chunhuhub but very possibly correct in formal Maya, though Cordemex agrees with me. The name, derived from the bird's call note, has been borrowed into Peninsular Spanish as *xcoc* or *xcoquita.* (Yucatán Spanish loves such multiple diminutives—compare the oft-heard *chiquitita* as an affectionate diminutive for almost any child or small animal.) There is also, probably, some influence from Spanish *coqueta* (coquette) here. This bird is known in Yucatán Spanish as *ruiseñor,* the formal Spanish name of the European Nightingale *(Luscinia megarhynchos).* This has led to considerable confusion. The Clay-colored Robin looks like a large nightingale and is related to the nightingale; its song is pleasant (though, to ENA's ears, not very close to the nightingale's in quality).

This robin is common in the town and orchards but was extremely hard hit by Hurricane Roxanne, dropping to 20 percent or less of its former abundance. It recovered rapidly. The name is extended to cover migrant and wintering thrushes, such as the Wood Thrush *(Hylocichla mustelina).*

Kolonte'. Large woodpeckers (Lineated, *Dryocopus lineatus,* and Guatemalan Ivory-billed [also known as Pale-billed and Flint-billed], *Campephilus guatemalensis).* These two species are similar and often nest near each other, so they tend to be lumped. Some people believe that the Lineated is the female of the Guatemalan. The term is sometimes used for large woodpeckers in general, such as the Chestnut-colored, *Celeus castaneus,* and Golden-olive, *Piculus rubiginosus,* though these are perhaps more often called *che'jun.*

Kooaak'ab (kooak'ab). Small owls. Focally, and usually, this name means specifically the Ferruginous Pigmy Owl *(Glaucidium brasilianum).* See also *chaxnuuk, jaap,* and *tojkaaxnuk.* Sometimes extended to the Vermiculated Screech Owl *(Otus guatemalae),* depending on the speaker. FMT uses it thus; he applied it to taped recordings of the Vermiculated Screech Owl made by Eugene Hunn.

J.E.S. Thompson poetically translates this name as "mad one of the night," which is etymologically possible, as are many other translations (cf. Cordemex: Barrera Vásquez 1980, 323), but Chunhuhub people prosaically translate it as "the one that calls *koo* at night."

Koos. Laughing Falcon *(Herpetotheres cachinnans)*. Extended to the rather similar Collared Forest-Falcon *(Micrastur semitorquatus)* and sometimes other birds of prey, such as the Gray-headed Kite *(Leptodon cayanensis)*. These extensions are rather ad hoc, since the latter birds are also called *ii'* and *ch'uuy*, but everyone recognizes the Laughing Falcon as *koos*.

Kox. Crested Guan *(Penelope purpurascens)*. Formerly common, now virtually extinct in the area under consideration. Said to persist in small numbers in extensive wild forest to the west, and is still found just south of our area. This bird is vulnerable to overhunting because its highly visible and noisy flocks can easily be located and shot out. Moreover, it requires extensive tracts of tall old-growth forest. It is unquestionably doomed in Quintana Roo unless far more stringent conservation measures are taken.

Kukut'kib. Large pigeons in general. Usually a syn. of *ucuch*.

Kulix. Red-lored Parrot. Apparently a synonym of *kocha'*, though possibly distinct in some way. We are not quite clear about this term.

Kulte'. Mottled Wood-Owl *(Ciccaba virgata)*. Sometimes used for other medium-sized owls. Identified by FMT from tapes made by Eugene Hunn and from pictures in the guidebooks.

Kusuun (kusaam, kosuum, kusuum). Swifts and swallows in general. Any back vowel seems to be usable in the name. This is the source of the name Cozumel *(kosuumil,* "place of swallows"). At least two swift and five or six swallow species exist locally, and no distinction is made among them.

Kusuy (sukuy, tsukuy). Groove-billed Ani. Rare syn. for the usual *chik bu'ul*.

Kuts (kuuts). Ocellated Turkey *(Agriocharis ocellata)*. Hocabá *kuutz*, but my ear and all other sources disagree; Hocabá may really have a distinctive usage here. This bird was once common in Chunhuhub but has been extirpated by hunting. We have found tracks and one feather in a very remote part of Chunhuhub's ejido land, but they were depressingly near a poacher's camp. This species, once abundant, is virtually extinct in all areas of the Yucatán

Peninsula because of relentless overhunting. It will be extinct everywhere in the very near future unless far more stringent measures are taken; existing reserves are either too small (El Eden, Tikal) or too poorly patrolled (Sian Ka'an, Calakmul) to offer it any real long-term protection. FMT remembers a time (some thirty years ago) when it abounded in Chunhuhub, with large flocks flushing up from abandoned milpas; earlier settlers remember turkeys displaying in what is now Chunhuhub's central plaza, at the time when Chunhuhub was settled in the early 1940s. See also *tuux.*

K'uubul. Oropendolas. Two species exist: the Montezuma Oropendola *(Psarocolius montezuma)* and the smaller Wagler's *(P. wagleri)*. These huge birds are local residents, disliked because of their fondness for orchard fruit. They nest in southern Chunhuhub.

K'uumil. Syn. of *ch'uyin.*

Kux (kultin, kuxtin). Trogons. Focally yellow-bellied ones. A variant *kultin* was recorded; the expectable link, *kuxtin,* is attested in early dictionaries. *Kux* is said to be the "real" Maya name for trogons, the usual term *uulum k'aax* being informal or, at least, not the traditional hach Maya. Through-out western Quintana Roo, however, it is the latter name that is standard.

Lechkal. Plovers in general. Name used to identify pictures in the guide-books; not elicited by seeing plovers in the field (no name was given when we saw actual plovers—to be exact, killdeers, *Charadrius vociferus*). This name must remain of uncertain application.

Loro. Sp.; parrots in general. A useful supplement to Yucatec Maya, which has no general term for parrots, and thus widely used.

Luisita. Sp.; White-collared Seedeater *(Sporophila torqueola)* and other small inconspicuous finches.

Lukupech. Cattle Egret *(Bubulcus ibis)*. Lit. "tickpecker." Eladio Chan Cantul supplied this unique name; it may be a mere descriptive phrase. The bird is not native, but it arrived in South America in 1937 from Africa and spread rapidly north, so it has been in southern Mexico for a long time. See also *aak'al* and *garza.*

Mankolom. Great Tinamou *(Tinamus major)*. Not found locally, but well known to residents who have been in southern Quintana Roo.

Mukuy. Ground doves. This name is so universally known that it has supplied the name of a Mérida hotel, among other features. Alicia Re Cruz (1996, 121–24) reports that in Yucatán state, migrant workers from the villages are called mukuy, because the ground dove, when it flies, always returns to (more or less) the same spot whence it started. The *"mucuy"* is mentioned in the *Ritual of the Bacabs*, for example, in the bird-rich and very long Charm 39 (for massaging for the placenta, to expel afterbirth), where the *"kak tan mucuy"* (i.e., *k'ak' tan mukuy*, "fiery-breasted ground dove") is mentioned (Arzápalo Marín 1987, 397).

The term is one of the few genuine folk generics. There are three recognized folk species:

Chak mukuy: Ruddy Ground Dove *(Columbina talpacoti)*. Lit. "red ground dove." Abundant locally.

Sojol mukuy: Common Ground Dove *(C. passerina)*. Lit. "leaf-litter ground dove" because it nests in leaf litter; the other two mukuy are said to nest in trees. Rare at the edge of town. Possibly increasing, as more land is cleared.

Tuch mukuy: Blue Ground Dove *(Claravis pretiosa)*. Lit. "ground dove that calls *tuch*." Fairly common in moist forest, usually second growth. "Tuch," which well represents the bird's characteristic call, means "navel."

Mut. Yellow-billed Cacique *(Amblycercus holosericeus)*. The word is the Yucatec Maya reflex of the widespread Maya root *mut* (bird). (*Ch'iich'* is a Yucatec Maya form that may reflect an ancient alternate root for birds or may simply be onomatopoeic.) We have no idea why the cacique became *the* bird par excellence in Yucatec, but, definitely, the bird has strange powers that fit it for the name. For example, the Cordemex dictionary lists what is almost certainly the cacique under *muan* (or *moan*)—a word that focally refers to the magical bird of the ancient Maya. The *mut* shows up in the creation myth in the Book of Chilam Balam of Chumayel (Roys 1933, 99), occupying a treetop as a *muan* bird would. Moreover, Hartig (1979; information from Edilberto Ucan Ek) calls the cacique *uay cot*, a term that literally means "eagle witch." Real eagle witches are still believed to exist, and cause fear in some areas (Re Cruz 1996). (The dictionaries list *kot* for "eagle," and Alicia Re Cruz [1996] records a belief in *way kot*, "eagle witches," for Chan Kom. We have not encountered *kot* in Chunhuhub.) In short, the cacique is not only *the* bird, it is also equated with the two mythically frightening birds of Maya folklore.

The cacique is common but seldom seen due to its residence in dense brush. However, it is one of the most eminently audible of local birds. Pairs duet, one giving loud whistles while the other answers with a woody chattering call. This is so typical that people assume one bird of the pair has died if a call is not answered. Perhaps this loud and sociable vocal pattern led to the bird receiving magical or religious attention.

Non (nom). Rufescent Tinamou *(Crypturellus cinnamomeus)*. The name comes from the beautiful single whistle that is the bird's call—one of the most characteristic sounds of the Chunhuhub area. Due to its secretive habits, the bird remains common, up to the very edge of Chunhuhub, in spite of being a well-appreciated game bird. Its whistled call is considered one of the most beautiful of natural sounds and can elicit great nostalgia and emotion in rural Maya. Color forms exist (*chak,* "red," *sak* "white," etc.). It is said that the whistle is sometimes imitated by predators, including foxes and snakes, trying to lure tinamous to their doom. No confirmation of this is available.

Ooxil. Yellow-green Vireo *(Vireo flavoviridis)*. Lit. "the one of the ramón trees." The bird is extremely common in summer in all large, leafy trees, including the ramón (*Brosimum alicastrum; oox* in Yucatec Maya). It migrates south in fall, returning in April. No one seems to notice this migration, probably because many similar vireos come during the winter. See also *ts'itkalants'i'.*

Pa'ap. Brown Jay *(Cyanocorax morio)*. The Yucatec Maya name is derived from the call. This large bird is one of the commonest, and certainly the most obvious, of forest birds. It is edible and much appreciated by some; Don Marcos Puc Bacab, the herbal doctor of Presidente Juarez, says it has the flavors of all seven common meat animals, from deer to chicken. He also uses it, toasted and powdered, to cure excessive coughing-and-spitting. However, it is rarely hunted. The *Ritual of the Bacabs* includes several chants that make reference to magical, varicolored *pa'ap* (Arzápalo Marín 1987). For instance, Chant XXVII refers to the red *"pahap"* and the white one, as well as to woodpeckers (p. 372); Chant XXXIX, for massaging for the placenta (i.e., to expel afterbirth), notes the *"pap"* and a probable synonym, *"ch'acat"* (p. 397). The religious and magical significance of this bird appears to have been great in pre-Columbian times, and it is interesting to see that a fragment of this significance still survives.

Pajaro gato. Sp.; catbird *(Dumetella carolinensis).* Winters in the area.

Pajaro tigre. Sp.; Barred Antshrike. See *pu'* and *sob.*

Pajaro tijera. Sp.; Fork-tailed Flycatcher *(Tyrannus savana).* A rare migrant.

Paloma de casa. Sp.; tame pigeon, Rock Dove (*Columba livia*). See *pichon.*

Panch'el. Collared Aracari *(Pteroglossus torquatus).* Extended by FMT to a White-necked Puffbird *(Bucco macrorhynchos)* we saw once in the forest. See also *pitoreal.*

Pato. Sp.; duck. Maya use this Spanish term, rather than *paatoj,* for ducks, even the Muscovy Duck *(Cairina moschata),* a native pre-Columbian domesticate that also occurs in the wild in the area. It is specified as *pato criollo, pato de pais,* or *pato indio.* Older sources list the tame Muscovy as *kuts ja',* "water turkey," an appropriate name in light of the red facial wattle, and the name is not entirely dead in current usage. Only the domestic birds have the red wattle, and it is unclear whether *kuts ja'* is extended to the wild ones.

P'eelank'eolij. Extended name for *k'eo.*

Perdiz. Local Sp.; tinamous. (In formal Spanish, it means "partridges"). See also *ke'el non, mankolom,* and *non.*

Pich' (pich'kulin). Melodious Blackbird (*Dives dives*—which is Latin for "rich man rich man"). One of the most familiar dooryard birds of the area. Loosely used for other small blackbirds. A bit of sympathetic magic is the prescription to eat *pich'* when young, to make the hair stay black in old age. See also *chikbu'ul.*

Pichon. Sp.; domestic pigeon, Rock Dove *(Columba livia).* The standard term for the bird. Also a standard euphemism for the human penis, routinely used by the Maya when speaking Spanish. See also *paloma de casa.*

Pico de espada. Sp.; Blue Honeycreeper *(Cyanerpes cyaneus).* Lit. "sword bill."

Piix. Applied to a Royal Flycatcher *(Onychorhynchus coronatus)* seen in the field, but rather tentatively; the Royal Flycatcher is usually called *juiiro*. This name needs further attention.

Pijije. Black-bellied Whistling-Duck *(Dendrocygna autumnalis)*. This name is used throughout all southern and eastern Mexico. The name, or versions of it, is attested in the earliest sources, at least for Nahuatl. It is a loan word into contemporary south Mexican Spanish. It is derived from the bird's characteristic whistled cry; thus, not surprisingly, more or less the same name is found in other indigenous languages of Mexico and Central America, including Nahuatl. It is not known whether the name is originally from Nahuatl or some other language(s), or was independently derived by all of them from the bird's cry.

Pitoreal. Sp.; Keel-billed Toucan *(Rhamphastos sulfuratus)*. Oddly, there is no Yucatec Maya name locally known for this common and obvious bird. It is always called by one of the two Spanish names (the other being *tucan*). Some call it *panch'el,* and it probably once shared this name with the usual panch'el, the Collared Aracari. Itzaj also lacks an indigenous name for the larger bird, however.

Pits'. Catchall term for small birds with notes that sound like the word. The Book of Chilam Balam of Chumayel speaks of a "pidzoy" bird (Roys 1933, 99).

Piupiu (gavilan piupiu). Nonstandard name used for the Bat Falcon *(Falco rufigularis)*, from the call. Probably a borrowing from Spanish; Mexican Spanish uses this as an echoic word for hawk calls. See also *keenkeenbak* and *kiris*.

Po'okin. Black Catbird *(Melanoptila glabrirostris)*. Very rare in Chunhuhub. One individual used it for the Spot-breasted Wren, usually called *yankotij;* he reserved the latter name for the Tropical House Wren.

Pu'. Barred Antshrike. Sometimes expanded to *chax pu'* or *mejex pu'.* See also *pajaro tigre* and *sob.*

Pu'ujuy (normally pronounced **pujuy**). Pauraque *(Nyctidromus albicollis)*. Extended to the other nightjars by those who do not know the name *tunki-iya*. The Spanish word *tapacamino* is also widely used as a term for all nightjars. Conversely, the Yucatec Maya name is sometimes Hispanicized as *pujuyero*. As in much of the world, nightjars are believed to be uncanny and spooky. Dried, they are used in magic; a powdered, dried *pu'ujuy*, or just the powdered head of one, may be thrown onto the head of someone, as love magic. (Hummingbirds are more standardly used for this, however.) When *pujuy* call and jump up repeatedly, someone will die. The birds do this every night—and, indeed, every night, someone dies somewhere in the world. This coincidence is enough to keep the belief alive. See also *jaap*.

Sakpakal (sakpakaal). White-winged Dove *(Zenaida asiatica)*. A common bird of open country and second growth. Often loosely applied to any dove with white in the wings, such as tame pigeons of this description. The White-winged Dove and Red-billed Pigeon both have calls that sound like "ku'uk tu tuusen" ("the squirrel tricked me"), and there are several variants of a folktale telling how the squirrel tricked the dove and ate her eggs or young (or tricked her into killing her young—which the squirrel then no doubt ate). This story makes use of the common knowledge that squirrels are nest-robbers. The bird is called torcaza or by other dove/pigeon names in Spanish.

Siete colores. Sp.; Painted Bunting *(Passerina ciris)*. Lit. "seven colors." Like other migrants, it has no Yucatec Maya name. The bird is a migrant in Chunhuhub, passing through rapidly, but is occasionally trapped and kept as a pet—as it often is in Yucatán state.

Sob. Barred Antshrike *(Thamnophilus doliatus)*. This bird is common and fairly well known but seems not to have a secure, familiar name. *Sob* appears standard; *pu'* is also used; the bird is sometimes lumped under other names. Even *chakts'its'ib* is heard (especially for the female, which looks vaguely like a female cardinal). See also *pajaro tigre*.

Sojlin. Ant Tanagers (applied to the two almost indistinguishable species, the Red-crowned, *Habia rubica*, and Red-throated, *H. fuscicauda*). These abundant and noisy birds are usually the most visible members of the forest-understory community.

Suus. A small, yellowish bird, observed in the field but unidentified.

Taadi'. White-crowned Parrot *(Pionus senilis)*. Rare in Chunhuhub but common farther south.

Takaay (xtakay, takay). Large flycatchers with yellow bellies. (Virtually always with shortened vowel, and with the diminutive: *xtakay*.) This is a cognitively interesting term because it appears to be a focus-and-extension term with two foci that are well recognized as distinct. The "real" or "typical" *takaay* is the Social Flycatcher *(Myiozetetes similis)* or the Couch's Kingbird *(Tyrannus couchii)*. Some informants focus on one or the other, but for most they are equally focal exemplars. The term is extended to cover the Great Kiskadee *(Pitangus sulphuratus)* and Boat-billed Flycatchers *(Megarhynchus pitangua)*; for some, these appear to be part of the focal set.

The term is more widely extended to any other similar flycatchers, such as the Brown-crested *(Myiarchus tyrannulus)*, Sulphur-bellied *(Myiodynastes luteiventris)*, Striped *(M. maculatus)*, and Piratic *(Legatus leucophaius)*, as well as other kingbirds. This creates a nomenclatural oddity—a group that is well recognized as several distinct birds serving as a category focus, with tentative and flexible extensions to another, larger group of birds. Moreover, many informants do not know the terms *yaj* and *juiiro*, and these people extend takaay to cover all flycatchers and indeed all medium-sized noisy birds with some yellowish color. Takaay is one of the few bird terms that essentially all Maya speakers, even young children, know. It is thus eminently available for such wide extension. We have encountered (and used) a mestiza-Maya diminutive form of *takaay*: *taquillo* (or, in Maya spelling, *takiyo*).

Takaay are magical birds. Their bickering around a house is taken by many as an omen of domestic troubles. Their brains are aphrodisiac—a very small amount being eaten. They are mentioned in several of the charms in the *Ritual of the Bacabs*, such as in Charm 39, for massaging for the placenta (to expel afterbirth), where the *"tacay"* is mentioned as an omen bird (Arzápalo Marín 1987, 397).

Tatak'che' (rarely **takak'che'** or **tak'anche'**). Woodcreepers (Dendrocolaptidae). Lit. "those who go 'tap-tap' on trees." Five very similar species exist in Chunhuhub and are not given separate names. Occasionally the name is applied loosely to the Smoky-brown Woodpecker *(Veniliornis fumigatus)*, which looks and acts more like a woodcreeper than like Chunhuhub's other woodpeckers. See also *chi'pirix*.

T'eel. Male domestic fowl, rooster, cock. Originally, the crest of any bird (Cordemex: Barrera Vásquez 1980, 835). See also *kaax*.

T'eel ja'. Jacana *(Jacana spinosa)*. Lit. "watercock." Common wherever there is open water in areas near Chunhuhub. See also *gallinola.*

Tojkaaxnuk. Ferruginous Pigmy Owl. See *chaxnuuk* and *kooaak'ab.*

Tooj. Turquoise-browed Motmot *(Eumomota superciliosa)*. The name is derived from the bird's call note, a characteristic sound of the Yucatán Peninsula (to which this species is endemic). This name is often extended in Chunhuhub to cover the Blue-crowned Motmot *(Momotus momota;* see *juj)*, which is poorly known. The Spanish name for both is *pajaro reloj* (clock bird), because the long tail with its round tip is often swung back and forth, producing a strikingly pendulumlike appearance.

Ts'aapim (ts'apin). Saltators. Black-headed *(Saltator atriceps)* and Grayish *(S. coerulescens)* occur commonly.

Tsiimink'aax. Black-faced Antthrush. Usually called *beech' lu'um.* Lit. "forest horse." Also *tsiiminchak* (see chapter 5).

Ts'itkalants'i' (ts'ikalantsi'). Yellow-green Vireo *(Vireo flavoviridis,* also known as *ooxil)*. From the song, the name being an excellent representation of a typical song phrase.

Ts'iu. Red-eyed Cowbird *(Molothrus aeneus)*. From the call note. This bird is probably a recent invader of Chunhuhub and is poorly known; it is often lumped with the Melodious Blackbird as a kind of *pich'.* See also *chikbu'ul.*

Ts'iu. Blue-black Grassquit *(Volatinia jacarina)*. From the song, a brief "dziu." This seems, from usage and from some enquiry on our parts, to be a quite different name from the preceding—a genuine homophone rather than a bizarre category lumping two dissimilar birds.

Tso'. Tom turkey.

Ts'unuun (ts'unu'un). Hummingbirds in general (Trochilidae). Hocabá *ts'unu'un,* but neither the Cordemex nor other sources hear it that way. It is recognized that there are many kinds—at least seven species occur—but no one wants to go to the effort of splitting this category. Hummingbirds are widely used in magic, as they were in pre-Columbian and colonial times. Most often, they are killed on a Tuesday or Friday, toasted till dry, and powdered. The powder—sometimes only from the head or heart—is then used in protective charms. Usually it is dusted onto the person in question. Most often, a boy throws it onto the head of a girl he wishes to have as a lover. However, hummingbird powder is also incorporated into medicinal powders for magical protection, to be dusted onto oneself. Boys sometimes carry dried hummingbirds as love charms, as elsewhere in Mexico. FMT's family came up with further possible ingredients of the powder: three drops of the hummingbird's blood; a toad heart; a *takaay* heart; or a drop of swallow's or swift's blood.

Tsutsuy (tsuutsuy). Doves, especially of the genus *Leptotila* (Sp. *tortolita*). (Hocabá *tsuutsuy*, probably formally correct but not so pronounced normally in Chunhuhub.) Three species (Caribbean, *L. jamaicensis,* Gray-headed, *L. rufaxilla,* and White-tipped, *L. verreauxi*) occur and are seen as slightly distinct but are not distinguished.

The White-tipped is by far the most common of these. These three are not separated by the Maya. The Ruddy Quail-Dove, *Geotrygon montana,* an uncommon forest bird, is *chak tsutsuy* or sometimes *k'ankab tsutsuy* (Lit. "red-dirt dove"). The word *tsutsuy,* like the Spanish *pichon,* is sometimes used for the penis—especially in a rather diminutive-affectionate way (used, for instance, by a mother or grandmother) for the penis of a small boy.

Tucan. Sp.; Keel-billed Toucan. See *pitoreal.*

Tunkiiya (t'unkiiya). Yucatán Nightjar *(Caprimulgus salvini),* whose call, a clear, sweet "tuk-tunkiiya," is a characteristic sound of spring nights. Extended to cover the Yucatán Poorwill *(Nyctiphrynus yucatanicus),* which is obscure and poorly known, though its call (a carefully enunciated "will!") is sometimes heard.

Tunkuruchu (tunkuluch'u). Great Horned Owl *(Bubo virginianus);* from the call. It is known that some Great Horned Owls say "tuncuruchu" while others say "tuncuruchu, hu, hu," but apparently no one realizes that the former is the male, the latter the female. This species is rare in the area. An extremely popular traditional Maya folk dance imitates, humorously, the courtship antics of these birds. It seems to be the main survivor of the animal-imitation dances referred to in early colonial Spanish documents. See also *bujk'aanij* and *xooch' xikin.*

T'uut' (usually xt'uut'). White-fronted Parrot *(Amazona albifrons).* Speakers not fluent in Yucatec bird nomenclature use it for all parrots except *k'ili'.* The White-fronted is by far the most common and obvious larger parrot of the area. Its numbers dropped by about 75 percent following Hurricane Roxanne but recovered fairly rapidly in the following year; probably most birds had not been killed, but had moved out of the area because of destruction of their food supply. However, by 2001, the parrot had not regained its pre-hurricane abundance, probably because the hurricane blew down so many nesting trees, and subsequent fires have consumed still more.

Tuux (tuxtuch). Hen turkey (either Ocellated or domestic). See also *kuts* and *uulum.*

Uukum (uukuch, ukuch, ukum). Red-billed Pigeon *(Columba flavirostris).* From the call. Used loosely to cover other similar pigeons, such as the Short-billed *(C. nigrirostris),* a very rare straggler. This bird, formerly exceedingly common and well known, became quite rare after Hurricane Roxanne, and the population has begun to recover only very slowly. See also *kukut'kib.*

Uulum. Domestic turkey *(Meleagris gallopavo).* Name almost certainly from the call note. See also *tux.*

Uulum k'aax. Trogons. Lit. "forest turkey," referring to the turkeylike call note. Three species occur. The commoner ones display in groups, and it is known that these are mating assemblages—the males gather to display to the females. However, if a trogon calls over and over for three days, this may be an omen of death. See also *kux.*

Wiij. Grayish Saltator (rarely used name; when used, *ts'aapim* is restricted to the Black-headed Saltator).

Xiich' (xooch'). Barn Owl *(Tyto alba).* From the call, a shriek that is a bad omen in Chunhuhub as almost everywhere else in the world.

Xooch' xikin. Great Horned Owl. Lit. "owl (with) ears." Some use this word; most use *tunkuruchu.* See also *bujk'aanij.*

Ya'ax bech' lu'um. Olive Sparrow *(Arremonops rufivirgatus)* and Green-backed Sparrow *(A. chloronotus)*—lumped by the Maya. These very similar birds are separated by habitat: the Olive Sparrow abounds in young second growth, while the Green-backed is equally (if not more) abundant in forest.

The name is an interesting example of term extension. These sparrows are explicitly recognized as being neither *beech'* nor *beech' lu'um*. Their name simply derives from the similarity of their head pattern to that of the *beech'*, and from their terrestrial habit. (The vowel in "be[e]ch" seems always short here.)

Yaj. Small dull-colored flycatchers. A catchall term with vague boundaries (few if any birds are more confusing and less culturally salient to the Yucatec). Focally, it means the Yucatán Flycatcher (Myiarchus yucatanensis) and the very similar Olivaceous Flycatcher (M. olivaceus). These are not distinguished. They both produce whistled notes that sound extremely melancholy and pained to the human ear, as if the bird were permanently complaining of its hurt; *yaj* means "pain" in Yucatec Maya. The name is extended to other small flycatchers, of which at least a dozen species occur as residents or migrants.

The calls are, not unnaturally, believed by some to presage sickness and ill luck, and the birds are said to be shot on occasion, though ENA has never actually observed or heard of a case of this. The sad calls, often given in autumn around the time of the Day of the Dead (All Saints' Day, November 1), announce the return of the souls of the deceased; some think the birds are souls—a thought that seems poetic to us but is frightening and uncanny to devout traditionalists. It is not surprising to find *yaj* associated with magic in both early texts and modern belief. In nearby Yucatán state, the Eastern Pewee—a North American migrant—is specifically distinguished as the *ch'ich'ij finados,* the Bird of Finados (All Souls' Day, November 2). The birds appear from North America about this time and sing "wiij! wiij!" ("Hungry! Hungry!"). This sounds like a prayer, so they are regarded as remembering the dead souls and are loved. This bird is not distinguished from the permanently resident Tropical Pewee; the belief is that the latter simply starts to sing at All Souls. In fact, the truth is that the Eastern arrives and sings; the Tropical has a quite different song.

Myiarchus flycatchers abounded in Chunhuhub through the 1990s but had unaccountably almost disappeared as of 2001, though they remained fairly common in other communities. Nest parasitism by the Red-eyed Cowbird is a possible cause, but purely speculative.

Yankotij (yankotil). Wrens in general (Troglodytidae). Several species occur, the most familiar being the Spot-breasted *(Thryothorus maculipectus)*. The focus, however, is clearly the Tropical House Wren *(Troglodytes aedon)*, for *yankotij* means "under the wall," referring to the House Wren's distinctive habitat—it forages and nests in the dry-laid stone walls *(kot)* that surround properties. The term is widely extended to other small brown birds, and, indeed, to any small skulking birds with loud voices that have no names of their own. Examples include the Gray-throated Chat *(Granatellus sallaei)* and gnatcatchers (two species of *Polioptila*).

Yuyum (yuuyuum, yuyuum). Orioles in general. Properly restricted to bright orange species and those that build large nests in the open. The focal species is the abundant Alta Mira Oriole (see *jonxa'anij*), whose nests, often more than a third of a meter in length, hang conspicuously from roadside trees. Hispanicized to *yuya* and widely used in this form, even by Maya speakers. Mentioned in the Book of Chilam Balam of Chumayel (Roys 1933, 99).

REPTILES AND AMPHIBIANS

There is no cover term for herps in Maya, nor is there a concept of them as a group. They are treated together here purely for convenience, not because they are thought of as a category in any sense. There are, however, life-form category names that correspond closely to Latin ordinal names for reptiles, and to the frog/toad subclass of amphibians:

Crocodiles (order Crocodylia, genus *Crocodylus*): *Ayin, aayin,* or *ayiin,* a "unique beginner" in Berlin's terms.

Lizards (order Squamata, suborder Sauria): Several terms (see below) are used as cover terms for small lizards. Iguanas have their own names, which are thus unique beginners.

Snakes (order Squamata, suborder Serpentes): *Kaan.* Snakes are rather uncommon in the Chunhuhub area, and thus many identifications must remain in some doubt. (See Campbell 1998; Lee 1980, 1996.) Scientific names are from Alvarez del Toro 1960, Bahena Basave n.d., Carr 1989, and Himmelstien n.d., but all are standardized to Lee 1996. Spanish equivalents of the Maya word are *culebra* and *serpiente,* both equally widely used. Some

Maya beliefs about snakes include the following: If snakes hiss a great deal, it will rain. Old temples are guarded by snakes.

Turtles (order Chelonia, a.k.a. Testudines): *Aak* (see below).

Frogs and toads (order Anura): The general term *muuch* (see below), focally "toad," is extended to cover this category. (Sp. *rana*, "frog"; *sapo*, "toad.")

Aak. Turtles and tortoises in general. The only one found in dry Chun-huhub is the pond turtle *(Pseudemys scripta),* which manages to find even small, transient ponds, and abounds on all permanent bodies of water. (See also *jicotea.*) Larger lakes have the foul-smelling musk turtles (*Kinosternon* spp.) and larger species of uncertain identity. Folk species of *aak* include (among others—forgotten by consultants):

Chak pool aak: Lit. "red-headed turtle." Usually the pond turtle.

Sak aak: Lit. "white turtle." Usually the pond turtle. *Dermatemys mawii*, the *tortuga blanca* of southern Mexico, occurs in Quintana Roo only as a very rare resident of the Rio Hondo on the Belize border.

Tu'kis aak: (*Kinosternon* spp.) Lit. "stinking-like-fart turtle," known in south Mexican Spanish as *pochitoque.*

Ayin (aayin, ayiin). Crocodiles in general (*Crocodylus* spp.). *C. moreleti* is the local species; the large *C. americanus* does not occur inland. These animals are found in most large bodies of water. They even managed to cross large stretches of open land to invade transient ponds left by the torrential rains of Hurricane Roxanne. They are rarely hunted.

Some works claim that caymans occur in Maya Mexico. This is wrong and is based on the fact that the Spanish word *caiman* is used to mean "crocodile" in Mexico. See also *lagarto.*

Baakinij. Young fer-de-lances whose white tails look like bone. Lit. "bone tail." See *cola de hueso* (under *cuatronarices*).

Barba amarilla. Sp.; Large yellow-chinned fer-de-lances *(Bothrops asper).* See also *k'an* (under *cuatronarices*) and *k'aanme'ex* (under *kan ni'*).

Boxkaan. Large dark snakes in general. Lit. "black snake."

Bujum. A small dark snake of the *ratonera* type. (See also *luk'ch'oo.*) Eats young chickens. *Chak bujum* is a red snake of this type. Name sometimes used for *Tantilla* species (which is far too small to eat even the smallest chickens). See also *ek'kunejij.*

Camaleon. Sp.; chameleon. A large lizard that lives in hollow trees; tongue is toasted and powdered to treat *nervios* leading to muteness. Obviously not a chameleon (being on the wrong continent), but identity unestablished.

Cascabel. Sp.; rattlesnake *(Crotalus durissus),* very rare in this area. See also *tsabkaan.*

Chajkaan. Coral snakes (*Micrurus* spp.), rather rare but widely present in the area. See also *coralillo* and *kalam.*

Chayikaan (cho'oyikaan). Any large constrictorlike snake; usually, and focally, the yellow-and-black-checkered *Spilotes pullatus.* (See also *ratonera.*) Other snakes, green or patterned, sometimes so called; this is a general term. See discussion in Carr 1989. She too identifies it as *Spilotes pullatus* (though sometimes also other species). This snake can turn into a *xtabay* (demon woman who haunts ceiba trees near wells), and what is probably the same snake is actually called *ixtabai* in Belize (Williams 1994). Some believe these snakes follow nursing mothers and suck their milk.

Chokaan (chohkaan). Geckos (Gekkonidae). Several species occur; the most visible are various introduced species, most or all Asian, that occur in houses. The identities of these are poorly worked out by scientists (M. Lascano, pers. comm.), let alone the Maya. The widespread belief that they are poisonous does not seem strongly established in the Zona Maya, but it is present. See also *ch'uk* and *geco.*

Ch'otkaan. A mythical snake that stings with its tail.

Ch'uk. House gecko. Echoic name. Several species occur, most or all introduced. Some people wrongly believe them to be poisonous. Most are aware of their beneficial insect-eating qualities. See also *chokaan* and *geco.* (Note that this is also a term used for large beetles.)

Coralillo. Coral snake (*Micrurus* spp.). This Spanish name is much more common than the Yucatec Maya one *(chajkaan).* Pacheco Cruz (1958) lists *chac ib caan* for these snakes; the Cordemex dictionary gives *kalam* and the mestiza-Maya compound *kóraleskaan.* See also *chajkaan* and *kalam.*

Cuatronarices. Fer-de-lances *(Bothrops asper)*. See also *baakinij, kan ni', kulimkaan, k'anch'aj,* and *nauyaca.* These deadly snakes are greatly feared and have killed a number of people in Chunhuhub and neighboring communities. They occur primarily in young second growth with grass and brush. They are largely crepuscular or nocturnal. A large number of snakebite "cures" are known, *Dorstenia contrayerva* and viperol (various spp. of Apocynaceous vines, esp. *Urechites andrieuxii*) being popular, but the reliability of these is, at best, not great. A number of incorrect folk beliefs about fer-de-lances are known: Some persons believe that there are flying fer-de-lances (apparently due to hearing at *nth* hand of the arboreal *B. schlegeli*), ones that sting with their tails, ones that leap appreciable distances to strike, and so on. Several folk species—actually, mere color variants of the one biological species—are distinguished by color:

Box: Lit. "black"—a dark form, seen, not uncommon.

Chak: Lit. "reddish"—dubiously a true name; probably just ad hoc description.

Cola de hueso (colihueso):—very young individuals, whose white tails appear like bone (see Bahena Basave n.d., 6). They are believed to sting with these tails. "Snake cotton" *(taman kaan),* a huge species of cotton, provides a cure for this, leaves and flowers being made into tea.

K'an: Lit. "yellow"—Yucatec Maya name of the *barba amarilla.* Thought to be the female of the darker species. Actually, it is probably only the freshly moulted form thereof.

Sak: Lit. "white"—doubtfully exists.

Ya'ax: Lit. "greenish"—not seen, and reported not to be in Chunhuhub. Said to be the worst, and to have a cross on its head.

Ek'kunejij (ek'konejij, ek'konejil). Any of a number of snakes with black heads, including *Ninia sebae* (the *rojillo,* observed several times in the field by ENA). The similar *Tantilla rubra* is called rojillo by Alvarez de Toro (1960), but Lee (1980, 1996) does not show *Tantilla rubra* as occurring in Quintana Roo. He shows range maps for several other *Tantilla* species, of which *T. moesta* seems the most likely to be the one in the Chunhuhub area, but it is not reddish. See also *bujum.*

Geco. Sp.; geckos. The usual term; few know the Maya names. See also *chokaan* and *ch'uk.*

Jajalxan. A large, thin, fast-moving lizard that sheds its tail when alarmed. Not seen by ENA.

Jicotea. South Mexican Sp.; pond turtle, slider turtle *(Trachemys scripta)*. One of these wandered into a garden near FMT's home, during a rainy period, and was kept as a pet. Its carapace was some thirty-five centimeters in length. See also *aak*.

Juuj. Iguana *(Ctenosaura similis)*. This lizard, so important in the economy of parts of Yucatán, does not occur in Chunhuhub and is rare in nearby areas. We have heard it was eaten out of existence in Chunhuhub. (An excellent and important, but alas unpublished, work on Maya use of iguanas is Batún Alpuche 1999.) See also *tool*.

Kaanibej. Lit. "snake of the road." A snake that bites one's shadow, causing one to waste away and die. One gets a headache and then becomes increasingly thirsty and thin. These symptoms sound like those of diabetes, which is not uncommon in the area. This snake is better known under the Spanish name *picasombra* (bite-shadow). Most people realize this animal does not exist and treat it as a joke. Some, however, believe it does exist. Its bite can be cured with stingless-bee honey. Cordemex identifies the Maya name with *Leptotyphlops*, the blind snake, no species of which is recorded for the Chunhuhub area. This is surely too specific and "real-world" an identification. However, a *Typhlops* does occur and is sometimes said to be a *kaanibej*. (See *lukumkaan*.) The term "snake of the road" is of interest; another bizarre animal, the *jijitsbeej*, also is associated with roads. "Road" is a standard Maya trope for life in general, or for one's life course, and has wide connotations. The whole complex of meanings and associations of *bej* need further exploration.

Kakmil. Unidentified. A name reported for an animal described as a pale lizard; not seen, and name not verified.

Kalam. Boas and constricting snakes in general. Rare syn. for *oochkaan;* also used for coral snakes. Term occurs in the *Ritual of the Bacabs*, probably for coral snakes. See also *chajkaan* and *coralillo*.

K'anch'aj. A small fer-de-lance that lives in hollows in rocks. See also *cuatronarices, kan ni',* and *nauyaca*.

Kan ni' (kan p'eej ni'). Fer-de-lances (*Bothrops* spp.). Lit. "four noses" and almost certainly just a translation into Yucatec Maya of *nauyaca/cuatronarices*. Also *k'aanme'ex*, "yellow beard" (possibly a translation of Sp. *barba amarilla*). See also *kulimkaan*.

Kulimkaan. Unidentified. A name occurring in the *Ritual of the Bacabs*; FMT thinks it is probably a kind of fer-de-lance. See also *cuatronarices, kan ni'*, and *nauyaca*.

Lagartito. Sp.; lizards in general. A useful generic, allowing people to refer to both iguanas and small lizards at once. See also *lagartito, meerech, sirwo'oj, t'arach, tolok,* and *tulub*.

Lagarto. Sp.; crocodiles in general. See *ayin*.

Luk'ch'oo. Rat snake. Lit. "rat swallower." Sp. *ratonera*. See also *bujum* and *chayikaan*.

Luk'much. A thin, brown, nonpoisonous water snake that eats frogs, whence the Maya name and its Spanish equivalent *ranera*. Lit. "frog swallower." See also *xokmis*.

Lukumkaan. Worm snake *(Typhlops microstomus)* and similar creatures. Said by some to be the *picasombra* (see also *kaanibej*). Others say no. The bite of the lukumkaan is not poisonous but is irritating and can get infected; there are thus specific herbal treatments for it. (This term is also used for earthworms.)

Meerech. Smallish lizards in general. *Tolok* (used to refer specifically to the basilisk in other areas, and sometimes in Chunhuhub; see also *t'ech tolok*) and *tulub (tulu')* are widely used as synonyms, the names being used interchangeably. See also *lagartito, sirwo'oj, t'arach, tolok,* and *tulub*. No one seems to care which lizards are which. Noteworthy local genera covered by these terms include the common and widespread *Sceloporus, Eumeces, Gerrhonotus, Cnemidophorus, Mabuya,* and *Anolis*.

Muuch (much). Toads in general. (Almost always *much*.) Folk species names are loosely used, and the first two cannot be pinned down to formal species.

Becerro muuch: toads with calls like a calf (Sp. *becerro*) bawling.

Carrillo muuch: a toad with a trilling call.

Chak muuch: a small red poisonous toad (possibly an arrow-poison treefrog?). Found in hollows in stones, and sometimes said to be found inside solid rocks.

Lek muuch: a toad that calls "lek, lek, lek."

O' muuch (wo' muuch): a huge toad (*Bufo marinus*) weighing up to five kilograms, common after rains.

Nauyaca. Fer-de-lances (*Bothrops* spp.). Hispanicized Nahuatl (from *nahuiyacatl*, "four nostrils," of which *cuatronarices* and probably the Maya *kan ni'* are straight translations; we thus have the word in both original and translated forms surviving in common usage).

Oochkaan. Boas and constricting snakes in general. Lit. "opossum snake," or, in more expanded translation, "snake that eats medium-sized mammals." Includes the *Constrictor constrictor* and also the large brown snake with black tail-tip *Drymarchon corais*. Both common. Boas have gotten rarer since the 1980s. See also *kalam*, a rare syn.

Picasombra. See *kaanibej*.

Rana. Sp.; frogs in general.

Ratonera. Sp.; harmless snakes in general. Lit. "rat snake." The commonest is the large black-and-yellow *Spilotes pullatus*. See also *bujum*, *chayikaan*, and *luk'ch'oo*.

Saalants'ak. A small lizard, unidentified.

Sirwo'oj (sirwu'uj). Lizards in general. Said to refer focally to a large pale lizard of uncertain identity. (Hocabá *sirwu'uj*, a genuine difference.) Pacheco Cruz (1958) identifies it as *Sceloporus* species, but that genus is *meerech* (or, more rarely, *tulub*) in Chunhuhub. *Sirwo'oj* (the focal one) is eaten, and the blood drunk, to get rid of phlegm and cough. ENA has rarely heard this term. Neither author has any strong sense of exactly how the term is used, but FMT does not apply it to *Sceloporus*. See also *lagartito*, *meerech*, *t'arach*, *tolok*, and *tulub*.

Ta'choyi. Vine snakes (Green, *Oxybelis fulgidus*, and Brown, *Oxybelis aeneus* or *O. acuminatus*).

T'arach (t'aara'ach). Small lizards. Yet another term used vaguely to cover any small species. More specifically, large *meerech* with patterned backs, such as *Gerrhonotus*, species of which are common. See also *lagartito, sirwo'oj, tolok,* and *tulub.*

T'ech tolok. Basilisk *(Basiliscus vittatus);* more specific than *tolok.* The basilisk is also called *tenterete,* which seems to be a local Spanish name.

Tiracola. Sp.; a "snake" that sheds its tail when alarmed. Since, in fact, only lizards do this, the animal in question is probably a legless lizard. Lit. "tail-thrower" or "tail-shooter." (ENA has not seen it.)

Tolok (toolok). Basilisk *(Basiliscus vittatus),* small lizards in general. (Hocabá *toolok,* probably correct formally, but not so pronounced in Chunhuhub.) Usually used as a general term for small lizards, in which case the basilisk is specially designated as *t'ech tolok.* See also *lagartito, meerech, sirwo'oj, t'arach,* and *tulub.*

Tool. Iguana. Rare syn. of *juuj.*

Tsabkaan (tsaa'kaan, tsabkan). Rattlesnake *(Crotalus durissus).* Hocabá *tsaa'kaan,* apparently a genuine difference or local pronunciation; Cordemex *tsabkan* from many sources. See also *cascabel.*

Tulub (tulu'). Smallish lizards in general. See also *lagartito, meerech, sirwo'oj, t'arach,* and *tolok.*

Uulum kaan. A small, harmless snake. Lit. "turkey snake."

Wolpoch' (woolpooch'). Cantil *(Agkistrodon bilineatus).* The thick, brownish cantil can strike a remarkably long distance and is thus greatly feared. It is believed to be very aggressive and to be able to strike so hard that it throws its body at the victim. It does not occur in the immediate area of Chunhuhub.

Xokmis (xookmiis). A kind of water snake or wetland snake, brown and thin, said to eat frogs. See also *luk'much.*

Ya'ax paasal. A large green lizard, similar to the iguana but smaller. (We have not seen this animal, at least not under this name; name reported from Presidente Juarez.)

FISH

Fish are rare in the Chunhuhub area, and few names exist. *Kay* is the Yucatec general term. *Pez* (plural *peces*) is formal Spanish, but everyone says *pescado* in ordinary Spanish.

Bocon. Sp.? Small food fish in general. Applied to various species of *Tilapia* and other genera stocked in local lakes. See also *chak chi.*

Chak chi. General term for small fish (esp. *Tilapia* spp.) with reddish near the mouth. Lit. "red mouth." See also *bocon.*

Luu' (lu'u, lu', hluu', hlub). Catfish in general. (Hocabá *lu';* Cordemex *lu', hluu', hlub;* evidently great minds can disagree on this one.) The rare native *Rhamdia* species of cenotes are not locally found. Various species of catfish are sold in markets occasionally and go by this name.

INSECTS

Yik'ej is the general Yucatec Maya term for insects; *insectos,* the Spanish. Yik'ej is usually applied to flying insects, and often used to mean bees specifically. In this section, Spanish names are supplied only when there is no local Yucatec Maya name.

Most of the terms below are of very general reference. Thus, for example, *aakach* means any tabanid fly or, by extension, any fly similar to a tabanid. Species identification of these names is rarely meaningful. Exceptions (largely bees) are noted below.

Not in the insect category are worms and other nonflying invertebrates, such as *urich* (snail) and *lukumkaan* (earthworm), though see the uncommon and nonstandard term *yik'ejwinik* below.

Wasp terminology is exceedingly rich. The many names recorded below need much further study. Ordinary people tend to apply them rather randomly and ad hoc. Identification of them to the species level is thus usually a mistake. However, some are quite specifically used. Jorge González Acereto has identified the common referents of the Yucatec Maya wasp and bee names and collected specimens; we rely on his identifications, for which see the main text (esp. chapter 3).

Aak'abpeepen. Moths in general. Lit. "night butterfly." See also *aak'abts'unuun* and *mahannajij.*

Aak'abts'unuun. Large moths—sphinx moths (Sphingidae) and perhaps some others. Lit. "night hummingbird." See also *aak'abpeepen* and *mahannajij.*

Aak'abxuux. An evening-flying wasp. Lit. "night wasp."

Aakach. Horseflies in general, covering exactly the semantic space of the English word, or the scientific term Tabanidae (though with occasional extensions to other large flies). Colors are noted (*box*, "black," *k'an*, "yellow," etc.).

Abeja. Sp.; bees in general. Often used in the Yucatán Peninsula only for the Old World honeybee, *Apis mellifera*, and especially to differentiate it from local bees. (The general Yucatec Maya name for bees is *yik'ejkab*, "honey insect." See also other bees covered in this section: *balankab, ek, ekjoj, joolom, kab, mu'ul, xnuk kab*, and *xunankab*.) The following subdivisions of *abeja* are noted:

   Abeja africana (africanizada): Sp.; African(ized) bees.

   Abeja europea (or) *abeja americana*: European bees. Still fairly common and cherished when found.

   Abeja india, abeja nativa, abeja sin aguda: Sp.; local stingless bees. The stingless-bee industry is maintained in only a few villages, primarily the extremely traditional ones that still make a point of finding native honey for ritual uses (de Jong 1999; Terán and Rasmussen 1994, 73–75).

Alkabej. Heliconia butterflies. Lit. "roadrunners," from their fast, straight flight, often down forest corridors. See also *peepen.*

Am. Spiders in general. A broad term. In the colonial dictionaries, many spider categories are given, but today very few are still current.

Avispa. Sp.; wasps in general. A very useful generic, since Yucatec Maya has no equivalent word, though *xuux* can be generalized for the purpose. See also other wasps in this section: *bech lu'um, bobote', chakmoolbej, chukukij, chukut'kib, chukute', chuuchukukij, ch'akat'bej, ek, joolom, k'an sak, k'otkanab, mamakaan, ts'eelem, ts'ibilnajij, tupchak, xanabchaak*, and *xnuk.*

Balankab. Large bumblebees that have savage stings. Lit. "jaguar honey (bee)." *Chak* (red) and *box* (black) ones exist. See *abeja* for a list of other bees covered in this section.

Bech lu'um. Lit. "ground quail." Usually a term for various small birds that look like quail, but also a black wasp that nests in the ground. See *avispa* for a list of other wasps covered in this section.

Bobote' (boobote', bobo'ote, booteh). Large black wasps, especially those with blue shining wings. Also black wasps with brown wings, apparently small tarantula hawks. See also *ch'akat'bej*. (Hocabá *booteh* is an evident genuine difference from Chunhuhub.) These, and the other large stinging wasps noted below, could be vespids, sphecids, and/or pompilids. The terms are generally used rather loosely, and excessive specification is a mistake, pending serious field study by an expert in wasp identification. See *avispa* for a list of other wasps covered in this section.

Bot'ooch (bot'o'och). A black grasshopper or cricket with red spots, very common in the forest, especially in late spring. (Hocabá *bot'o'och.*) See also *chapulin, maas,* and *saak'.*

Cha'che'. Clothes moths.

Ch'akat'bej (chak'at'bej). Big black wasps, including tarantula hawks (*Hemipepsis* spp.?) and other very large ones but also any smaller dark wasp with a savage sting. See *avispa* for a list of other wasps covered in this section.

Chak iste'. A red gnat. See also *us.*

Chakmoolbej. Velvet ants (Mutillidae). This is a family of wasps in which the female is wingless. The Maya name means, literally, "road jaguar"—from the habitat, coloration (the typical one is black with yellow spots or streaks), and savage sting. Velvet ants are tireless and fierce hunters, and are thus used in dog training for sympathetic-magical reasons (see under *peek',* in the Mammals section). See also *avispa* for a list of other wasps covered in this section.

Chamalk'iin. Caterpillars. The name means "sun cigarette." It is known that these *nook'ol* (worms) turn into *peepen.*

Chapat'. Grubs and caterpillars. The *gallina ciega*—huge burrowing grubs of beetles—are one class. Another is a stinging caterpillar. Another is a two-headed worm that is said to get in one's head and eat the brain. The adult beetles that the grubs become are also *chapat'*.

Chapulin. Sp. (from Nahuatl); grasshoppers in general. Usually used as a cover term for the group, but more specifically used by FMT and some others for green grasshoppers, to distinguish them from other colors. See also *bot'ooch, koochol, saak',* and *sit'riyo.*

Chi'ichibej. A bright orange centipede, smaller than *chimes.*

Chi'ikmak. Large spiders in general. See also *chiiwol.*

Chiiwol. Tarantula spiders (Theraphosidae). *Chi'ikmak* and *chiintun* also heard for large spiders.

Ch'ik. Fleas in general.

Chik'ich. Chigger (actually a mite). Lit. "redbug." *Coloradillo* or *coloradilla* in Spanish.

Chimes (chiimes). Millipedes and larger centipedes in general.

Chincha. Bedbug (*Cimex* spp.). From Spanish *chinche.*

Chipitin. Cicadas (Cicadidae) whose calls are more or less like the word "chipitin" often repeated and then running into a long trill. Its call is an omen of dry weather, while that of the *choochlin* presages rain. This belief was recorded by Morris Steggerda in the 1930s (Steggerda 1977, 117). It is still current. See also *k'ix.*

Choochlin. Cicadas (Cicadidae) that are not *chipitin.* Name derived from call. See also *k'ix.*

Chuchiits'inij. Certain true bugs (Hemiptera). Lit. "the one that takes care of its younger sibling." They occur in swarms, and little ones often wind up riding on the backs of larger ones. See also *kisaay.*

Ch'uk. Large beetles, including Scarabaeids. (Also the house gecko.) See also *escarabajo, kaarax,* and *xo'.*

Chukukij (chujukij). Small and black, but very fierce, wasps that hang a small, bell-shaped paper nest from *subin* trees (*Acacia cornigera, A. gaumeri,* and similar spp.) or in caves. This wasp, when disturbed, burrows into one's hair (or an animal's fur) and stings repeatedly. It is one of the least appreciated animals in the Maya world.

It is noteworthy that so many wasp names begin with *chukuk-* or *chukut-*. At a wild guess, this might have something to do with *chukul* (anguish), but further research is needed. See *avispa* for a list of other wasps covered in this section.

Chukute'. A large wasp. See *avispa* for a list of other wasps covered in this section.

Chukut'kib (chukut'kibij). A wasp with a bad sting. Also used, loosely, for dead-leaf butterflies—probably just a mistake. See *avispa* for a list of other wasps covered in this section.

Chuuchukukij. A small wasp. See *avispa* for a list of other wasps covered in this section.

Ch'uuiche'. A black ant, smaller than a *weex*. Lit. "tree lifter"? It makes big termitelike nests in trees. See also *sinik*.

Ch'uuitunich (ch'uitun). Large wood-boring beetles (some at least are Cerambycidae). Lit. "stonelifter." They cling to the substrate when one tries to pick them up, and people are fond of letting them cling to small pebbles, then lifting them into the air, pebbles and all. See also *escarabajo, makech,* and *xo'*.

Coloradilla. Sp.; chiggers. See *chik'ich*.

Conchuela. Sp.; small pestiferous beetles of various kinds (Coleoptera). See also *cuclilla* and *xo'*.

Cuclilla. Sp.; small pestiferous beetles in general (Coleoptera), and perhaps other pests. See also *conchuela* and *xo'*.

E'jool (echol, ekjol, e'wool). A type of stingless bee. Carrillo Magaña (1990, 4, under the name *e'wool*) identifies it as tribe Trigonini, especially *Cephalotrigona capitata*. Medellín Morales and Campos López (1990), using identifications from Jorge González Acereto, identify it as *C. capitata capitata* (the subspecies identification is surely a bit of overprecision).

Ek. A wasplike bee (or honey-producing wasp). Its nest, known in Spanish as *panal real* (royal hive), is a very popular food. When one is found, people build a smoky fire and smoke the hive till the bees are tranquil. The larvae, and the small amount of honey, are then eaten from the broken-up nest. The authors of this work disagree on the gourmet qualities of this adventure; FMT finds it a high point among foods, while ENA finds the typical *ek* nest unbearably smoky and greasy. See *abeja* for a list of other bees covered in this section, and *avispa* for a list of other wasps covered in this section.

Ekjoj (eek jo'oj, ek jol). Colonial ground bees. This name probably comes from *eek jool,* "*eek* of holes." See also *mu'ul* and see *abeja* for a list of other bees covered in this section. This name may be a variant of *e'jool,* but it is used for a very different sort of animal.

Escarabajo. Sp.; large beetles (not just Scarabaeids). See also *ch'uuitunich, ch'uk, kaarax, kuklin,* and *xo'.*

Gallina ciega. Sp.; White grubs of beetles. Lit. "blind hen." A common food elsewhere in Mexico but rarely eaten in the peninsula. These emerge from the ground in abundance after rains in early fall and are sometimes fed upon by poultry. See also *chapat'.*

Gorgojo. Sp.; weevils (Coleoptera of various seed-eating and plant-eating families of characteristic appearance). Has been borrowed into Maya, which has no current exact equivalent. Weevils are major pests. Particularly serious are various small dark bruchid weevils that are the common, and devastating, pests of stored corn. They are particularly damaging when the maize is poorly stored, and especially when it is damp. Dry storage in the husk usually prevents serious damage, unless the maize is left for a long time (more than a year). Nobody minds slightly weevily maize, but extensively nibbled ears are given to the chickens and pigs. Maize was traditionally protected by being stored in insect-repellent branches and leaves, and by having insect-repellent leaves dried, powdered, and scattered among the ears. Today, insecticides, including some that are exceedingly dangerous to humans, are all too often used in the same way. Fortunately, insecticides are expensive, and it is rarely worth using much, since it conveys little advantage over and above the protection provided by careful storage alone.

Seed ears, as well as beans and other seeds, are saved from weevils by being hung from the roof above the *k'oben* (hearth or fireplace); the smoke offers virtually complete protection.

Gusano ganadero. Sp.; botfly or screwworm. Formerly a major pest of mammals, now eliminated from the area by a highly successful government campaign. The area was saturated with publicity, and cattle (the main hosts) were sprayed with insecticide if botflies were present. Vigilance is maintained at the Belize border to prevent reintroduction from the south.

Gusarapo. Sp.; mosquito larva.

Iisij. Lit. "sweet-potato bug." A soft, pale, mushy insect of uncertain affiliation.

Ili'bej. An ant, one centimeter long, with black head and abdomen, and pale sandy red thorax and legs. See also *sinik*.

Iswajij. Large pale yellow butterflies (sulphur butterflies of the family Pieridae). A perhaps informal or nonstandard name. The color of *is waj* (green corn tortillas). Also used for yellow hoverflies, which are the color of green corn and fly at the time it is ready. See also *peepen*.

Jooch' (jooch'ok', xooch'). Very large biting/stinging ants, including (and probably focally) ponerines. See also *sinik*.

Joolom. A large black wasp, said to fly at night. Also, more commonly or usually, carpenter bees and large ground-nesting bees (similar to bumblebees). The small black carpenter bees that nest in the poles of Maya houses are probably the most commonly encountered *joolom*. (*Joloom* in Carrillo Magaña 1990, 5, but not identified.)

A typical example of Maya care for animals occurred when Don Jacinto Cauich carefully repaired a ground nest after breaking it somewhat open to show us. See *abeja* for a list of other bees covered in this section, and *avispa* for a list of other wasps covered in this section.

Jueex (weex). A black ant with a gray abdomen about five millimeters in length. It is the commonest large forest ant, being found in large groups or files throughout all forest environments. It loves fruit, honeydew, and indeed any concentrated food source. See also *sinik*.

Kaarax. Dung beetles (Scarabaeidae). Syn. for *kuklin*. See also *ch'uk*, *sacuchero*, and *xo'*.

Kab. Honey; sometimes used for bees. See *abeja* and *yik'ejkab*.

K'amas. Termites (Isoptera). Focally, this refers to the common tiny termites that build huge, hard nests of chewed wood pulp on trees in the forest. These nests are usually at least the size of a volleyball and may reach bushel-basket size or larger. They are collected, broken up, and given to poultry, which pick the small termites out as they appear; this is a very high-quality poultry food. The smoke of the smoldering nests is a good mosquito repellent, and the inside of the nests is a source of dry tinder if the forest is rain-wet. See also *tuyul*.

K'an ixi'im. A beetle the color, shape, and size of a local *nalt'eel* (maize kernel). Lit. "yellow corn."

K'an kub (k'ank'ub, k'ankab, k'ankabij). A fierce yellowjacket. See *avispa* for a list of other wasps covered in this section.

K'an kuk. A large yellowjacket with a hivelike nest. See *avispa* for a list of other wasps covered in this section.

K'an sak. A wasp that likes to hang its nest under the lips of cave mouths. These nests are oddly shaped and made of mud. See *avispa* for a list of other wasps covered in this section.

Ka'pech. A black seed tick. See also *pech*.

Kisaay. True bugs (Hemiptera). Exactly the entomologist's category of true bugs. Described by color, such as *chak kisaay* (red bugs). See also *chuchi-its'inij*.

K'ix. A cicada (Cicadidae) that says "k'ix."

Koochol. Jerusalem Crickets and similar ground-dwelling pests. Sometimes used for earwigs. One grasshopper or cricket of this name calls "hichi." See also *chapulin*, *maas*, and *saak'*.

Kookay. Fireflies (Lampyridae). This word is very often heard in the Hispanicized form *cocaina*. Sometimes misused for other flying beetles and bugs. At least two, and probably more, species of fireflies exist in Chunhuhub: a cool-weather one with a single long flash, and a hot-weather one with a double flash. No one has stepped forward to identify these.

K'ooxol (k'oxol). Mosquitoes (Culicidae) in general. Commonest are nuisance mosquitoes of the genus *Culex.* An extremely revealing incident about the Maya attitude toward animals is told by Betty Faust (1998, 110): "I complained about the nastiness of mosquitoes and was reprimanded with the reminder that biting people is, after all, the 'work' of mosquitoes." Every animal has its place, and no animal can be blamed for acting accordingly!

Folk species include

Box k'ooxol: common mosquito. Lit. "dark mosquito."

Puuts k'ooxol: huge mosquitoes.

Ts'unuunk'oxol: very large forest mosquitoes. Lit. "hummingbird mosquito."

K'otkanab (k'otkanal). A large wasp with a fierce sting. See *avispa* for a list of other wasps covered in this section.

Kuklin. Dung beetles, scarabs (Scarabaeidae). See Kim de Bolles (1973, 7) for a hilarious Maya folktale from central Yucatán state about these animals. Syn. for *kaarax.* See also *ch'uk* and *xo'.*

Kulsinik, sinik subin. Ants of *subin* trees. These live in the spines of subin (*Acacia cornigera* and similar spp.), the spines being specially hollow for the purpose. The acacia bears special nutrient bodies just for the ants, which pay it back by ferociously biting anything that bothers the tree. The subin is thus allowed to flourish in places where other plants are eaten down, such as heavily stocked cattle pastures. The ants are used in medicines, especially to restore male potency; subin roots and ants are boiled together for this. The ferocious thorniness of the subin and the fiery courage and savage bite of the ants suggest potency, believed to be transferred to the human male. Subin ants with bech' lu'um (here, a black wasp that nests in xaan trees), *chukukij* wasps, and sometimes other stinging creatures, serve to disenchant a man bewitched by a woman to keep him faithful and/or weakly sexed. The brew makes him capable of wanting others again. It is thought by many to work on women, too. A great deal about morality in rural areas is learned from this set of beliefs. See also *sinik.*

Kuruch. Cockroach (Blattidae; the present name is focally *Periplaneta* spp.); from Spanish *cucaracha*—or, just possibly, the Spanish may be from the Maya. Yet more funny stories, featuring the cockroach, are in Kim de Bolles (1973). See also *naats'ul.*

K'uulsinik. A biting ant, tiny and very common. See also *sinik.*

Libélula. Sp.; dragonfly, damselfly. Often used, though mainly to explain *turix.*

Maas. Crickets in general (Gryllidae). The commonest one makes a noise like a tiny hammer hitting metal and is therefore known by the mestizo-Maya terms *martillo maas* (little hammer cricket) and *herrera maas* (blacksmith cricket). See also *bot'ooch* and *koochol.*

Mahannajij. Black Witch Moth *(Otosema odorata).* Sometimes extended to other large dark moths, but the term is normally very specific. The name literally means "house borrower," because the Black Witch loves to come into houses and roost on the walls. This moth is regarded as a bad omen in much of Mexico and (at least formerly) the United States (hence its English name), but to our knowledge it has no ominous connotations among the Yucatec. See also *aak'abpeepen* and *aak'abts'unuun.*

Makech (mak'ech). Mottled brown wood-boring beetles. (Often *mak'ech,* but apparently this is not the normal pronunciation.) One large species is commonly used in Mérida as a living ornament: costume jewelry is glued to its back, and it is chained to a brooch base which is pinned to a lady's evening dress; the insect crawls around, flashing the jewelry. See also *ch'uuitunich.*

Malamosca. Sp.; a fly with a very dangerous, ulcerating bite. Known elsewhere as the *chiclero fly.* The ulceration is due to cutaneous leishmaniasis, a serious disease vectored by the fly. While rarer than in the past, this disease is still not uncommon. Adriano and Manuel Dzib came down with it from bites of chiclero flies in fall 2001, but fortunately were soon well after prompt treatment with antibiotics and topical gentian violet at the local government clinic—offering evidence that Mexico's rural health care system is excellent, effective, and a true life-or-death matter for countryfolk.

Mamakaan. Tarantula hawk wasps (*Hemipepsis* spp.). Lit. "snake mother." Ones seen were huge (ca. seven centimeters long, much larger than the *ch'akat'bej*), and brilliant blue-green. See *avispa* for a list of other wasps covered in this section.

Minador. Sp.; leafminers. Minor but annoying pests of vegetable crops.

Mu'ul. Colonial ground bees. Carrillo Magaña (1990, 6) identifies *mu'ul kaab* as *Trigona fulviventris*. See also *ekjoj* and see *abeja* for a list of other bees covered in this section.

Naats'ul. Cockroach (Blattidae). Rare term. Full range of meanings needs further research. See also *kuruch*.

Niitkij (niitkib, niit' kaab). Lime bee. Called the "lime bee" from its smell. Medellín Morales and Campos López (1990, 11) list it as *Lestrimelitta limao*; so does Carrillo Magaña 1990, 7, who calls it *niit' kaab*.

Nukuch anka. A large moth. See also *aak'abts'unuun* and *mahannajij*.

Pech (peech). Ticks in general. (Hocabá *peech*, but note *peech'* below. Vowel length is phonemic here; apparently Hocabá usage confounds these two names.) See also *ka'pech*.

Peech'. A ground-dwelling bug. Its bite is a good counterirritant for sore knees. FMT has tried it with good results.

Peepen. Butterflies in general. This is one of the most widely known Maya animal terms and even tends to replace *mariposa* in Yucatán Peninsula Spanish. See also *alkabej* and *iswajij*.

Pik. Giant waterbugs (Belostomatidae) and other large bugs, including *Triatoma* species, whose fierce bite is known.

Pulgón. Sp.; cucumber beetle and similar medium-sized beetle pests. Rarely serious, but annoying pests of squash and related plants.

Pu'pus lu'um. Ant lions (Neuroptera). Syn. of *wech lu'um*.

Puuk' ha'. Water beetles in general.

Saak'. Grasshoppers in general. See also *bot'ooch*, *koochol*, *chapulin*, *saak'*, and *sit'riyo*.

Saakal. Army ant, specifically small black ones and large red ones (contrasts with *xuulab* for large black ones, *Eciton* spp.). Also, any large black ants that occur in large swarms or files. A mestizo-Maya version of the word is *sacalaca*. See also *sinik*.

Saay. Leafcutter ants in general (*Atta* spp.). Red ones are *chak saay*. The huge nests of these common ants are a characteristic feature of the forest. The ants become a major pest of isolated orchards near forest; a colony can defoliate and kill a small orchard of orange trees in a few months. These nests are hard to eradicate. Sometimes, desperate cultivators resort to dynamite, or douse the nest with gasoline and set it alight. The problem in Chunhuhub was virtually eliminated, for a while at least, by Hurricane Roxanne, which drowned most of the colonies. The nests are called *saayeras* in mestiza-Maya. See also *sinik*.

Don Juan Sanchez, yerbatero of Gavilanes, tells us that if you take four cargo-carrying *saay* and three going in the opposite direction for more cargo, mix them with corn dough, make a tortilla of it and feed it to a dog, the dog will be a better hunter. We have not tried this.

Sacuchero. Sp.; large dung beetles. See also *ch'uk, escarabajo, kaarax, kuklin,* and *xo'.*

Sats'. Large, strikingly patterned tree caterpillars. Also used for the huge white beetle grubs that emerge from the ground in late summer and early fall after rains. These can be ten to fifteen centimeters long. They eat roots and can kill trees. See also *chamalk'iin, chapat',* and *gallina ciega.*

Sina'an. Scorpions in general.

Sinik (siinik). Small ants in general. Large species have their own particular names. However, *sinik* can be loosely used for any and all ants. See *ch'uuiche', ili'bej, jooch', jueex, kulsinik, k'uulsinik, saakal, saay,* and *xuulab.*

Sit'riyo. Katydids, large green or brown grasshoppers. Lit. "jumper." Also applies to the local Mexican jumping bean, animated by an active larva in the seed. See also *chapulin* and *saak'.*

Tatak'ch'iibij. A yellowjacket, approximately one centimeter long, that builds small paper nests in hollow trees. Tame and unaggressive. The larvae are used to make a poultice for sore or swollen penises of young boys.

Tok'tux. A large black fly, deerfly. Bites. Probably a small tabanid.

Ts'awayek' (ts'awayak). Praying mantises. Lit. "giver of dreams," specifically of strange or ominous dreams; attested in the colonial dictionaries. Certainly the insects look nightmarish enough. They grow to a large size in the forest. Magical beliefs attributed to them seem to have existed and may persist. Name extended to stick insects (Phasmatidae).

Ts'eelem. A common smallish wasp. See *avispa* for a list of other wasps covered in this section.

Tse'ets (ts'ets'). A wild bee. Medellín Morales and Campos López (1990, 11) and other sources list it as *Melipona yucatanica*. In the past, this was an important honey source. See *abeja* for a list of other bees covered in this section.

Ts'ibilnajij. A fierce wasp. Lit. "the one of the house with what looks like writing on it," from the patterned nest. See *avispa* for a list of other wasps covered in this section.

Tsintsin (tziintzin). Common green flies. This old term appears in the *Calepino de Motul* and elsewhere. (Hocabá *tziintzin* may be more correct.)

Tsitsek. Large edible woodworms (beetle larvae).

Tso'ots nookol. Hairy caterpillars. Lit. "hairy worm." May be merely a descriptive phrase rather than a regular reference name. See also *chamalk'iin* and *chapat'*.

Tuch mukuy. Lit. "blue ground dove." This bird name is applied to a species of stinging caterpillar. See also *chamalk'iin* and *chapat'*.

Tuk'uch. A beetle that makes a noise like "tuk."

Tupchak. A wasp. See *avispa* for a list of other wasps covered in this section.

Turix (tulix). Dragonflies in general. Libellulids. See also *libélula*.

Tuus (tuusij). Cocoon, pupa, larva.

Tuyul. Silverfish, termite. See also *k'amas*.

Uk'. Lice in general.

Us (uus). Gnats. (Hocabá has *us*, so *uus* may be an overcorrection.) A mestizo-Maya form is *usito*. *Taan us* is one type of biting gnat. See also *chak iste'*.

Wech lu'um. Ant lion larvae, doodlebugs (Neuroptera); also used for sowbugs (Isopod crustacea). Lit. "earth armadillo." Used as a poultice for cracks between toes. Syn. for *pu'pus lu'um*.

Xaanchij. A large cockroach. Not a kind of *kuruch*. See also *naats'ul* and *xo'*.

Xanabchaak (xana'chaak). A category of savage wasps. *Xana'* means "shoe" and refers to the shoe-shaped nests characteristic of this group. Others explain the name as correctly *xa'anajchak* (red one of the palmetto), with reference to this wasp's habit of hanging its nest under palmetto leaves. The second part of this explanation (chak) must be an error, however, for the animal is yellow with brown bands and wings, not red. It makes a paper nest with various cells. Its sting can give you a fever for two days. See *avispa* for a list of other wasps covered in this section.

Xi'ik'. A bee. Medellín Morales and Campos López (1990, 11) list it as *Tetragonisca friseomelitta nigra*. See *abeja* for a list of other bees covered in this section.

Xnuk, xnuk kab. Various small wasps and bees. Lit. "old bees." One species, identified in Medellín Morales and Campos López (1990, 11), is *Partamona cupira*. This is a bee that makes a paper nest; small amounts of honey are produced but rarely considered worth bothering to take. See *abeja* for a list of other bees covered in this section, and *avispa* for a list of other wasps covered in this section.

Xo'. Beetles in general (Coleoptera); loosely used also for cockroach. See also *ch'uuitunich*, *ch'uk*, *conchuela*, *cuclilla*, *escarabajo*, *kaarax*, *kuklin*, *kuruch*, *makech*, *naats'ul*, *puuk' ha'*, *sacuchero*, and *xaanchij*.

Xunankab. Native stingless bees *(Melipona beecheii)*. Lit. "fine lady honey (insects)." See *abeja* for a list of other bees covered in this section.

Xuulab. Army ants, specifically darker ones. The common black army ants, *Eciton* spp., are *box xuulab*. A red one is *chak xuulab*. See also *saakal* and *sinik*.

Xuux. Wasps in general. It is possible to include all the various types of wasp under this term, in which case it becomes a sort of folk family or perhaps folk supergeneric. However, it is more usually confined by experts to smallish wasps that build paper nests; its use as a general term is primarily by people nonexpert in animal terminology. *Box xuux* is the term for black wasps of this description. See *avispa* for a list of other wasps covered in this section.

Ya'ax ich. A small wild bee. Minor honey source. See *abeja* for a list of other bees covered in this section.

Ya'axkach. Housefly. (Note that by comparison with *aakach*, we might expect a root *kach*, but none is attested in any dictionary.) Other flies of similar color (gray) are called the same name, by extension. Included in this extension are the interesting flies that hover over army ant swarms, eating the insects scared up by the ants. These are called "dogs of the army ants" and are thought by some to be deliberately driving the insects into the army ants' clutches.

Yik'ejixi'im. Pests of maize in general. Lit. "maize insect."

Yik'ejkab. Honeybees. Lit. "honey insect." See *abeja* for a list of other bees covered in this section.

Yik'ejwinik. Roundworms. Lit. "insect of humans." Possibly should be in the worm life-form category and indicates that these two categories are not very distinct. See also *lukumwinik* in the Worms section below.

WORMS

Nook'ol is only vaguely distinct from *yik'ej*. Caterpillars and other larvae are *nook'ol*, though they are known to turn into flying *yik'ej*.

Lukumkaan. Earthworms. (This term also refers to worm snakes.)

Lukumwinik. Roundworms. Lit. "worm of people." See also *yik'ejwinik*.

Urich (ulich, uul). Snails in general. (Hocabá *uul*.) Dubiously in the *nook'ol* category; perhaps better analyzed as a separate life-form entirely.

BIRDS OBSERVED IN
CHUNHUHUB AND ENVIRONS

E. N. ANDERSON

This is a complete list of all birds I identified in the area from Polyuc south to Nueva Loria, February–July 1991, January–June 1996, and September–November 2001. All birds were identified visually, on the basis of careful observation in the field, except for the Mottled Wood-Owl, which Eugene Hunn and I identified by voice when it answered his recordings, and the Guatemalan Screech-Owl, which we first identified that way and which I later heard in the town.

Scientific and Maya names are provided. The Maya names are patterned as follows: *CAPITALS* (italicized) designate the focal species of names that are routinely extended. *Ordinary italics* designate names that are not extended, and also ordinary extensions of focal names. *[Bracketed italics]* designate names that are loose, casual, or ad hoc extensions rather than regular names. I have not bothered to note the routine extension of *chinchinbakal, yankotij,* and *k'ok'* to winter visitors that are small, obscure, and otherwise nameless (see the Bird section in appendix I).

Abundant. Several found during an hour of birding in suitable habitat.

Common. One or a very few found per one to two hours of birding in suitable habitat.

Uncommon. Can usually be found by search, but requires several hours of search.

Occasional. Not common; unpredictable.

Rare. Not usually found; only one to a few records. "Finding" a bird includes hearing it; many birds are almost impossible to see but are extremely vocal (e.g., the Rufescent Tinamou and some night birds). Birds listed for a given habitat will usually turn up occasionally in similar habitat; casual occurrences of this kind have not been noted. Most forest birding was done at dawn or soon after. Forest birds quiet down early and are then difficult to find.

Scientific and popular name usage follows Barbara MacKinnon, *Check List of the Birds of the Yucatan Peninsula* (1992). See also Stephen Howell and Sophie Webb, *A Guide to the Birds of Mexico and Northern Central America* (1995). Both these works have been consulted on matters of abundance and distribution. The Maya names are found in the main body of this work and in appendix I.

Wet forest. This is the *Selva mediana subperennifolia* of Mexican maps.

Dry forest. *Selva caducifolia* in Mexican terminology, growing on rocky hills with very little soil.

Forest. The above collectively; refers to birds equally common in both types. (Most birds prefer one or the other.)

Second growth. The *huamil* of Mexican Spanish. Regrowing weeds, brush, and young trees. The birds confined to this formation tend to move out in a few years (about five), when the trees get tall enough to be a woodland and the species composition approximates standard dry-forest conditions.

Fields. Actively cultivated fields and associated grassland.

Town. Chunhuhub itself—a large area of buildings set among planted trees, most of them fruit trees. There is no dense housing in the town; all yards have fruit trees and gardens. Town birds are about equally characteristic of Presidente Juarez, Polyuc, and other smaller towns.

Most of the water birds do not normally occur in Chunhuhub itself—it has no surface water—but visited during 1996, when they were attracted to ponds left by the torrential rains of Hurricane Roxanne. Large transient ponds also formed in many other areas, especially Presidente Juarez and the Rancho el Corozo area. These ponds, covering fertile land (often maize fields!), were rich in nutrients and attracted many more species and individuals of water birds than most of the large (and rather oligotrophic) lakes did. In general, there were far more water birds in 1996 than in 1991. Intermediate conditions existed in 2001 (following a major tropical storm, with heavy rain, in August), and many water birds were seen in the Juarez-Corozo area. The major centers of water bird abundance in the area in drier years are the huge marshy lakes at Rancho el Corozo, Altamirano, and Piedras Negras.

This list is of some interest partly because it extends some ranges, and partly because it records the effects of a major hurricane on the bird life. I noted significant reductions of several species in 1996 and was informed that the hurricane was responsible for most of this change.

Rufescent Tinamou *(Crypturellus cinnamomeus). Non.* Abundant in forest. Less common after Roxanne, according to my experience and local agreement.

Least Grebe *(Tachybaptus dominicus).* Common on nearby lakes.

Olivaceous Cormorant *(Phalacrocorax olivaceus). CAMACHO* (probably a Hispanicization of the Maya name *mach* heard elsewhere). Common near water areas.

Anhinga *(Anhinga anhinga). Camacho.* Common in small numbers near water areas.

Magnificent Frigatebird *(Fregata magnificens).* Rare; one seen flying over after a storm on May 24, 1991. Regular on large lakes nearby, and abundant on the coast.

Pinnated Bittern *(Botaurus pinnatus). Garza.* Rarely seen but evidently resident in nearby marshes. Fairly common visitor to the transient ponds left by Roxanne.

Bare-throated Tiger-Heron *(Tigrisoma mexicanum). Garza.* Rare; found in huge lake-marsh complex at Altamirano.

Great Blue Heron *(Ardea herodias). Garza.* Abundant winter visitor and common breeder at large nearby lakes and flooded savannahs.

Great Egret *(Casmerodius albus). Garza.* Common, especially in winter, near lakes.

Snowy Egret *(Egretta thula). Garza.* Same as Great Egret.

Little Blue Heron *(Egretta caerulea). Garza.* Same as Great Egret.

Tricolored Heron *(Egretta tricolor)*. *Garza.* Occasional on lakes and abundant in coastal areas not far off. Like other herons, much more evident in 1996 and 2001 than in 1991.

Cattle Egret *(Bubulcus ibis)*. *LUKUPECH, aak'al, garza.* Abundant in permanent fields, especially with cattle, but not necessarily associated with them.

Green-backed Heron *(Butorides striatus)*. *Garza.* Common near water, especially in winter.

Black-crowned Night Heron *(Nycticorax nycticorax)*. *Garza.* Uncommon; found near marshy areas in winter. Noted at Rancho el Corozo and at ponds left by Roxanne.

Yellow-crowned Night Heron *(Nycticorax violacea)*. *Garza.* Uncommon; found near marshes and lakes, especially in winter. Somewhat erratic in distribution.

White Ibis *(Eudocimus albus)*. Not seen in 1991. Rare visitor to ponds left by Hurricane Roxanne, in 1996; also in 2001. Especially often noted along main road near Rancho el Corozo.

Roseate Spoonbill *(Ajaia ajaja)*. *Garza.* Same as White Ibis (observed with it, but even less often).

Wood Stork *(Mycteria americana)*. *SAK CH'OOM.* Not seen in 1991. A flock of about forty birds—probably always the same flock—observed frequently in 1996 and 2001. The birds fed in an Altamirano marsh and lake, and in flooded areas in Presidente Juarez or near Rancho el Corozo and as far south as Vallehermosa, and were often observed flying overhead between these sites or in the area around.

Black-bellied Whistling-Duck *(Dendrocygna autumnalis)*. *Pijije.* Same as Wood Stork. Sometimes seen flying over forests and other areas between lakes. Common in 2001 in flooded savannahs around Vallehermosa.

Muscovy Duck *(Cairina moschata)*. *Pato, pato criollo, pato de pais, pato indio.* Rare, but probably breeding; found near an Altamirano lake.

Blue-winged Teal *(Anas discors)*. *Pato.* Irregular, locally common, winter visitor.

Black Vulture *(Coragyps atratus). Box pool ch'oom.* Abundant everywhere.

Turkey Vulture *(Cathartes aura). Chak pool ch'oom.* Abundant everywhere.

King Vulture *(Sarcorhamphus papa). Batab ch'oom.* Rare resident of the area. A pair lives in the area, usually nesting in the forest preserved at the Nueva Loria archaeological site. Two adults with an immature were seen together in 1991 and 1996, and again on subsequent visits. They forage along roads in the vicinity.

Osprey *(Pandion haliaetus).* Rare winter visitor to large lakes.

Gray-headed Kite *(Leptodon cayanensis). Ii', ch'uuy.* Rare. A few pairs in central Quintana Roo; wide-ranging and sometimes flies or hunts through Chunhuhub.

Hook-billed Kite *(Chondrohierax uncinatus). Ii, ch'uuy.* Rare but widely distributed, from forests to fields to towns.

White-tailed (Black-shouldered) Kite *(Elanus leucurus). Ii, ch'uuy, keen-keenbak.* Common in fields. A pair is resident in large permanent-field areas south of town. Consultants agree this is a recent invader. It seems to be getting more common.

Snail Kite *(Rostrhamus sociabilis). Ch'uuy.* Rare; found at nearby bodies of water.

Plumbeous Kite *(Ictinia plumbea). Ii', ch'uuy, keenkeenbak.* Rare migrant. Does not seem to breed in area, though seen later than normal migration time.

Marsh Hawk *(Circus cyaneus).* Rare migrant. Noted only in fall.

Common Black Hawk *(Buteogallus anthracinus). Ch'uuy,* rarely *ii'.* Rare to uncommon resident near lakes. A pair was seen in an orchard in Chunhuhub on June 11, 1991.

Great Black Hawk *(Buteogallus urubitinga). Ch'uuy, ek' pip.* Rare; found at lakes. One seen May 26, 1991, in wet forest.

Gray Hawk *(Buteo nitidus). II'* (sometimes, but nonstandardly, *ch'uuy).* Common everywhere, especially in fields.

Roadside Hawk *(Buteo magnirostris)*. *CH'UUY, ii'*. Uncommon; found in fields. Locally common in permanent orchard areas.

Short-tailed Hawk *(Buteo brachyurus)*. Rare visitor. The bird is a fairly common resident in areas just north and east where there is more open country.

Zone-tailed Hawk *(Buteo albonotatus)*. Rare transient in spring. Noted in fall just outside the area in 2001.

Black Hawk-Eagle *(Spizaetus tyrannus)*. *EK' PIP*. Rare. Most often seen near Presidente Juarez, where it probably breeds (pair seen displaying).

Ornate Hawk-Eagle *(Spizaetus ornatus)*. *Ek' pip*. Rare but probably resident in the area, in deep forest. Both adult and immature birds seen.

Crested Caracara *(Polyborus plancus)*. Rare transient, open country.

Laughing Falcon *(Herpetotheres cachinnans)*. *KOOS*. Uncommon; found in fields. More common in nearby areas north and east where there is more open country.

Barred Forest-Falcon *(Micrastur ruficollis)*. *Ii', ch'uuy*. Rare; found in forest.

Collared Forest-Falcon *(Micrastur semitorquatus)*. *Ii', ch'uuy, koos*. Rare; found in wet forest. Observed as a pair in same general area, so probably resident in remote parts of the ejido. As of fall 2001, a pair had set up residence at the edge of Chunhuhub and raised a family, so the birds were easy to find—especially when giving evening calls, which carry well over a mile in still weather.

American Kestrel *(Falco sparverius)*. *Keenkeenbak*. Uncommon winter visitor to fields. Almost to common status in 1991, and common nearby where open country is more extensive. In 1996 it was rare.

Bat Falcon *(Falco rufigularis)*. *KEENKEENBAK, kiris, piupiu*. Uncommon or locally common, mostly in dry forest but hunts widely. At least one pair resident, nesting near Chunhuhub in 1991 and near Nueva Loria in 1996 and 2001.

Plain Chachalaca *(Ortalis vetula)*. *Bach*, rarely *kobi*. Abundant in forest. Numbers reduced by Hurricane Roxanne; considerable recovery by 2001.

Great Curassow *(Crax rubra). K'aambuul, faisan.* Rare transient. One observed at fruiting trees, southeastern corner of Chunhuhub, May 1996. A pet bird, locally caught, was in Chunhuhub in 1991.

Ocellated Turkey *(Agriocharis ocellata). Kuts.* Not seen alive, but tracks (identified by both authors) and a feather were found in remote southwestern corner of Chunhuhub in 1996.

Singing Quail *(Dactylortyx thoracicus). Chibilub.* Rare but resident in dry forest. Not noted in 2001, and reported to have gotten much rarer; since the Yucatán Bobwhite is commoner than ever, both the Maya and I suspect changes in habitat as the cause. The Singing Quail lives in less-disturbed hill forest, the Bobwhite in second growth.

Yucatán Bobwhite *(Colinus nigrogularis). Beech', codorniz.* Uncommon to locally common in second growth and brushy fields. Spectacularly successful breeding in 2001 made this bird abundant in second growth around town.

Ruddy Crake *(Laterallus ruber). Gallinola.* Status unclear. Occurs, at least occasionally, in marshes at Rancho el Corozo, but whether resident or transient is unknown.

Gray-necked Wood-Rail *(Aramides cajanea). Gallinola.* Rarely observed but resident in marshland. Quickly moved into the transient pools left by Hurricane Roxanne, where it foraged in drowned cornfields and other atypical habitats.

Sora *(Porzana carolina). Gallinola.* Uncommon to locally common in winter; found near large marshes.

Purple Gallinule *(Porphyrula martinica). Gallareta.* Rare resident in water areas.

Common Moorhen *(Gallinula chloropus). GALLARETA.* Locally abundant in winter; uncommon resident in water areas. Usually confined to large lakes with marshland, but occurred in small ponds left by Roxanne.

American Coot *(Fulica americana). Gallareta.* Irregular and local in winter; found in water areas, including ponds left by Roxanne.

Limpkin *(Aramus guarauna). Correa.* Uncommon; found near large bodies of water, especially lakes with emergent vegetation.

Killdeer *(Charadrius vociferus). Lechkal.* Rare; migration and winter; found in fields near water, especially cattle pastures.

Black-necked Stilt *(Himantopus mexicanus).* Uncommon; found in transient pools, such as those left by Roxanne and by storms of 2001.

Jacana *(Jacana spinosa). GALLINOLA, t'eel ja'.* Common to abundant on local waters. The most widely distributed resident marsh bird, occurring on every body of water from tiny waterholes to huge lakes.

Solitary Sandpiper *(Tringa solitaria).* Rare in winter; rare to uncommon migrant; found at bodies of water with shady wooded margins.

Common Snipe *(Gallinago gallinago).* Rare; found in winter on wet fields.

Laughing Gull *(Larus atricilla).* One seen after a storm on June 9, 1991, flying over Chunhuhub. Uncommon visitor to large local lakes. (Common on the coasts.)

Rock Dove *(Columba livia). Pichon, paloma de casa.* Abundant in town. Occasionally kept as domesticated bird.

Scaled Pigeon *(Columba speciosa). Chuukij* (the only name specific to this bird; the rest are extensions), *kukut'kib, uukum.* Rare, but widespread, in wet forest. Commoner east and south.

Red-billed Pigeon *(Columba flavirostris). UUKUM.* Abundant in forest. Often seen flying over all areas. Hurricane Roxanne reduced the abundance of this bird by 80–90 percent in Chunhuhub; numbers were slowly increasing again by spring of 1996, but the bird was still far less common in 2001 than in 1991, here and (to a lesser extent) throughout Quintana Roo.

Short-billed Pigeon *(Columba nigrirostris). Uukum, kukut'kib.* Rare, but widespread, in forest. Noted at edge of town, March 21, 1991, and in deep forest locations in 1996. This represents a slight northwestward extension of range for this bird.

White-winged Dove *(Zenaida asiatica). Sakpakal.* Abundant in second growth. Often seen flying through other habitats.

Mourning Dove *(Zenaida macroura)*. Rare winterer.

Common Ground Dove *(Columbina passerina)*. *Sojol mukuy*. Uncommon and local in second growth; occasional in orchards. Found at the edges of towns and villages, in dryish young second growth. Slightly commoner in 2001, with opening of the country.

Ruddy Ground Dove *(Columbina talpacoti)*. *Chak mukuy*. Abundant everywhere, particularly in town and associated fields and second growth.

Blue Ground Dove *(Claravis pretiosa)*. *Tuch mukuy*. Uncommon resident of damp areas with much underbrush (in wet forest or second growth).

White-tipped Dove *(Leptotila verreauxi)*. *TSUTSUY* (but not really distinguished from other *tsutsuy*). Abundant everywhere.

Gray-headed Dove *(Leptotila rufaxilla)*. *Tsutsuy*. Rare and local in southern part of area; observed at Rancho el Corozo and heard in other spots.

Caribbean Dove *(Leptotila jamaicensis)*. *Tsutsuy*. Rare; found in wet forest, especially medium-age young forest near large bodies of water.

Ruddy Quail-Dove *(Geotrygon montana)*. *Chak tsutsuy, k'ankab tsutsuy*. Rare; found in wet forest.

Olive-throated (Aztec) Parakeet *(Aratinga nana)*. *K'ili'*. Abundant everywhere (as much in the center of town as in the remote forest).

White-fronted Parrot *(Amazona albifrons)*. *T'UUT'*. Abundant everywhere in 1991. Numbers reduced about 75 percent by Hurricane Roxanne. (Personnel at Sian Ka'an Reserve reported the same rate of reduction there; pers. comm.) Numbers were increasing sharply by late spring 1996, and apparently the birds had moved out rather than dying out. Still, even in 2001, it was less common than before.

Yucatán (Yellow-lored) Parrot *(Amazona xantholora)*. *Ek'xikin*. Rare or uncommon resident, usually seen with the White-fronted Parrot. Same comments on changes as for the White-fronted, though perhaps proportionately less reduced.

Red-lored (Yellow-cheeked) Parrot *(Amazona autumnalis)*. *Kocha', kulix*. Rare; found in wet forest. Though rarely seen, it was well known to local people. A pet bird had been obtained locally. Observed nesting in tall dead trees in the higher forest in the southern part of the area. Northern limit of breeding range seems to be around Presidente Juarez. Commoner in Margaritas, just south of our area.

Mangrove Cuckoo *(Coccyzus minor)*. Rare; found in forests near water and at the edge of town.

Squirrel Cuckoo *(Piaya cayana). Kipchoo'.* Common in forest. Occasional in second growth and orchards.

Striped Cuckoo *(Tapera naevia). Baakenchulul.* Rare; found in weeds in extensive old-field habitat. I am certain that this is a new bird to the area. The local people do not know it. It seems to have colonized as pastures and extensive fields have spread.

Pheasant Cuckoo *(Dromococcyx phasianellus). BAAKENCHULUL.* Uncommon to locally common in forest. Primarily a bird of dense half-grown damp forests. Hard to see, but very vocal in spring, and answers to calls; FMT can call it so well that we have had the bird flying around our heads. Easily found (if this method is used) in second-growth forests along the highway, in the southern part of Chunhuhub ejido lands.

Lesser Roadrunner *(Geococcyx velox). Baakenchulul.* Rare; found in second growth. So poorly known to the local people that I suspect it is a recent invader, as the second-growth habitat has increased following expansion of cultivation. Increasing—commoner in 2001 than before.

Groove-billed Ani *(Crotophaga sulcirostris). CHIKBU'UL,* rarely *kusuy.* Abundant in fields and second growth, but can turn up anywhere. Increasing with clearing of land and expansion of cattle industry.

Barn Owl *(Tyto alba). Xiich'.* Rare resident. Commoner in 2001; probably expanding due to clearing of land.

Guatemalan Screech Owl *(Otus guatemalae). [Kooaak'ab.]* Heard April 17, 1991, in wet forest, responding to tape-recording of call. Also heard at night in town. Probably resident.

Ferruginous Pigmy Owl *(Glaucidium brasilianum). Xnuk, chaxnuuk, kooaak'ab.* Common in dry forest, town, and orchards; rare in other habitats.

Mottled Wood-Owl *(Ciccaba virgata). Kulte'.* Uncommon but evidently resident (pair easily heard at one site); wet forest.

Lesser Nighthawk *(Chordeiles acutipennis).* Rare migrant; flock passed through on May 12, 1991; individuals and small groups (some possibly the following species, *C. minor*) observed during migration time in all three years.

Common Nighthawk *(Chordeiles minor).* Rare migrant; at least one bird, May 25, 1991, flying over Chunhuhub; white bars at center of outer part of wing.

Pauraque *(Nyctidromus albicollis). Pu'ujuy.* Common to abundant everywhere except depths of wet forest.

Yucatán Poorwill *(Nictiphrynus yucatanicus). Tunkiiya.* Uncommon; found in dry forest.

Tawny-collared Nightjar *(Caprimulgus salvini). TUNKIIYA.* Uncommon to locally common in dry forest.

Common Potoo *(Nyctibius griseus). Jaap.* Resident. Not observed in 1991, but in 1996 a bird had taken up residence near the Chunhuhub cemetery—appropriately for a bird of such ominous connotations to the Maya. The attraction was the street lamp at the cemetery, which attracted large insects, in pursuit of which the potoo would make spectacular flights in the evenings.

Chimney Swift *(Chaetura pelagica). Kusuun.* Apparently a rare migrant. Status unclear due to difficulty in distinguishing from Vaux's Swift.

Vaux's Swift *(Chaetura cf. vauxi). Kusuun.* Abundant everywhere. Gaumer's Swift, the abundant Yucatán swift, is very possibly a separate species. Howell and Webb inaccurately map this bird as occurring only in northern Quintana Roo. It occurs abundantly throughout the state.

Little Hermit *(Phaethornis longuemareus). Ts'unuun.* Locally common in the high forest at the Nueva Loria archaeological site. This is probably a northwestward range extension for this bird. It does not occur away from high forest, in my experience.

Wedge-tailed Sabrewing *(Campylopterus curvipennis).* Ts'unuun. Uncommon to locally common in forest.

Fork-tailed Emerald *(Chlorostilbon canivetii).* Ts'unuun. Common resident of second growth, orchards, and gardens.

White-bellied Emerald *(Amazilia candida).* Ts'unuun. Common in wet forest.

Rufous-tailed Hummingbird *(Amazilia tzacatl).* Ts'unuun. Rare resident of orchards and gardens. Seems primarily or wholly a human commensal in this area. It probably has come with human settlement. Appeared somewhat commoner in 2001.

Buff-bellied Hummingbird *(Amazilia yucatanensis).* Ts'unuun. Uncommon to locally common resident of gardens and second growth. Not noted in 2001.

Cinnamon Hummingbird *(Amazilia rutila).* Ts'unuun. In 1991 and 1996, rare to locally uncommon; found in orchards in and around town. Appears to be strictly a human commensal in Chunhuhub. Rare to absent elsewhere. By 2001 it was very common in Chunhuhub and evident in other towns. It has clearly increased with urbanization, and appears to have supplanted the Buff-bellied.

Ruby-throated Hummingbird *(Archilochus colubris).* Ts'unuun. Uncommon migrant and winterer in town and in second growth; locally elsewhere in the area.

Black-headed Trogon *(Trogon melanocephalus).* Kux, uulum k'aax. Uncommon to locally common in wet forest; uncommon in dry forest.

Violaceous Trogon *(Trogon violaceus).* Kux, uulum k'aax. Common but erratic in forest.

Collared Trogon *(Trogon collaris).* Kux, uulum k'aax. Uncommon; found in deepest and tallest parts of wet forest. Rare and local in less tall wet forest.

Blue-crowned Motmot *(Momotus momota).* Juj. Common in wet forest; uncommon or locally common in dry forest.

Turquoise-browed Motmot *(Eumomota superciliosa). Tooj.* Abundant resident of town; nests primarily in outer orchards. Uncommon in second growth and dry forest.

Ringed Kingfisher *(Ceryle torquata). Martin pescador.* Uncommon to common in winter; possibly rare resident (Rancho el Corozo, etc.); found at lakes and ponds. Commoner in 1996 and 2001, when it could be easily if somewhat erratically found at Rancho el Corozo and in transient pools left nearby by Roxanne; almost certainly breeding. Occasional at other lakes.

Green Kingfisher *(Chloroceryle americana).* Common at a Rancho el Corozo lake in 1991, and occasional elsewhere. Not seen anywhere in the area in 1996 or 2001. Hurricane Roxanne had apparently wiped out the Rancho el Corozo population.

White-necked Puffbird *(Bucco macrorhynchos). [Panch'el.]* Very rare transient. Seen at close range in remote part of wet forest, April 28, 1991.

Collared Aracari *(Pteroglossus torquatus). Panch'el.* Common in forest.

Keel-billed Toucan *(Ramphastos sulfuratus). Tucan, pitoreal.* Common in forest.

Red-vented (Yucatán) Woodpecker *(Melanerpes pygmaeus). Che'jun.* Uncommon; found in forest and orchards.

Golden-fronted Woodpecker *(Melanerpes aurifrons). CHE'JUN.* Common everywhere in 1991; abundant in areas with scattered trees, especially orchards. Far less common in 1996; numbers down perhaps 90 percent. Hurricane Roxanne blew down most of the trees and snags in which the bird had lived. No other woodpecker appeared to be seriously affected by Roxanne (the other species do not prefer high, isolated dead trees, as the Golden-fronted does). Appeared completely recovered by 2001. Unlike, say, the parrots, which remain rare, this species can excavate its own holes, and thus is not decimated by blowdown of big hollow trees.

Ladder-backed Woodpecker *(Picoides scalaris). CHI'PIRIX.* Uncommon resident of dry forest and orchards.

Smoky-brown Woodpecker *(Veniliornis fumigatus). [Tatak'che'], chi'pirix.* Uncommon; found in forest. Considerably more numerous in wet forest than in dry.

Golden-olive Woodpecker *(Piculus rubiginosus). [Che'jun.]* Uncommon; found in forest.

Chestnut-colored Woodpecker *(Celeus castaneus). Che'jun, kolonte'.* Uncommon; found in wet forest.

Lineated Woodpecker *(Dryocopus lineatus). KOLONTE'.* Uncommon to locally common, anywhere with trees. Comes into the center of town to feed in dooryard trees.

Pale-billed Woodpecker (also known as Guatemalan Ivorybill or Flint-billed Woodpecker; *Campephilus guatemalensis). KOLONTE'.* Uncommon; found in forest with large trees (i.e., mature forest, especially the wet forest). Often associates with Lineated Woodpecker.

Rufous-breasted Spinetail *(Synallaxis erythrothorax).* Rare resident of dense underbrush in wet forest.

Plain Xenops *(Xenops minutus). [Yankotij.]* Rare; found in wet forest. Locally uncommon; found in particularly wet, dense forest.

Tawny-winged Woodcreeper *(Dendrocincla anabatina). Tatak'che'.* Rare resident of wet forest.

Ruddy Woodcreeper *(Dendrocincla homochroa). Tatak'che'.* Uncommon; found in forest.

Olivaceous Woodcreeper *(Sittasomus griseicapillus). Tatak'che'.* Uncommon; found in wet forest. Commonest of the woodcreepers. With the Ruddy Woodcreeper, typically at army ant swarms.

Barred Woodcreeper *(Dendrocolaptes certhia). Tatak'che'.* Rare resident of wet forest.

Ivory-billed Woodcreeper *(Xiphorhynchus flavigaster). Tatak'che'.* Uncommon; found in forest (both wet and dry). All the woodcreepers like to hunt above army ant swarms; this species is one that is fond of ant-following.

Barred Antshrike *(Thamnophilus doliatus). PU', pajaro tigre, sob.* Abundant in all brushy places (second growth and dense forest underbrush).

Black-faced Antthrush *(Formicarius analis). Tsiimink'aax, beech' lu'um.* Abundant in wet forest. Uncommon; found in dry forest (locally common in thick, moist areas thereof).

Greenish Elaenia *(Myiopagis viridicata). Yaj.* Uncommon; found in wet forest.

Yellow-bellied Elaenia *(Elaenia flavogaster). Yaj.* Rare but probably resident; found in orchards. Perhaps a recent colonizer.

Northern Bentbill Flycatcher *(Oncostoma cinereigulare). Yaj [Yankotij].* Apparently a summer resident. First noted May 8, 1991; came at about the same time in 1996. After arrival, uncommon to locally common in wet forest.

Yellow-olive (White-eyed) Flycatcher *(Tolmomyias sulphurescens). Yaj.* Uncommon resident in tall wet forest or near water.

White-throated Spadebill *(Platyrinchus mystaceus). Yaj.* Rare to locally uncommon resident in deep and shady parts of wet forest.

Northern Royal Flycatcher *(Onychorhynchus coronatus). Juiiro, yaj.* Uncommon; found in tall wet forest. Found only in forest high and thick enough to have a well-developed middle story, as at Nueva Loria and in the remote southwestern corner of Chunhuhub. Here this beautiful, fearless bird is one of the most attractive and lively features of the forest.

Eye-ringed Flatbill *(Rhynchocyclus brevirostris). Yaj.* Fairly common in the high forest at the Nueva Loria archaeological site. Otherwise not recorded. Apparently requires very tall forest with well-developed story structure.

Sulphur-rumped Flycatcher *(Myiobius sulphureipygius). Yaj.* Rare; found in wet forest.

Olive-sided Flycatcher *(Contopus borealis). Yaj.* Rare migrant, but seen in 1991 and 1996 (easily identified by conspicuous white patches on flanks).

Eastern Wood Pewee *(Contopus virens). Ch'ich'ij finados, yaj.* Uncommon migrant; found in forest.

Tropical Pewee *(Contopus cinereus). Ch'ich'ij finados, yaj.* Uncommon to locally common resident in wet forest.

Yellow-bellied Flycatcher *(Empidonax flaviventris). Yaj.* Fairly common migrant; apparently rare winter visitor. Status unclear, especially in winter, because I feel less than confident in my ability to distinguish this species from, for example, the Acadian Flycatcher. However, many fall migrants in particular were quite clearly this species.

Acadian Flycatcher *(Empidonax virescens). Yaj.* Rare migrant.

Least Flycatcher *(Empidonax minimus). Yaj.* Abundant winterer everywhere (and no question of this identification).

Vermilion Flycatcher *(Pyrocephalus rubinus).* Rare but easily seen resident of wet savannahs, as at Rancho el Corozo. Possibly a recent invader of the area; the Howell and Webb (1995) range map does not show it for this area.

Bright-rumped Attila *(Attila spadiceus). JUIIRO, pak'sak'al.* Rare but widely distributed; found in forest.

Yucatán Flycatcher *(Myiarchus yucatanensis). YAJ.* Uncommon or locally common resident of forest, especially dry forest.

Dusky-capped (Olivaceous) Flycatcher *(Myiarchus tuberculifer). YAJ.* Common in forest, especially wet forest. Not noted in 2001 in Chunhuhub, in spite of more and more diligent looking; remained fairly common in the surrounding communities. The reasons for the collapse of the population are mysterious. Perhaps the expansion of the Red-eyed Cowbird is the cause; it is possible that this flycatcher is a preferred victim.

Brown-crested Flycatcher *(Myiarchus tyrannulus). Takaay.* Uncommon resident throughout most of area; locally common, as at edge of Chunhuhub. Like the Dusky-capped Flycatcher, not noted in 2001.

Great Kiskadee *(Pitangus sulphuratus). Takaay.* Common to abundant everywhere.

Boat-billed Flycatcher *(Megarhynchus pitangua). Takaay.* Common everywhere.

Social Flycatcher *(Myiozetetes similis). TAKAAY.* Abundant everywhere.

Streaked Flycatcher *(Myiodynastes maculatus). Takaay.* Very rare summer visitor. Nesting observed in a milpa in southwestern Chunhuhub, near both Sulphur-bellied and Piratic Flycatcher nests, in late spring 1996.

Sulphur-bellied Flycatcher *(Myiodynastes luteiventris). Takaay.* Summer resident. Arrives at beginning of May, after which common in areas with large trees near open patches. All gone by early September.

Piratic Flycatcher *(Legatus leucophaius).* Very rare summer visitor. Pair observed displacing orioles from their nest, in milpa where both the Streaked and the Sulphur-bellied were also nesting, in late spring of 1996.

Couch's Kingbird *(Tyrannus couchii). TAKAAY.* Abundant everywhere.

Eastern Kingbird *(Tyrannus tyrannus).* Rare migrant.

Fork-tailed Flycatcher *(Tyrannus savana). Pajaro tijera.* Rare migrant.

Gray-collared Becard *(Pachyramphus major). [Juiiro].* Uncommon resident in forest.

Rose-throated Becard *(Pachyramphus aglaiae). Juiiro.* Uncommon resident in forest, especially dry forest.

Masked Tityra *(Tityra semifasciata). K'EO, p'eelank'eolij, puerquito.* Common resident in forest. Often comes into orchards.

Black-crowned Tityra *(Tityra inquisitor). K'eo.* Uncommon resident in wet forest.

Red-capped Manakin *(Pipra mentalis).* Rare to uncommon resident in wet forest.

Purple Martin *(Progne subis). Kusuun.* Migrant. Occasionally numerous.

Gray-breasted Martin *(Progne chalybea). Kusuun.* Abundant summer resident, primarily in the town, where it nests in large numbers on the ruined colonial church and elsewhere. First noted mid-April; date unclear due to difficulty of separation from the Purple Martin. Begins to move out in mid-September; gone by mid-October.

Tree Swallow *(Tachycineta bicolor). Kusuun.* Common migrant and winter visitor in more open and/or wet habitats.

Mangrove Swallow *(Tachycineta albilinea)*. *Kusuun*. Common resident at lakes.

Ridgway's Rough-winged Swallow *(Stelgidopteryx ridgwayi)*. *Kusuun*. Uncommon migrant. Breeds just north of our area.

Rough-winged Swallow *(Stelgidopteryx serripennis)*. *Kusuun*. Common migrant, at least in fall; spring status unclear due to confusion with Ridgway's Rough-winged Swallow; certainly much less common in spring than in fall of 2001, when vast flocks passed through.

Barn Swallow *(Hirundo rustica)*. *Kusuun*. Abundant migrant.

Green Jay *(Cyanocorax yncas)*. *Ya'ax ch'eel*. Common in wet forest. Uncommon in dry forest. (See under ch'eel in appendix I.)

Brown Jay *(Cyanocorax morio)*. *Pa'ap*. Abundant in forest.

Yucatán Jay *(Cyanocorax yucatanica)*. *Ch'eel*. Abundant in dry forest. Often in other habitats with trees. Much less evident in nesting season, though presumably as numerous as ever; birds pair off and become very shy.

Spot-breasted Wren *(Thryothorus maculipectus)*. *Yankotij*. Abundant everywhere except in fields and central part of town. Particularly abundant in second-growth scrub.

Carolina (White-browed) Wren *(Thryothorus ludovicianus)*. *Yankotij*. Rare resident of dry second growth.

Tropical House Wren *(Troglodytes aedon)*. *YANKOTIJ*. Abundant in town. Around houses wherever they may be.

White-bellied Wren *(Uropsilla leucogastra)*. *Yankotij*. Common in forest.

White-breasted Wood-Wren *(Henicorhina leucosticta)*. *Yankotij*. Common in the high forest at the Nueva Loria archaeological site. It may be readily found here by anyone familiar with its notes, and observed at close range. This apparently represents a considerable northward extension of range for this bird, which seems to be an obligatory high-forest species. Certainly, saving the isolated population of this interesting and delightful bird is one of the major benefits that would come from better protection of the Nueva Loria site.

Long-billed Gnatwren *(Ramphocaenus melanurus,* separated by recent authors as *R. rufiventris). Yankotij.* Common in wet forest; probably summer only, since first noted April 17, 1991, and slightly later in 1996. As with the Northern Bentbill, this bird appeared to migrate into Chunhuhub, arriving quite suddenly and being easily found thereafter, but the literature does not list it as a migrant. Young birds were still seen, from a late nesting, in October of 2001, but the birds all appear to have migrated by November. Local (?) movements of this kind need further investigation.

Blue-gray Gnatcatcher *(Polioptila caerulea).* Abundant resident in second growth and dry forest. During winter, far more abundant and occurring everywhere.

Tropical Gnatcatcher *(Polioptila plumbea).* Uncommon; found in wet forest.

Swainson's Thrush *(Catharus ustulatus).* Rare migrant.

Wood Thrush *(Hylocichla mustelina). K'ok.* Rare winterer; found in forest.

Clay-colored Robin *(Turdus grayi). K'OK'.* Abundant in town and around houses. Occurs everywhere but almost strictly a human commensal. Numbers greatly reduced by Hurricane Roxanne, but back up to normal by 2001.

Gray Catbird *(Dumetella carolinensis).* Uncommon winter visitor, primarily in underbrush in wet forest.

Black Catbird *(Melanoptila glabrirostris). Po'okin.* Very rare visitor or possibly resident of dense forest near water.

Tropical Mockingbird *(Mimus gilvus). Chiik, chica.* Abundant wherever people have gone. Primarily a human commensal, but occurs everywhere.

White-eyed Vireo *(Vireo griseus).* Abundant winter visitor. Most abundant in dry forest, second growth, and town. Possibly the most numerous bird in the area during winter.

Mangrove Vireo *(Vireo pallens).* Common, especially in second growth but also in dry forest with brush.

Yellow-throated Vireo *(Vireo flavifrons).* Fairly common winter visitor, in forest and town trees. Visibly less common in 1996 and 2001 than in 1991, either due to local fluctuation or to the very rapid decline in numbers of this bird throughout its range.

Red-eyed Vireo *(Vireo olivaceus).* Common migrant.

Yellow-green Vireo *(Vireo [olivaceus] flavoviridis). Ooxil, ts'itkalants'i'.* Common summer visitor to forest. First noted April 12, 1991. Locally abundant in areas with large wide-canopied trees near open country. Gone by early September.

Tawny-crowned Greenlet *(Hylophilus ochraceiceps).* Rare (locally uncommon) resident in dense underbrush in the densest wet forest.

Lesser Greenlet *(Hylophilus decurtatus).* Abundant in wet forest. Uncommon in dry forest.

Rufous-browed Peppershrike *(Cyclarhis gujanensis). Ch'uyin.* Abundant in second growth and brushy parts of forest.

Blue-winged Warbler *(Vermivora pinus).* Uncommon migrant.

Tennessee Warbler *(Vermivora peregrina).* Rare migrant.

Northern Parula Warbler *(Parula americana).* Uncommon to locally common winter visitor, primarily in wet forest.

Yellow Warbler *(Dendroica petechia).* Abundant migrant.

Magnolia Warbler *(Dendroica magnolia).* Abundant winter visitor wherever there are trees.

Yellow-rumped Warbler *(Dendroica coronata).* Rare winterer; found near water (especially at Rancho el Corozo).

Black-throated Green Warbler *(Dendroica virens).* Common winter visitor wherever there are trees. Commoner in migration, especially in town.

Yellow-throated Warbler *(Dendroica dominica).* As for the Black-throated Green Warbler. Notably a town bird.

Black-and-white Warbler *(Mniotilta varia).* Abundant in winter; found in forest and orchards.

American Redstart *(Setophaga ruticilla).* Abundant winter visitor everywhere.

Prothonotary Warbler *(Protonotaria citrea).* Uncommon winter visitor and migrant, primarily in wet forest but also in town and orchards.

Worm-eating Warbler *(Helmitheros vermivorus).* Not noted in 1991 but fairly common in winter in wet forest in 1996 and 2001. This rather dramatic difference cannot be due simply to inadequate observation in 1991, since I visited repeatedly, and watched carefully, in areas where the bird was common in later years. The increase is almost certainly due to Hurricane Roxanne and the rains of 2001, which filled low places in the forests with water, and thus produced a flush of insects. The Worm-eating Warblers seen in 1996 were seen in such wet forest areas.

Swainson's Warbler *(Limnothlypis swainsonii).* Rare. One record, winter 1996, in a dry second-growth forest in Polyuc.

Mourning Warbler *(Oporornis philadelphia).* Rare fall migrant.

Ovenbird *(Seiurus aurocapillus).* Uncommon migrant.

Northern Waterthrush *(Seiurus noveboracensis).* Abundant winter visitor in areas with water.

Common Yellowthroat *(Geothlypis trichas).* Abundant in winter in brush, weedy growth, and orchards throughout.

Hooded Warbler *(Wilsonia citrina).* Common to abundant in winter, primarily in orchards and town. Much commoner in 1991 than in 1996, again for reasons obscure.

Golden-crowned Warbler *(Basileuterus culicivorus).* Uncommon resident in densest, shadiest parts of wet forest, in areas with much undergrowth. Locally common (several resident pairs, easily found and keeping to regular territories) in dense green brush along a dirt road branching east off the main highway, 7.8 miles south of Chunhuhub center. This may represent a range extension for this somewhat little-known bird. The note, much like that of a Ruby-crowned Kinglet, must be learned if one is to find it.

Yellow-breasted Chat *(Icteria virens).* Rare. One migrant bird noted on April 4, 1991, near water just south of Chunhuhub.

Gray-throated Chat *(Granatellus sallaei). Yankotij.* Uncommon to locally common resident of dry forest. Occurs wherever there is considerable brush or undergrowth (e.g., in tall second growth or in underbrush in forest). Seemed less common in 1996, perhaps because of Hurricane Roxanne;

recovered by 2001. An inveterate ant follower, most often seen with ant armies.

Red-legged Honeycreeper *(Cyanerpes cyaneus)*. Common around flowering trees, in wet forest. Resident (contra map in Howell and Webb 1995).

Scrub Euphonia *(Euphonia affinis)*. *CHINCHINBAKAL*. Uncommon resident in wet forest and orchards.

Yellow-throated Euphonia *(Euphonia hirundinacea)*. *CHINCHINBAKAL*. Uncommon or rare resident in wet forest.

Blue-gray Tanager *(Thraupis episcopus)*. Common in towns. Purely a town bird in Chunhuhub. Probably a recent invader to the region, following humans and their fruit-tree plantings. (The range map in Howell and Webb 1995, based on earlier data, does not show the bird in this area.)

Yellow-winged Tanager *(Thraupis abbas)*. Uncommon. Purely a town bird. Almost always seen with the Blue-gray Tanager.

Gray-headed Tanager *(Eucometis penicillata)*. Rare resident in forest.

Black-throated Shrike-Tanager *(Lanio aurantius)*. Rare or occasional. One record in dry forest, March 2, 1991.

Red-crowned Ant-Tanager *(Habia rubica)*. *Sojlin*. Uncommon resident in forest. Status somewhat unclear due to difficulty of distinguishing this from the Red-throated.

Red-throated Ant-Tanager *(Habia fuscicauda)*. *Sojlin*. Common to abundant in wet forest; uncommon, or locally common, where there are many ants, in dry forest.

Summer Tanager *(Piranga rubra)*. *Chakts'its'ib*. Abundant migrant and winter visitor in town. Common winter visitor everywhere except open fields.

Scarlet Tanager *(Piranga olivacea)*. Rare migrant.

Grayish Saltator *(Saltator coerulescens)*. *Ts'aapim*, rarely and tentatively *wiij*. Common in dry forest, second growth, and on edges of town; abundant in woodland/orchard/town ecotone areas.

Black-headed Saltator *(Saltator atriceps)*. *Ts'aapim*. Abundant everywhere.

Common (Northern) Cardinal *(Cardinalis cardinalis). Chakts'its'ib.* Common in second growth, in young dry forest with brush. Uncommon in dry forest.

Rose-breasted Grosbeak *(Pheucticus ludovicianus).* Uncommon migrant.

Blue Bunting *(Cyanocompsa parellina).* Uncommon; found in forest.

Blue Grosbeak *(Guiraca caerulea).* Common winter visitor throughout; abundant, especially in migration, in second growth and weeds around fields.

Indigo Bunting *(Passerina cyanea). Azulejo.* Abundant winter visitor everywhere except in deep forest, and not infrequent even there.

Painted Bunting *(Passerina ciris). Siete colores.* Uncommon migrant.

Olive Sparrow *(Arremonops rufivirgatus). Ya'ax bech' lu'um.* Abundant in second growth. Rarely seen in other habitats, but occasionally enters fields or town.

Green-backed Sparrow *(Arremonops chloronotus). Ya'ax bech' lu'um.* Abundant in dry forest. Common in wet forest in openings regrowing to brush and small trees. Can turn up anywhere.

Blue-black Grassquit *(Volatinia jacarina). Ts'iu.* Abundant in fields and second growth.

White-collared Seedeater *(Sporophila torqueola). Luisita, chinchin.* Abundant in fields. Rarely seen in any other habitat.

Yellow-faced Grassquit *(Tiaris olivacea).* Abundant everywhere. Most common in fields. Occurs even in the deep forest, but usually only along roads or at openings (though it abounds even in well-regrown openings).

Red-winged Blackbird *(Agelaius phoeniceus).* Abundant winterer and common breeder in marshes and flooded fields.

Melodious Blackbird *(Dives dives). Pich'.* Abundant everywhere, but prefers the company of humans.

Great-tailed Grackle *(Quiscalus mexicanus). K'aau.* Abundant in town and around houses. Common everywhere, but definitely preferring human-created environments—the more artificial these environments are, the more grackles. Numbers reduced by Hurricane Roxanne; the day after it, "the square was littered with dead grackles," as one person told me. In a year the numbers were back to normal, and the bird was commoner than ever in 2001.

Bronzed (Red-eyed) Cowbird *(Molothrus aeneus). Pich', ts'iu.* Common in and around town. Flies widely throughout the ejido, especially when seeking nests to parasitize, but otherwise strictly a bird of artificial habitats and domestic stock. Poor knowledge of this bird by locals is fairly conclusive evidence that it is a recent invader, since almost all other birds, even very rare ones, are well known to local people. Steady, rapid increase noted during time of research, perfectly tracking expansion of livestock. Possibly implicated in decline of other birds: Could it be the cause of the disappearance of *Myiarchus* flycatchers?

Giant Cowbird *(Scaphidura oryzivora).* Very rare transient or possibly resident; seen with oropendolas, its preferred hosts, near their nesting colony, so may be breeding or planning to breed.

Black-cowled Oriole *(Icterus dominicensis). Yuyum.* Common in forest.

Orchard Oriole *(Icterus spurius).* Common winterer in forests around flowering trees; abundant in town in fruit trees.

Hooded Oriole *(Icterus cucullatus). JONXA'ANIJ.* Uncommon resident, primarily in town, but also in dry forest.

Yellow-backed Oriole *(Icterus chrysater). Yuyum.* Rare; found in forest.

Yellow-tailed Oriole *(Icterus mesomelas). Yuyum.* Uncommon to locally common in brushy damp places and regrowing wet forest near open country. Seems to be increasing with increase of this habitat.

Orange Oriole *(Icterus auratus). Jonxa'anij.* Uncommon resident of dry forest; sometimes other habitats with open stands of trees, including orchards.

Alta Mira Oriole *(Icterus gularis). YUYUM.* Abundant everywhere except open fields and the depths of the wet forest (and occurs even there). Much less common in 1996, having evidently sustained massive damage from Hurricane Roxanne, and perhaps other causes, such as the drought of 1994. Recovered within a year.

Northern Oriole *(Icterus galbula).* Rare to uncommon winterer, primarily in town. More numerous in migration. All identifiable birds were of the "Baltimore" form (now often listed as a separate species, under the scientific name given).

Yellow-billed Cacique *(Amblycercus holosericeus). Mut.* Common resident of taller second growth, and shorter, denser parts of dry forest. Birds are rarely seen, but the loud and striking antiphonal duetting of pairs of this bird is one of the most characteristic sounds of regrowing milpa areas.

Wagler's Oropendola *(Psarocolius wagleri). K'uubul.* Rare; generally with Montezuma Oropendola.

Montezuma Oropendola *(Psarocolius montezuma). K'uubul.* Erratically common wanderer. Nests where there is good habitat (large trees, fields, water).

Lesser Goldfinch *(Carduelis psaltria). CHINCHINBAKAL.* Rare in winter. Uncommon and erratic migrant. Usually absent but sometimes common in summer. (The seasonal movements of this bird would be interesting to study.)

NOTES

CHAPTER 1: IN THE FIELD IN QUINTANA ROO

1. I have the cynical feeling that the only real function of assigning blame in such vexed cases is to get the blamer off the hook. One should always be extremely cautious of people who are quick to blame others for a problem. One may consider the Mexican elite's tendency to blame the United States for all Mexico's problems—a tendency that is, at least, more understandable than the United States elite's current fondness for blaming Mexico, and especially immigrants therefrom, for United States' problems.

2. The proper and polite address and reference style for a Maya head of household is Don or Doña followed by the first name. My wife and I are Doña Barbara and Don Eugenio to all the town. This address form has a long and honorable history. The Yucatec Maya, a proud and independent people, simply refused to be addressed with contempt by the Spanish colonial overlords. The Maya eventually succeeded in their insistence on being addressed by the aristocratic title of Don. The Spanish, though they at first laughed incredulously at this demand, eventually had to accede. The tradition still holds strong, and no one has forgotten its origin. I maintain it out of politeness, but also because I honor the Maya's deep self-respect and quiet but implacable resistance.

3. Northern Quintana Roo had suffered similarly from Hurricane Gilbert in 1988; the southern part from Janet in 1955. It is widely believed by both scientists and local Maya that hurricanes are getting more frequent and serious. Many scientists ascribe this to global warming.

4. It seems hard to doubt that some Maya actually do practice black magic in the sincere belief that it works. We have both seen examples to the point—Don Felix far more than I, of course. Don Felix and I differ not so much on how extensive these practices are as on how preternaturally effective we believe them to be.

5. The above discussion distills a considerable amount of theoretical reading on development (including sustainable development and ecodevelopment), conservation, and world systems. Theoretical discussion is outside the scope of the present work, which is intended to report the working conclusions of a team of field

investigators. More sustained theoretical discussion will appear in forthcoming volumes on Chunhuhub. However, the basics are in the above account.

CHAPTER 2: THE MAYA AND THE ANIMAL WORLD

1. ENA has observed a Classic Maya cup, painted with figures of masked dancers, described in a museum display as doubtless commemorating some solemn and holy ritual. Unfortunately for the creators of this romantic label, the dancers were costumed as an armadillo, a rabbit, and an opossum—three animals that the Maya regard as hilarious. Clearly, the cup immortalized the town's comedy team. Karl Taube (pers. comm.) thinks they were probably elite youths masked for ritual but amusing dancing.

2. Perhaps the oldest decipherable text in lowland eastern Mesoamerica is an inscription in "pre–proto-Zoque" on a statuette of a priest or shaman dressed as a giant duck. The inscription includes a line, "the animal soul is powerful," which includes an ancestor of the glyph that in Maya would be pronounced *way* (Gossen 1996, 533; Justeson and Kaufman 1993, esp. 1703). The religious officiant's costume, now strongly evocative of Disneyland, seems to ENA to fit well into the Mesoamerica-wide use of water birds as symbols of water, and may also be related to the Nahuatl wind god Ehecatl, who sports a duck's bill. Cormorants, limpkins, and herons in Classic Maya art are obviously used as water symbols, often paired with crocodiles and turtles or opposed to evocative land creatures such as Ocellated Turkeys. Compare the use of the phrase *kuts ja'*, "water turkey," or more precisely, "Ocellated Turkey of the water," for duck in Yucatec Maya—implying a complementarity.

APPENDIX I: THE ANIMAL CLASSIFICATION OF THE MAYA OF CHUNHUHUB AND AREA, QUINTANA ROO

Author's Note: The section on birds was originally published in a much different form as "Maya Knowledge and 'Science Wars,'" *Journal of Ethnobiology,* 20, no. 2 (2000):129–58. Reprinted by permission.

REFERENCES

Acosta Bustillos, Luz Elena. 1995. Estudio sobre el uso y manejo de plantas forrajeras para cría de animales dentro del solar en una comunidad Maya de Yucatán. Tesis, Universidad Nacional Autónoma de México.

Alcocer Puerto, Elias Miguel. 2001. Manejo sustentable de recursos naturales y culturales por parte de una comunidad Maya de Yucatán: El caso de Yaxunah. Licenciado tesis, Universidad Autónoma de Yucatán.

Alcorn, Janis. 1984. *Huastec Maya ethnobotany.* Austin: University of Texas.

Almanza Alcalde, Horacio. 2000. Percepciones locales de la naturaleza en el área de protección de flora y fauna "Yum Balam" en Quintana Roo. Licenciada tesis, Universidad Autónoma de Yucatán.

Alvard, Michael. 1995. Intraspecific prey choice by Amazonian hunters. *Current Anthropology* 36:789–818.

Alvard, Michael, and Lawrence Kuznar. 2001. Deferred harvests: The transition from hunting to animal husbandry. *American Anthropologist* 103:295–311.

Alvarez, Cristina. 1980. *Diccionario etnolingüístico del idioma Maya Yucateco colonial.* México: Universidad Nacional Autónoma de México.

Alvarez del Toro, Miguel. 1960. *Reptiles de Chiapas.* México: Govt. of Chiapas.

_____. 1991. *Los mamíferos de Chiapas.* 2nd ed. Tuxtla Gutierrez: Govt. of Chiapas.

Anderson, E. N. 1996. *Ecologies of the heart.* New York: Oxford University Press.

———. 2000. Maya knowledge and "science wars." *Journal of Ethnobiology* 20:129–58.

———. 2001. Traditional knowledge of plant resources. Paper presented at the Maya Conference, University of California, Riverside.

———. 2003. *Those who bring the flowers: Ethnobotany of the Maya of Western Quintana Roo.* Chetumal: Ecosur.

———. 2003. Traditional knowledge of plant resources. In *The lowland Maya area: Three millennia at the human-wildland interface,* ed. A. Gómez-Pompa, M. F. Allen, S. L. Fedick, and J. J. Jiménez-Osornio, 533–50. Binghamton, NY: Haworth Press.

Anderson, E. N., with Aurora Dzib, Felix Medina Tzuc, and Pastor Valdez. n.d. The lords of the forest, unpublished manuscript.

Andrade, Manuel, and Hilaria Maas Colli. 1990–1991. *Cuentas Mayas Yucatecos.* Mérida: Universidad Autónoma de Yucatán.

Andrews Heath de Zapata, Dorothy. 1980. *Vocabulario de Mayathan.* Mérida: Universidad Autónoma de Yucatán.

Arzápalo Marín, Ramón. 1987. *El ritual de los Bacabes.* México: Universidad Nacional Autónoma de México.

———. ed. 1996. *Calepino de Motul.* México: Universidad Nacional Autónoma de México.

Atran, Scott. 1990. *Cognitive foundation of natural history.* Cambridge, UK: Cambridge University Press.

———. 1993. Itza Maya tropical agro-forestry. *Current Anthropology* 34: 633–700.

———. 1999. Itzaj Maya folkbiological taxonomy: Cognitive universals and cultural particulars. In *Folkbiology,* ed. Douglas Medin and Scott Atran, 119–204. Cambridge, MA: MIT Press.

Atran, Scott, Douglas Medin, Norbert Ross, Elizabeth Lynch, John Coley, Edilberto Ucan Ek, Valentina Vapnarsky. 1999. Folk ecology and the commons: Management in Maya lowlands. *Proceedings of the National Academy of Sciences* 96:7598–7603.

Avila, Gilberto. 1996. Evaluación de los aprovechamientos tradicionales de venado en Quintana Roo. Pp. 152–57 In *V simposio sobre venados de México,* ed. María Magdalena Escamilla Guerrero and Ana Palmira

Raña Garibay, 152–57. Chetumal: Universidad Nacional Autónoma de México, Govt. of Quintana Roo, and Asociación Nacional de Ganaderos Diversificados.

Bahena Basave, Humberto. n.d. [ca. 1995]. *Reptiles venenosos de Quintana Roo.* Chetumal, QR: Consejo Nacional para la Cultura y las Artes, Programa de Apoyo a las Culturas Municipales y Comunitarias (PACMYC).

Barrera Marín, Alfredo, Alfredo Barrera Vásquez, and Rosa Maria Lopez Franco. 1976. *Nomenclatura etnobotanica Maya.* Mérida, Yucatán: Centro Regional de Sureste, Instituto Nacional Antropologia y Historia.

Barrera Vásquez, Alfredo. 1975. *Horoscopos Mayas.* Mérida, Yucatán: Area Maya/Mayan Area (Jose Diaz Bolio).

———. director. 1980. *Diccionario Maya Cordemex.* Mérida, Yucatán: Cordemex. (Current 4th edition was published in 2001 by Editorial Porrúa.)

Batún Alpuche, Adollfo Iván. 1999. Importancia de algunos especies de la familia Iguanidae en el area Maya precolombina. Licenciada tesis, Universidad Autónoma de Yucatán.

Benedict, F. G., and Morris Steggerda. 1936. *The food of the present-day Maya Indians of Yucatan.* Contribution 18, Publication 456. Washington, DC: Carnegie Institution of Washington.

Benitez, Fernando. 1986. *Ki: El drama de un pueblo y de una planta.* México: Fondo de Cultura Económica.

Benson, Elizabeth P. 1997. *Birds and beasts of ancient Latin America.* Gainesville: University of Florida Press.

Berlin, Brent. 1992. *Ethnobiological classification.* Princeton, NJ: Princeton University Press.

Berlin, Brent, Dennis Breedlove, and Peter Raven. 1974. *Principles of Tzeltal plant classification.* New York: Academic Press.

Boster, James. 1987. Agreement between biological classification systems is not dependent on cultural transmission. *American Anthropologist* 89: 914–20.

Boster, James, Brent Berlin, and John O'Neill. 1986. The correspondence of Jivaroan to scientific ornithology. *American Anthropologist* 88:569–83.

Boster, James, and Roy d'Andrade. 1989. Natural and human sources of cross-cultural agreement in ornithological classification. *American Anthropologist* 91:132–42.

Bourdieu, Peter. 1977. *Outline of a theory of practice.* Cambridge, UK: Cambridge University Press.

———. 1990. *The logic of practice.* Stanford, CA: Stanford University Press.

Bowes, Anne LaBastille. 1964. *Birds of the Mayas.* Big Moose, NY: West-of-the-Wind Publications. (First edition used, because it has more Mayan names. A second edition, 1993, is authored by Anne LaBastille, and published by the same publisher but in Westport, NY.)

Bricker, Victoria, Eleuterio Po'ot Yah, and Ofelia Dzul de Po'ot. 1998. *A dictionary of the Maya language as spoken in Hocabá, Yucatán.* Salt Lake City: University of Utah Press.

Brown, Cecil. 1979a. Folk zoological life-forms: Their universality and growth. *American Anthropologist* 81:4:791–817.

———. 1979b. Growth and development of folk botanical life forms in the Mayan language family. *American Ethnologist* 6(2):366–85.

———. 1982. Folk zoological life-forms and linguistic marking. *Journal of Ethnobiology* 2:95–112.

Brown, Cecil, and Stanley Witkowski. 1982. Growth and development of folk zoological life-forms in the Mayan language family. *American Ethnologist* 9:97–112.

Bulmer, Ralph. 1967. Why is the cassowary not a bird? A problem of zoological taxonomy among the Karam of the New Guinea highlands. *Man* 2:5–25.

Burger, Joanna, Elinor Ostrom, Richard Norgaard, David Policansky, Bernard D. Goldstein, eds. 2001. *Protecting the commons.* Washington, DC: Island Press.

Burns, Allen. 1983. *An epoch of miracles.* Austin: University of Texas Press.

Callicott, J. Baird. 1995. *Earth's insights.* Berkeley: University of California Press.

Campbell, Jonathan. 1998. *Amphibians and reptiles of northern Guatemala, the Yucatan, and Belize.* Norman: University of Oklahoma Press.

Carr, Helen Sorayya. 1989. Changing referents of certain snake terms in Yucatec Maya; or, the adventures of a zooarchaeologist on a foray into folk biology. Paper presented at the annual meeting of the Society of Ethnobiology, Riverside, CA.

———. 1991a. The Maya medicinal turtle, *xkokak,* and a suggested alternate reading of two Yucatec ethnomedical texts. *Journal of Ethnobiology* 11:187–92.

———. 1991b. Precolumbian Maya exploitation and management of deer populations. Paper presented at the Conference on Ancient Maya Agriculture and Biological Resource Management, University of California, Riverside.

Carrillo Magaña, Felipe. 1990. *Glosario de terminologías Maya-Yucatecas referentes a la cría de abejas indígenas.* Mérida, Yucatán: Sostenibilidad Maya.

Chávez Guzmán, Mónica. 1995. *Dzibilchaltun: Flora y fauna.* Mérida, Yucatán: Biocenosis.

Chicchón, Avecita. 2000. Conservation theory meets practice. *Conservation Biology* 14:1368–69.

Coe, Michael. 1996. *The Maya.* 4th ed. London: Thames and Hudson.

Colchester, Marcus. 2000. Self-determination or environmental determinism for indigenous peoples in tropical forest conservation. *Conservation Biology* 14:1365–67.

CONACULTA. 1999–2001. *Cocina tradicional e indígena.* 54 vols. México: CONACULTA.

Conrado de Ucán, Teresa de Jesús, José del Carmen Ucán Ek, Sergio Medellín Morales, and Jorge González Acereto. 1992. *La cría de la abeja xunan kab en el litoral oeste de Yucatán: tradición oral y problemática de la actividad.* Mérida, Yucatán: Yik'el Kab A.C. (issued by Sostenibilidad Maya).

Cruikshank, Julie. 2000. *The social life of stories.* Lincoln: University of Nebraska Press.

de Jong, Harriet. 1999. The land of corn and honey: The keeping of sting-less bees (meliponiculture) in the ethno-ecological environment of Yucatan (Mexico) and El Salvador. PhD diss., University of Utrecht, Netherlands.

de Rosado, Engracia. 1992. *Los pájaros eran diferentes entonces (leyendas Mayas).* Mérida: Govt. of Yucatán. (Orig. pub. 1946.)

Durkheim, Emile, and Marcel Mauss. 1963. *Primitive classification.* Trans. Rodney Needham. London: Cohen and West. (Fr. orig. 1903.)

Editorial Porrúa. 1995. *Leyes y códigos de México: Legislación forestal y de caza.* México: Editorial Porrúa.

Ehnis Duhne, Alberto. 1996. Primer ensayo de liberación de venados en eji-dos forestales de Quintana Roo. In *V simposio sobre venados de México,* ed. María Magdalena Escamilla Guerrero and Ana Palmira Raña Garibay, 125–29. Chetumal: Universidad Nacional Autónoma de Méx-ico, Govt. of Quintana Roo, and Asociación Nacional de Ganaderos Diversificados.

Ellen, Roy. 1993. *The cultural relations of classification.* Cambridge, UK: Cambridge University Press.

Emmons, Louise. 1990. *Neotropical rainforest mammals: A field guide.* Chicago: University of Chicago Press.

Escamilla Guerrero, María Magdalena, and Ana Palmira Raña Garibay, eds. 1996. *V simposio sobre venados de México.* Chetumal: Universidad Nacional Autónoma de México, Govt. of Quintana Roo, and Asociación Nacional de Ganaderos Diversificados.

Faust, Betty. 1998. *The plumed serpent and Mexican rural development.* West-port, CT: Bergin and Garvey.

Fedick, Scott, ed. 1996. *The managed mosaic.* Salt Lake City: University of Utah Press.

Figueroa Esquivel, Elsa Margarita. 1994. Estudio avifaunístico de la región sur del Estado de Quintana Roo, México. Biología Tesis, Universidad Nacional Autónoma de México.

Flores, J. Salvador. 1984. *Algunas formas de caza y pesca usadas en Meso-américa.* Xalapa, Veracruz: Instituto Nacional de Recursos Bióticos.

Flores, J. Salvador, and Edilberto Ucan Ek. 1983. *Nombres usados por los Mayas para designar a la vegetación.* Xalapa, Veracruz: Instituto Nacional de Recursos Bióticos.

Forth, Gregory. 1996. Nage birds: Issues in the analysis of ethnoornithological classification. *Anthropos* 91:89–109.

Foucalt, Michel. 1971. *The order of things.* New York: Pantheon Books.

Geertz, Clifford. 1963. *Agricultural involution.* Berkeley: University of California Press.

Gómez-Pompa, Arturo. 1987. On Maya silviculture. *Mexican Studies/ Estudios Mexicanos* 3(1):1–17.

Gómez-Pompa, Arturo, Jose Salvador Flores, and Victoria Sosa. 1987. The "Pet Kot": A man-made tropical forest of the Maya. *Interciencia* 12: 10–15.

González, Roberto. 2001. *Zapotec science.* Austin: University of Texas Press.

González Acereto, Jorge, and Victor Cámara González. 1991. *Comparación entre la producción de miel entre colonias de* Melipona beecheii *Bennett alojadas en troncos ahecados (jobones) y cajas modernas (PNN, PA-1 e INPA-1) a las cuales se suministró alimentación energética durante cuatro meses.* Mérida, Yucatán: Sostenibilidad Maya.

González Acereto, Jorge, and Sergio Medellín Morales. 1991a. *La división artificial en la abeja xunan kab: Manual.* Mérida, Yucatán: Yik'el Kab A.C. (issued by Sostenibilidad Maya).

_____. 1991b. *Manual práctico para criar abejas nativas sin aguijón.* Mérida, Yucatán: Yik'el Kab A. C. (issued by Sostenibilidad Maya).

Gossen, Gary. 1994. From Olmecs to Zapatistas: A once and future history of souls. *American Anthropologist* 96:553–70.

_____. 1996. Maya Zapatistas move to the ancient future. *American Anthropologist* 98:528–38.

Goulet, Jean-Guy. 1998. *Ways of knowing.* Lincoln: University of Nebraska Press.

Greenberg, Laura S. Z. 1992. Garden hunting among the Yucatec Maya: A coevolutionary history of wildlife and culture. *Etnoecologica* 1:23–33.

Grube, Nicolai, and Werner Nahm. 1994. A census of Xibalba: A complete inventory of *way* characters on Maya ceramics. In vol. 4 of *The Maya vase book: A corpus of rollout photographs of Maya vases,* Justin Kerr, 686–715. New York: Kerr Associates.

Gutierrez, Efrain. 1987. Plantas comestibles de una comunidad Maya de Quintana Roo, México, unpublished manuscript.

Hanks, William. 1990. *Referential practice.* Chicago: University of Chicago.

Hardin, Garrett. 1968. The tragedy of the commons. *Science* 162:1243–47.

Hartig, Helga-Maria. 1979. *Las aves de Yucatán: Nomenclatura en Maya-Español-Inglés-Latin.* Mérida: Fondo Editorial de Yucatán.

Himmelstien, Jeff. n.d. *Observations and distribution of amphibians and reptiles in the state of Quintana Roo, Mexico.* Pamphlet supplied by author. (Originally an article in *Bulletin of the New York Herpetological Society* 16:2; reprinted without date, presumably ca. 1979 because that is the date of the latest reference cited, and the fundamental work of Lee 1980 is not cited.)

Hofling, Charles A. 1991. *Itzá Maya texts.* Salt Lake City: University of Utah Press.

Hofling, Charles, and Felix F. Tesucún. 1997. *Itzaj Maya-Spanish-English dictionary.* Salt Lake City: University of Utah Press.

Hostetler, Ueli. 1997. Milpa agriculture and economic diversification: Socioeconomic change in a Maya peasant society of central Quintana Roo, 1900–1990s. PhD diss., University of Berne, Switzerland.

Houston, Stephen, and David Stuart. 1989. *The* way *glyph: Evidence for "co-essences" among the classic Maya.* Research Reports on Ancient Maya Writing, no. 30. Washington, DC: Center for Maya Research.

Hovey, Kevin. 1997. Maya continuity: The contemporary, historic, and prehistoric practice of gopher trapping and consumption. Paper presented at the James Young Memorial Colloquium, Riverside, CA.

Hovey, Kevin, and Dominique Rissolo. 1999. The process and sociocultural significance of gopher trapping in a modern Yucatec Maya community. *Journal of Ethnobiology* 19:261–76.

Howell, Stephen, and Sophie Webb. 1995. *A guide to the birds of Mexico and northern Central America.* New York: Oxford University Press.

Humphries, Sally. 1993. The intensification of traditional agriculture among Yucatec Maya farmers: Facing up to the dilemma of livelihood sustainability. *Human Ecology* 21:87–102.

Hunn, Eugene. 1977. *Tzeltal folk zoology.* New York: Academic Press.

———. 1982. The utilitarian factor in folk biological classification. *American Anthropologist* 84:830–47.

———. 1991. Yucatec Maya zoological dictionary, unpublished manuscript.

———. 1992. The use of sound recordings as voucher specimens and stimulus materials in ethnozoological research. *Journal of Ethnobiology* 12: 187–202.

INEGI [Instituto Nacional de Estadística Geografía e Informática]. 1994. *Felipe Carrillo Puerto, estado de Quintana Roo: Cuaderno estadístico municipal, 1993.* Aguascalientes: INEGI.

Jones, Grant. 1989. *Maya resistance to Spanish rule.* Albuquerque: University of New Mexico Press.

Jorgensen, Jeffrey. 1993. Gardens, wildlife densities, and subsistence hunting by Maya Indians in Quintana Roo, Mexico. PhD diss., University of Florida.

———. 1994. La cacería de subsistencia practicada por la gente Maya en Quintana Roo. In *Madera, chicle, caza y milpa: Contribuciones al manejo integral de las selvas de Quintana Roo, México,* ed. Laura K. Snook and Amanda Barrer de Jorgensen, n.p. Chetumal: Ecosur.

———. 1998. The impact of hunting on wildlife in the Maya forest of Mexico. In *Timber, tourists, and temples: conservation and development in the maya forest of Belize, Guatemala, and Mexico,* ed. Richard B. Primack, David Bray, Hugo A. Galletti, and Ismael Ponciano, 179–94. Washington, DC: Island Press.

Juárez, Ana. 2002. Ecological degradation, global tourism, and inequality: Maya interpretations of the changing environment in Quintana Roo, Mexico. *Human Organization* 61:113–24.

Justeson, John, and Terrence Kaufman. 1993. A decipherment of Epi-Olmec hieroglyphic writing. *Science* 293:1703–11.

Kearney, Michael. 1996. *Reconceptualizing the peasantry.* Boulder: Westview.

Kendall, Jonathan. 1992. The thirteen volatiles: Representation and symbolism. *Estudios de Cultura Nahuatl* 30:99–131.

Kim de Bolles, Alexandra. 1973. *Mayan folk tales.* Komchhen, Yucatán: D. Bolles.

Krech, Shepard. 1999. *The ecological Indian: Myth and reality.* New York: W. W. Norton.

Kronenfeld, David B. 1996. *Plastic glasses and church fathers.* New York: Oxford University Press.

Landa, Fray Diego de. 1978. *Yucatan before and after the conquest.* Trans. and ed. William Gates. New York: Dover. (Orig. pub. 1937, translating a work of 1566.)

Lawrence, T. E. 1935. *Seven pillars of wisdom.* New York: MacMillan.

Lee, Julian C. 1980. *An ecogeographic analysis of the herpetofauna of the Yucatán Peninsula.* Miscellaneous Publication No. 67, Museum of Natural History. Lawrence, KS: University of Kansas.

———. 1990. Creatures of the Maya. *Natural History,* January, 44–50.

———. 1996. *The amphibians and reptiles of the Yucatan Peninsula.* Ithaca, NY: Comstock Cornell.

Lenkersdorf, Carlos. 1996. *Los hombres verdaderos.* México: Siglo veintiuno Editores.

Lévi-Strauss, Claude. 1962. *La pensée sauvage.* Paris: Plon.

Linares, Olga. 1976. Garden hunting in the American tropics. *Human Ecology* 4:331–50.

Litzinger, William, and Robert Bruce. n.d. [ca. 1994]. The significance of Lacandon Maya animal and plant onen or spirit-beings and their potential importance for interpreting ancient Mayan art and iconography, unpublished manuscript.

Llanes Pasos, Eleuterio. 1993. *Cuentos de cazadores.* Chetumal: Govt. of Quintana Roo.

López Ornat, Arturo, James F. Lynch, and Barbara MacKinnon de Montes. 1989. New and noteworthy records of birds from the eastern Yucatán Peninsula. *Wilson Bulletin* 101:390–409.

Love, Bruce. 1994. *The Paris codex: Handbook for a Maya priest.* Austin: University of Texas Press.

Maas Colli, Hilaria, ed. 1993. *Leyendas Yucatecas.* Mérida: Universidad Autónoma de Yucatán.

MacKinnon, Barbara. 1992. *Check list of the birds of the Yucatan Peninsula.* Cancún, Quintana Roo: Amigos de Sian Ka'an.

Mandujano, Salvador, and Victor Rico-Gray. 1991. Hunting, use, and knowledge of the biology of the white-tailed deer (*Odocoileus virginianus* Hays) by the Maya of central Yucatan, Mexico. *Journal of Ethnobiology* 11:175–86.

Marmolejo Monsiváis, Miguel Ángel. 2000. *Fauna alimentaria de la Península de Yucatán.* México: Instituto Nacional Indigenísta.

Martin, Paul S., and Christine R. Szuter. 1999. War zones and game sinks in Lewis and Clark's West. *Conservation Biology* 13:36–45.

———. 2002. Game parks before and after Lewis and Clark: Reply to Lyman and Wolverton. *Conservation Biology* 16:244–47.

Martinez López, J. F., ed. 1946. *Primera convención apicola peninsular: Memoria.* Mérida, Yucatán: Zamna, with aid of the state governor.

Medellín Morales, Sergio. 1991. *Meliponicultura Maya: Base bibliográfica.* Mérida, Yucatán: Sostenibilidad Maya with collaboration of Yik'el Kab A.C.

Medellín Morales, Sergio, and Enrique Campos López. 1990. *La meliponicultura Maya: Perspectivas de su sostenibilidad.* Mérida, Yucatán: Sostenibilidad Maya.

Medellín Morales, Sergio, Enrique Campos López, Enrique Campos Nuñez, Jorge González Acereto, and Victor Cámara González. 1991. *Meliponicultura Maya: Perspectivas para su sostenibilidad.* Reportes de Sostenibilidad Maya #2. Mérida, Yucatán: Sostenibilidad Maya.

Medellín Morales, Sergio, and Jorge González Acereto. 1991a. *La cría de abejas nativas: Una alternativa tradicional para comunidades marginadas.* Mérida, Yucatán: Yik'el Kab A.C. (issued by Sostenibilidad Maya).

———. 1991b. *La cría de la abeja xunan kab: Ayer y hoy.* Mérida, Yucatán: Yik'el Kab A.C. (issued by Sostenibilidad Maya).

Medellín Morales, Sergio, and Maria Mercedes Cruz Bojorquez. 1992. *Xunan kab: Una experiencia etnoecológica y de transferencia de tecnología tradicional en una comunidad Maya de Yucatán.* Mérida, Yucatán: Sostenibilidad Maya.

Medin, Douglas, and Scott Atran, eds. 1999. *Folkbiology.* Cambridge, MA: MIT Press.

Murphy, Julia. 1990. Indigenous forest use and development in the "Maya Zone" of Quintana Roo, Mexico. Master's thesis, York University, Ontario, Canada.

Navarro L., Daniel. 1992. *Los mamíferos de Quintana Roo en peligro de extinción.* Chetumal: Centro de Investigaciones de Quintana Roo.

Niiler, Eric. 2001. Into the jaguar's den. *Scientific American,* September, 22–24.

Nyerges, A. Endre, ed. 1997. *The ecology of practice.* New York: Gordon and Breach.

Olson, Mancur. 1965. *The logic of collective action.* Cambridge, MA: Harvard University Press.

Ostrom, Elinor. 1990. *Governing the commons.* New York: Cambridge University Press.

Pacheco Cruz, Salvador. 1958. *Diccionario de la fauna Yucateca.* Mérida, Yucatán: Salvador Pacheco Cruz.

Paine, Richard R., and AnnCorinne Freter. 1996. Environmental degradation and the Classic Maya collapse at Copan, Honduras (AD 600–1250): Evidence from studies of household survival. *Ancient Mesoamerica* 7:37–48.

Paredes, Americo. 1970. *Folktales of Mexico.* Chicago: University of Chicago.

Peraza Lopez, Maria Elena. 1986. Patrones alimenticios en Ichmul, Yucatán. Licenciada Tesis, Universidad Autónoma de Yucatán.

Peterson, Roger Tory, and Edward Chalif. 1973. *A field guide to Mexican birds.* Boston: Houghton Mifflin.

———. 1989. *Aves de México: Guía de campo.* México: Diana.

Primack, Richard B., David Bray, Hugo A. Galletti, and Ismael Ponciano, eds. 1998. *Timber, tourists, and temples: Conservation and development in the Maya forest of Belize, Guatemala, and Mexico.* Washington, DC: Island Press.

Ramos Elorduy de Conconi, Julieta. 1991. *Los insectos como fuente de proteínas en el futuro.* México: Noriega Limusa.

Ramos Elorduy de Conconi, Julieta, and José Manuel Pino Moreno. 1989. *Los insectos comestibles en el México antiguo.* México: Agt Editor.

Re Cruz, Alicia. 1996. *The two milpas of Chan Kom.* Albany: State University of New York.

Redfield, Robert, and Alfonso Villa Rojas. 1934. *Chan Kom: A Maya village.* Report no. 448. Washington, DC: Carnegie Institution of Washington.

Redford, Kent, and Jane A. Mansour, eds. 1996. *Traditional peoples and biodiversity conservation in large tropical landscapes.* Arlington, VA: The Nature Conservancy.

Redford, Kent, and Steven E. Sanderson. 2000. Extracting humans from nature. *Conservation Biology* 14:1362–64.

Redman, Charles. 1999. *Human impact on ancient environments.* Tucson: University of Arizona Press.

Reid, Fiona. 1997. *A field guide to the mammals of Central America and Southeast Mexico.* New York and Oxford: Oxford University Press.

Remolina Suárez, José Francisco. 1996. Producción estabulada de venado colablanca en la región Maya de Quintana Roo. In *V simposio sobre venados de México,* ed. María Magdalena Escamilla Guerrero and Ana Palmira Raña Garibay, 186–94. Chetumal: Universidad Nacional Autónoma de México, Govt. of Quintana Roo, and Asociación Nacional de Ganaderos Diversificados.

Ridington, Robin. 1988. *Trail to heaven.* Iowa City: University of Iowa Press.

Robicsek, Francis. 1981. *The Maya book of the dead: The ceramic codex.* Charlottesville, VA: University of Virginia Art Museum.

Roys, Ralph. 1933. *The book of Chilam Balam of Chumayel.* Washington, DC: Carnegie Institution of Washington.

Salazar, Gabriel. 2000. Geography of the lowlands. (Orig. Sp. 1620.) In *Lost shores, forgotten peoples*, ed. Lawrence H. Feldman, 20–54. Durham, NC: Duke University Press.

Santamaria, Francisco X. 1988. *Diccionario general de Americanismos.* 2nd ed. Villahermosa: Government of the State of Tabasco.

Schwartzman, Stephan, Adriana Moreira, and Daniel Nepstad. 2000. Rethinking tropical forest conservation: Perils in parks. *Conservation Biology* 14:1351–57.

Schwartzman, Stephan, Daniel Nepstad, and Adriana Moreira. 2000. Arguing tropical forest conservation: People versus parks. *Conservation Biology* 14:1370–74.

Seler, Eduard. 1961. Die tierbilder der Mexikanischen und der Maya-Handschriften. In *Gesammelte abhandlungen zur Amerikanischen sprach-und altertumskunde*, vol. 4, Eduard Seler, 453–758. Graz, Austria: Akademische Druck J. Verlagsanstalt. (Originally appeared serially in *Zeitschrift fur Ethnologie*, 1909:2–6 and 1910:1–2.)

Sharp, Henry. 1987. Giant fish, giant otters, and dinosaurs: 'Apparently irrational beliefs' in a Chipewyan community. *American Ethnologist* 14: 226–35.

Sheridan, Thomas. 1988. *Where the dove calls.* Tucson: University of Arizona Press.

Sillitoe, Paul. 2002. Contested knowledge, continguent classification: Animals in the highlands of Papua New Guinea. *American Anthropologist* 104:1162–71.

Silveira Silveira, Raul. 1990. *Catálogo de plantas nectar poliníferas de la Peninsula de Yucatán.* Mérida, Yucatán: Sostenibilidad Maya.

Simonian, Lane. 1995. *Defending the land of the jaguar: A history of conservation in Mexico.* Austin: University of Texas Press.

Smith, David M. 1998. An Athapaskan way of knowing: Chipewyan ontology. *American Ethnologist* 25:412–32.

Sosa, Victoria, J. Salvador Flores, Victor Rico-Gray, Rafael Lira, and J. J. Ortiz. 1985. *Etnoflora Yucatanense, fascículo 1: Lista florística y sinonimia Maya.* Xalapa, Veracruz: Instituto Nacional de Recursos Bióticos.

Souza Novelo, Narciso, Victor M. Suarez Molina, and Alfredo Barrera Vásquez. 1981. *Plantas melíferas y poliníferas de Yucatán.* Mérida: Fondo Editorial de Yucatán.

Steggerda, Morris. 1977. Rasgos personales y actividades diarias de los Mayas de Yucatán. In *Enciclopedia Yucatanense,* 2nd ed., 93–131. Mérida: Govt. of Yucatán.

Steward, Julian. 1955. *Theory of culture change.* Urbana: University of Illinois Press.

Stonich, Susan. 1993. *"I am destroying the land!" The political ecology of poverty and environmental destruction in Honduras.* Boulder: Westview.

Sullivan, Paul. 1989. *Unfinished conversations.* Berkeley: University of California Press.

Taube, Karl. 1989. Ritual humor in classic Maya religion. In *Word and image in Mayan culture,* ed. William Hanks and Donald Rice, 351–82. Salt Lake City: University of Utah Press.

Tedlock, Dennis. 1985. *Popol Vuh: The Mayan book of the dawn of life.* New York: Simon and Schuster.

_____. 1993. *Breath on the mirror.* New York: HarperCollins.

Terán, Silvia, and Christian Rasmussen, eds. 1992. *Relatos del centro del mundo/U tsikbalo'obi ch'umuk lu'um.* 3 vols. Mérida: Govt. of Yucatán.

_____. 1994. *La milpa de los Mayas.* Mérida: Govt. of Yucatán.

Terborgh, John. 2000. The fate of tropical forests: A matter of stewardship. *Conservation Biology* 14:1358–61.

Tozzer, Alfred M., and Glover M. Allen. 1910. *Animal figures in the Maya codices.* Peabody Museum Papers 4:3. Cambridge, MA: Peabody Museum of Harvard University.

Várguez Pasos, Luis A., ed. 1981. *La milpa entre los Mayas de Yucatán.* Mérida: Universidad de Yucatán.

Vayda, Andrew P. 1996. *Methods and explanations in the study of human actions and their environmental effects.* Jakarta: CIFOR and World Wildlife Fund.

Vayda, Andrew P., and Bradley Walters. 1999. Against political ecology. *Human Ecology* 27:167–79.

Villegas Maldonado, Lorenzo. 1996. Huellas y cualidades del venado en Quintana Roo. In *V simposio sobre venados de México*, ed. María Magdalena Escamilla Guerrero and Ana Palmira Raña Garibay, 130–31. Chetumal: Universidad Nacional Autónoma de México, Govt. of Quintana Roo, and Asociación Nacional de Ganaderos Diversificados.

Vogt, Evon Z. 1969. *Zinacantan*. Cambridge, MA: Harvard University Press.

Weaver, Nevin, and Elizabeth C. Weaver. 1980. Beekeeping with the stingless bee *Melipona beecheii* by the Yucatecan Maya. *Bee World* 62:7–19.

Weber, Max. 1930. *The Protestant ethic and the spirit of capitalism*. New York: Harper.

———. 1963. *The sociology of religion*. Boston: Beacon. (German orig. 1922.)

White, Christine D. 1999. *Reconstructing ancient Maya diet*. Salt Lake City: University of Utah Press.

Whitmore, Thomas, and B. L. Turner. 2001. *Cultivated landscapes of middle America on the eve of conquest*. New York: Oxford University Press.

Williams, Teo. 1994. *Teo's way*. Comp. Annabel Ford. Santa Barbara: Cori/MesAmerican Research Center, University of California.

INDEX

Abeja Africana. See Africanized bees

Acacia cornigera. See Subin trees

Achras sapota. See Sapote trees

Africanized bees, 43, 46, 47, 183. *See also* Bees

Afterbirths, 40

Agkistrodon bilineatus, 181

Agouti paca, 26, 70, 135. *See also* Pacas

Agoutis, 70

Agriocharis ocellata. See Ocellated Turkeys

Alakbij, 105

Alouatta pigra, 141

Alux, 91

Alvarez, Cristina, 107

Amazona: albifrons, 172; *autumnalis,* 160; *xantholora,* 155

Amblycercus holosericeus, 164

American bees, 58. *See also* Bees

Amphibians: less common, 119

Ancient Mayas: animals, 128–30

Anemia, 35

Animal names: authorities, 127–28; use of Maya by urban elite, 98

Animals: aesthetic function, 35; ancient Maya, 127–30; in Chunhuhub, 77; conservation rules, 71–72; densities, 84, 88; as food, 34, 63; humor, 35; ill omens, 37; "life-form classes," 104; in magic, 35, 38; and milpa cycle, 64; negative feelings towards, 36; persons, 38; pests, 37; populations, 68; spirit companions, 40; symbiotic relationships with humans, 8; transformations, 39; treatment of, 32

Anisette liquor: of Yucatán, 46

Anser anser. See Geese

Ant Lion larvae, 195. *See also* Insects

Ants, 184, 186, 188, 190, 191, 193; Maya medicine, 190. *See also* Insects

Ant Tanagers, 168. *See also* Birds

Apis mellifera. See Honeybees

Aramus guarana, 155

Aratinga nana, 160

Arremonops: chloronotus, 172; *rufivirgatus,* 172

Ateles geoffroyi, 132, 146

Atran, Scott, 100–101, 106, 116

Ba'alch'e, 104

Baalche'. See Stingless bees

ABOUT THE AUTHORS

E. N. ANDERSON is professor of anthropology at the University of California, Riverside. He teaches cultural and political ecology, ethnobiology, and medical anthropology. He has done field work in Hong Kong, Malaysia, British Columbia, and southeast Mexico, and shorter projects in several other countries. He and his wife, Barbara Anderson, live in San Bernardino, California.

FELIX MEDINA TZUC was born in rural Yucatán state, Mexico, in 1942. As a young man he moved to the area of Chunhuhub, then largely a trackless old-growth forest. He married Elide Uh May, and they spent most of their lives subsistence farming on an isolated plot of land south of Chunhuhub. Eventually they moved to town, planting orange trees on their parcel of land. Don Felix has served a term as justice of the peace for Chunhuhub. He has a biologist's eye for the natural world and has devoted a lifetime to learning about plants, animals, farming, and field skills in Quintana Roo's tropical forests.